Ursula Burton

1990.

THIS BOOK
BELONGS TO

Ursula Burton
Kilmuir

A NEW VISION OF REALITY

BEDE GRIFFITHS

A NEW VISION
OF REALITY

Western Science, Eastern Mysticism
and Christian Faith

Edited by Felicity Edwards

COLLINS
8 Grafton Street, London W1
1989

William Collins Sons & Co. Ltd
London · Glasgow · Sydney · Auckland
Toronto · Johannesburg

First published 1989

BRITISH LIBRARY CATALOGUING IN PUBLICATION DATA

Griffiths, Bede
A new vision of reality: western science, eastern
mysticism and Christian faith.
1. Religion. Theories
I. Title   II. Edwards, Felicity
200′.1

ISBN 0-00-215363-7

Photoset in Linotron Baskerville by
Rowland Phototypesetting Ltd
Bury St Edmunds, Suffolk
Printed and bound in Great Britain by
William Collins Sons & Co. Ltd, Glasgow

CONTENTS

FOREWORD

There is no need to say how much this book owes to Fritjof Capra, whose *The Tao of Physics* first gave me an insight into the new movement in science today, and from whose book *The Turning Point* the title of this book is taken. So also my debt to Ken Wilber who has opened up Western psychology to the insights of Eastern wisdom is no less evident. But I owe special thanks to Rupert Sheldrake and Michael von Brück, who have kindly read through the book and made suggestions to make it more accurate. But above all I have to thank Dr Felicity Edwards who after a visit to our ashram offered to transcribe the tapes on which these talks were recorded and to edit them for publication. Her editing has been not merely in giving precision to the language, especially in the more scientific parts, but also in contributing her own insights. Assistance from the Publication Committee of Rhodes University where she works is also gratefully acknowledged, and special thanks are due to Mrs G. Emslie and Miss P. Ndemka for their cheerful and efficient secretarial help.

BEDE GRIFFITHS
SHANTIVANAM
INDIA

1

The New Physics, the New Biology and the Evolution of the Material Universe

The world today is on the verge of a new age and a new culture. Over a period of nearly three centuries in the West the philosophy of materialism has come to permeate every level of society. This materialist philosophy may be explicit, as in Marxist dialectical materialism, or it may be implicit, as it is in most Western scientific theory and above all in popular thinking. So pervasive has it been that most people in one way or another have come under its influence. This fundamental materialist philosophy arose from an understanding of the universe which was based on a mechanistic model. The development of this mechanistic understanding can be traced in the Western science of the last three centuries.

As an interpretative model in science it prevailed until the present century, and in certain quarters it is still strongly supported. In the last hundred years however, and mainly in the last fifty, it has been radically undermined by a new understanding of science and particularly by new physics. Fritjof Capra's *The Tao of Physics* (1975) did much to awaken public attention to the breakthrough, while in a later book, *The Turning Point* (1982), Capra showed how this new vision of the universe affects not only physics but also biology, medicine, psychology, sociology and economics. We are, Capra asserts, on the verge of a paradigm shift. A new vision of reality is penetrating the scientific world.

P. 1

Another element in the change of paradigm is in psychology. Western psychology, which began with Freud on an entirely materialistic basis, has now begun to open up. The first stage was through the work of Jung, who introduced a more spiritual aspect, but recently it has developed much further with the emergence of transpersonal psychology. This new area within psychology has begun to discover and explore levels of consciousness far above or beyond normal mental consciousness. At this point Western psychology has begun to open itself to oriental thought and to Eastern psychology. We are now reaching an understanding not only of the conscious and unconscious levels of mind but also of a whole "spectrum of consciousness" as Ken Wilber calls it. Wilber is prominent among the new transpersonal theorists and is one of the leading authorities on this range of psychological development. He traces the stages of development from the elementary psychology of the child and of primitive man, right through to the supreme consciousness, which is the awareness of Ultimate Reality as known in Hindu and Buddhist mysticism. So the whole horizon has opened up vastly in the last century, from a very limited materialist philosophy of life to a philosophy based on science and psychology but open now to the whole transcendent reality of existence as known both in the East and in the West.

Until the sixteenth century there was a universal philosophy not only in Europe but also throughout the civilised world. This is usually referred to in the West as "the perennial philosophy". It was found in China in the development of Taoism and Confucianism which came to a head in the neo-Confucianism of the seventeenth and eighteenth centuries; in India in the development of Vedanta; in the rest of Asia in Mahayana Buddhism; in Islam in both the philosophical development of Islam and in Sufism; and finally in Europe in the whole development of medieval

Christianity. This universal wisdom, or perennial philosophy, prevailed from about AD 500 to about AD 1500 and is part of our inheritance. It was based on the belief in a material world which was studied scientifically with considerable accuracy, although of course modern science has gone far beyond its limited achievements. What was distinctive about the universal wisdom was its understanding that the material world was pervaded by, and would find its explanation in, a transcendent reality. This transcendent reality was known in China as the Tao, in Mahayana Buddhism as the Void, the *Sunyata*, in Hinduism as the Brahman, and in Islam as *al Haqq*, the Reality. In Christian doctrine it was known as the Godhead (as in Dionysius and Eckhart) or simply as the Supreme Being. In this there is to be found a universal philosophy which is the inheritance of all mankind. For various complex reasons this philosophy began to be gradually undermined in the Europe of the sixteenth century. Widespread developments took place at that point and the new materialist philosophy began to emerge, coming to a head in the nineteenth century.

Materialism has become a major component of our inheritance and all our attitudes to life are determined, at least partially and very often unconsciously, by a materialist view of reality. What is needed now is to discover that we are conditioned in that way and to move on to recover the elements of the more universal and profound vision, within the context of the scientific thought of today. It is very significant that the new physics and other branches of the new science are helping us to get a renewed vision of reality which takes us back to aspects of the ancient wisdom, and in the process assists the development of our new vision in even more profound and far-reaching directions. What is now important is to see how Christianity accords with this new paradigm in science. In the course of examining this it

11

will become apparent that the new paradigm affects in many ways our Christian understanding of the world.

Modern materialist philosophy began with Descartes. It had been evolving over several centuries from the Aristotelian philosophy which had long dominated the Western world. Aristotelism had come to prevail for at least five centuries not only within Christianity but also in Islam. The great Muslim philosophers, Avicenna and Averroes, were both Aristotelians. The medieval thinkers and theologians, St Thomas Aquinas, Bonaventure and Duns Scotus, were all basically Aristotelian philosophers. What is characteristic of Aristotelian philosophy is the belief that human knowledge is based on the evidence of the senses. It was this understanding which came to dominate philosophy after the sixteenth century to the exclusion of the more profound view of Plato. In the fourteenth and fifteenth centuries Aristotelian philosophy began to take a new direction. It was this new understanding which emerged into full light in the sixteenth century and began the path of a new philosophy which eventually became the materialistic philosophy we know today.

Descartes was a key figure in the development of materialism in that he was the first to make a complete separation between mind and matter. In Aristotle mind and matter, or form and matter, were considered to be always interdependent in a dynamic interrelationship. The human being was a body-soul. The soul for Aristotle was the form of the body, so that the human being was an integrated whole. Descartes's understanding was radically different in that he separated body and mind, and maintained that matter, including the body, is reality extended outside of us, *res extensa*, totally separate from mind. The mind is, as it were, an observer which looks out on this universe extended outside of us. Descartes was a great mathematician and he believed that through mathematics one could come to a perfect understanding of the universe. The whole universe was to him a mechanism governed by mathematical law. Once the laws of mathematics had been discovered the whole material universe could be known. Within this system each individual person was a separated entity, a *res cogitans*, a thinking reality, over against material reality, *res extensa*. The Cartesian view, then, continued to feed into Western thought operating with two separate realities, *res cogitans* and *res extensa*, mind and matter. This separation of mind from matter marks the beginning of all modern philosophy.

A second stage which was very important in this development was the work of Francis Bacon, the English philosopher, who saw the value of its main features for practical purposes. He was one of the first to declare that the goal of science is not simply to understand the universe but to control it. This meant using mathematical and scientific knowledge to change nature and to reconstruct matter. The whole of modern technology flows from the idea that by the scientific enterprise not only can the structure and properties of matter be understood but this knowledge can be applied for practical purposes.

There is no need to say how profound the effect of all this has been. It has transformed our world, giving us a different understanding of the universe and vastly changing the condition of human life through technology. But on the other hand this development had grave defects which have only gradually come to light.

The next stage was that of Galileo, who is famous for his discoveries in astronomy and who was also a mathematician and philosopher of science. Galileo maintained that matter itself had to be studied only in its quantitative aspect. Mass and motion were the main characteristics of matter and these could be measured quantitatively. The understanding grew that the only real knowledge is that which can be measured and therefore mathematically understood. All else

13

is subjective. Matter is extended substance, *res extensa*, obeying mathematical laws. Being quantitative it can be known only by quantitative methods. Beyond that all sense qualities, sight, sound, touch, taste, smell, and even more, all emotional aspects of life, all art, morality and religion, were considered to be purely subjective. The extended mathematical system represented the only objective reality. Moreover, the whole of this reality was seen as an exclusively mechanical system. At that time many new types of clock were appearing and the clock seemed to be the most appropriate model of reality. A clock could be built as a more or less perfect mechanism, and on the model of the clock the universe as such was assumed to be a perfect mechanism. Further, once the working of the mechanism was understood, it could be controlled and used. That was the fundamental idea and from it arose modern technology.

The next stage developed with Isaac Newton, whom some consider the greatest scientist that ever lived. Newton built an understanding of the universe, complete as far as it went, which was so successful that until the present century it was accepted by all scientists. It was a marvellous achievement, for it really showed how the universe worked as a system in terms of the mechanisms with which he was concerned. But it was also crude in a sense, because for Newton matter was extended in space, and reality consisted of concrete objects moving in space and time. Measurement of mass, motion and other properties, and their interrelationships, provided the model of the universe for the succeeding centuries.

It must be remembered, however, that both Descartes and Newton were Christians with a definite belief in God. For Descartes, although the matter of the material universe was extended substance without mind, man himself, or rather the mind of man, possessed knowledge by what Descartes called "innate ideas". Ideas did not arise from matter; they arose in the human mind as innate ideas which came ultimately from God. In Descartes's view God was the supreme reality who enlightened the mind of the scientist, enabling him to explain the material universe.

Newton's position was even more interesting. He was a great philosopher and theologian, and many so-far unpublished manuscripts of his have been discovered in which he explores elements of the paranormal. He was very interested in alchemy and astrology, as Richard Westfall shows in his *Never at Rest* (1980), and his vision of the universe was profoundly religious. He believed that it was God who had created the universe and that God continues to pervade it. It was the presence of God which constituted space and time and which ordered the motions of material objects. In itself it was an extremely interesting system. The sequel, however, was this. In the eighteenth century the Newtonian system was not only accepted in physics but became the standard for science generally. Because the method of Newtonian mechanics was so highly successful and yielded such impressive results it became extrapolated into metaphysics. It was assumed philosophically that Newtonian physics provided not only a complete picture of reality but the only picture of reality. The result was that everything that was not amenable to measurement by Newtonian methods was systematically excluded from consideration. Theology, ethics and aesthetics, for instance, were dropped from this new world view. Descartes, Bacon and Newton were not materialists as such. All believed in God as the supreme reality governing the universe. In fact in Newton's case the irony was that philosophically he himself was not a mechanist at all; he believed the universe to be a body, an organism, rather than a machine.

But by the eighteenth century these aspects of reality had been eliminated and the mechanistic system alone remained. Thorough-going materialism, then, combined with mechanism, was the philosophy which prevailed into and during the nineteenth century. It was gradually extended from inorganic matter (as in physics and astronomy) to include life and life processes. Biological science went ahead to attempt to explain life and living phenomena in terms of mechanical causality, using the concepts of physics and chemistry. It must be said that at the present time this development in the form of modern molecular biology and palaeontology, coupled with neo-Darwinian evolutionary theory, has been enormously successful. Molecular biology has made extraordinary discoveries about the nature and function of genetic material, for instance, and in the area of genetic engineering immense new visions have opened up, all within the framework of this mechanistic system. Life itself, then, came to be explained exclusively in terms of mechanism.

The next stage in this development was in the sphere of psychology. In cosmology and the natural sciences generally the existence of a God was no longer necessary, and now in psychology the existence of a soul was considered superfluous. The whole human being could be explained in terms of mechanistic causality. The great pioneer in this work was Freud. He had been trained in neurology and his original idea was that all human psychology could be accounted for in terms of neurochemistry, the chemistry of the nervous system. He gradually transcended that view but always retained this basically mechanistic model. Freud was the first to explore the unconscious, and it is one of the great pioneering discoveries of modern times that there is a whole world of the unconscious beneath the conscious experience of the mind. Freud maintained, however, that the unconscious was governed by mechanistic laws and he explained the process in terms of forces. Just as there are forces in nature which move the various bodies in the world, so there are forces in the unconscious, in the form of instincts and impulses, appetites and desires, which move the human being.

In particular, Freud discovered that many of these appetites and desires resulted from repressed feelings. Repression, by the conscious part of the mind, of desires, emotions and sexual feelings resulted in these repressed elements becoming forces in the unconscious which drove the person to action, and could account not only for human action but also for the processes of human thought. All human thought, all knowledge, all morality and all religion could thus be explained in terms of these forces in the unconscious. Freud's disciple Jung, however, broke with Freud on this issue, and discovered in the unconscious not only repressed emotions and desires but also creative principles which he called archetypes. These were formative principles in the unconscious which opened the human mind to other levels of reality. From this Jung was led to conceive the "collective unconscious" as the repository of the inherited experience of humanity, manifesting itself particularly in dreams and in the myths of ancient man.

In spite of the prevailing materialist philosophy, developments in contemporary science are arising which support the basic principles of the "perennial philosophy". In physics, for instance, there has recently been the discovery that the material universe is essentially a field of energies in which the parts can only be understood in relation to the whole. A related and most profound idea which has been introduced in physics is that the whole is in some way present in every part and, further, that every part is interconnected with every other part. This principle applies to the whole universe and everything in it. In physics the nature of the electron itself exemplifies this. The electron is spoken of in terms of a wave-function which is information about the probability of locating the electron in a certain area of space. That wave-function spreads out to fill the entire universe, so that a certain electron which is identifiable as being at point x has a very tiny fraction of itself spreading billions and billions of light years away. Further, the electron which is here at point x is also the product of all the other billions and billions of electrons that fill the universe. One of the interesting consequences of this is that if the physicist tries to contain this electron by, say, building a box around it, this cannot be done completely because the electron has part of itself extending outside the box. The effect of that is the so-called Tunnelling Process or Tunnelling Effect whereby, after a little while, the electron will defy all the forces that attempt to hold it and will gradually "leak" out, tunnelling through the wall. It transcends itself, in a sense, to fill the entire universe. The Tunnelling Effect is well verified experimentally. It is common in modern technology and is a central idea in contemporary quantum mechanics.

The discovery that the whole is present in every part and that within the whole all parts are interconnected has been further corroborated by the work of the physicist, David Bohm. Bohm is a good example of a modern physicist who is open to the spiritual dimension of reality, and is known as a disciple of Krishnamurti. As a physicist Bohm is well-known and well-respected and his philosophical theories are based on his work in physics, but at the same time he is exploring spiritual reality through meditation and other spiritual practices. Particularly important is his introduction of the theory of the implicate order (*Wholeness and the Implicate Order*, 1980). According to Bohm's theory the whole universe is originally implicated, or folded up together, and what we observe in the everyday world is the explicate order, i.e. that which has been explicated or unfolded. The implicate order is continually unfolding, becoming explicate. But behind the explicate order the implicate is always present, so in that sense the whole universe is implicated behind every explicit

18

form. This has extraordinarily interesting results. It is held now that the universe came into being about fifteen billion years ago with what is known as the Big Bang, an explosion of matter at an extremely high temperature. Even in that original explosion, which could best be described as an explosion of energy in the form of light in which there were as yet no forms, all the atoms and molecules, organs and organisms of the whole universe were already implicit, from the very beginning. This does not mean that particular forms were pre-determined. Rather, there was an infinite potential present in the very origin of the universe and one aspect of that potential came to be actualised at each moment of development. In other words, the universe could have developed along a whole variety of different potential routes and we perceive only one of those possible pathways. Because the explicate universe is unfolding from the implicate order where all possible interconnections are latent, everything at the level of the implicate order is interrelated. This means that we are living in a universe which is co-ordinated and integrated as a whole. And that opens up a new vision of reality. It needs to be added that this new aspect of Bohm's work is essentially philosophical though at the same time it relates to experimental physics. In fact the theory of the implicate order is in the same philosophical tradition as that of Einstein. Einstein was particularly disturbed by the philosophical implication of quantum mechanics that the world, at the sub-atomic level at least, is by its very nature unknowable. Bohm is affirming, in the spirit of Einstein, a fundamental wholeness, interconnectedness and intelligibility.

Another rapidly-moving area in the new science is that of biology, where an important set of ideas have been advanced by the Cambridge biologist Rupert Sheldrake. Working in the forefront of theoretical evolutionary biology, Sheldrake published in 1981 a book entitled *A New Science of Life: The*

Hypothesis of Formative Causation in which he maintains that the attempt to explain the phenomena of life in terms of physics and chemistry alone cannot ultimately succeed. Molecular biology is extremely successful at the moment at its own level of operation but, Sheldrake holds, it is simply not adequate to explain the main features of life, in particular the process of morphogenesis, the development of new forms of life, and their regulation and regeneration. Sheldrake's contribution here has been the introduction of a theory of "formative causation" based on the hypothesis of morphogenetic fields. The theory that has prevailed up to now is basically neo-Darwinian and it asserts that the evolutionary development of living organisms is to be accounted for in terms of random mutations, Mendelian genetics and natural selection. Monod, the French Nobel laureate, speaks for his colleagues in molecular biology in his recent work *Chance and Necessity* (1972), and the account he gives is an explicit statement of this thoroughgoing mechanistic position. There are many features of the natural world, however, that this mechanistic theory does not explain. How is it, for example, that electrons, protons and so on are organised into an atom? How is it that atoms are organised into molecules and again into more and more complex molecular structures? How is it that molecules are organised into increasingly complex forms in the living cell? How are cells organised into more and more complex forms, into plants, into animals and into the human body? Higher levels of organisation arise by constant development of increasingly complex forms. Sheldrake's thesis is that, although there are fields of energy in the universe, the universe cannot be explained in terms of energy alone; there has also to be formative power. This formative power exists as non-physical, non-energetic fields which Sheldrake calls "formative causes" or "morphogenetic fields". The Greek word *morphe* means a form, hence "morphogenetic" is that which produces forms. With this theory Sheldrake has reintroduced a notion very similar to that of Aristotle who held that the universe is made not merely of matter but of matter and form. In Aristotle's understanding matter is potential energy. It has no existence in itself; it is the potentiality to exist. Matter is structured by what Aristotle called form, *eidos*. The Greek word *eidos* meant first a form in the literal sense, the shape of a tree or an animal or anything else, and then it came to mean the organising power of the tree or the animal. So there is matter which is indeterminate and unstructured, which is the source of all the indeterminacy and the unpredictability of the material world. This is observable; there is an element of the indeterminate, the unpredictable, an element of sheer chance, in matter. But the indeterminate and unpredictable does not explain the universe. It has to be recognised that matter is being organised by form or, in Sheldrake's terms, by morphogenetic fields. Sheldrake introduces here the concept of morphic resonance. This means that each living or non-living entity develops its particular form as a crystal or organ or plant or animal because it is within a particular morphogenetic field which is structuring it, and which is in resonance with all similar organisms. The field thus contains an inherent memory.

To illustrate the difference between the mechanistic view and his own position Sheldrake uses the analogy of a radio. The radio is a mechanistic system and it has to be in working order, but when the mechanism is correctly set up it works by being tuned into events from outside. The materialistic view would be that everything can be explained in terms of the mechanism of the radio. If, for instance, you were to take a radio to a primitive tribe in Africa and play it to the people, they might well think that the voices they were hearing were coming from the radio set itself. What is more, they would be able to prove it because the moment the set went wrong the voices would stop and as soon as the set

21

was repaired the voices would come on again. So it would be all too easy to conclude that the voices could be explained in terms of the mechanism. In the mechanistic model of the universe it is quite true that when the mechanism goes wrong, when for instance the brain fails, then the mind stops acting, but that does not mean that the mind can be reduced to the brain, or, in the case of the phenomenon of the voices, that the voices can be reduced without remainder to what happens inside the radio. Rather, the signals giving rise to the voices come from outside the radio and are of a different order to that of the radio set. Similarly, in the evolutionary process there is a material, mechanistic aspect of matter which works according to mechanistic laws, like the radio set itself, but there are also formative causes, the effect of which is to organise matter. Each different kind of matter tunes in, as it were, to its own particular field. As an organism starts to develop it begins to resonate to a certain field, and the more the organism follows that particular path the more it becomes habituated and goes on developing within that field to its final form. Morphogenetic fields are thus seen to be an important component in the explanation of the course of evolution.

In the evolutionary process there were at first elementary particles, then simple atoms like hydrogen and helium, then the more complex atoms of the whole range of chemical elements. The atoms of each element are structured by mathematical laws, the exact number of protons and electrons structuring each type of atom determining the properties of each particular element. When living cells evolved, the chromosomes in each nucleus and the genes on them each have their own particular structure. The universe thus formed can be seen to have developed through two forces working together. On the one hand there is energy/matter, which is unstructured, and on the other there is form, which is the principle of structure in the universe. These two forces

22

work together so that the organism is opening itself all the time to new form.

Of special interest here is the work of Ilya Prigogine, for which he won the Nobel Prize in 1977. Prigogine, a Russian-born physical chemist, discovered that within certain chemicals there are systems which he termed "dissipative structures". These maintain their order, and develop it further, by breaking down other structures in the process. The entropy or disorder which results is dissipated in the form of waste products. The self-organisation within these chemical systems is so like that of living organisms that it has been suggested that they may represent a link between non-living and living matter.

In a similar way, at the level of the cell there is continual interchange; the cell is taking in matter/energy from the environment and giving out matter/energy at the same time at the expense of increasing entropy, or disorder. The cells of our bodies, and our bodies themselves, are being built up in that way, day by day, hour by hour, in constant interchange with their environment. This whole wave of energies is a dynamic process. Everything is in a state of flux and change at every moment and two forces are at work. On the one hand an organism tends to go out of itself, to open itself to other forms around, and on the other hand it tends to organise itself, to centre on itself. The actual forms that we know are the result of the balance between these two tendencies. What frequently happens is that the tendency to go out of itself, to transcend itself, increases and a disequilibrium takes place. If that disequilibrium is allowed to go too far then the entity disintegrates. That can happen at every level from chemical to living cell. On the other hand, the self-organising power within the organism is always tending to reconstruct itself, so that as the disequilibrium takes place and the organism starts to go out of order it begins to reconstruct, and a new form comes into being and begins to tune in to a new morphogenetic field. It needs to be noted that at present the theory of formative causation as put forward by Sheldrake is still hypothetical; it has not so far been verified experimentally. Like Bohm in physics when he is speaking of the implicate order, Sheldrake here does not represent mainstream thinking in his field. Should experimental support be forthcoming, however, Sheldrake's work would constitute a major breakthrough beyond the mechanistic explanations of present-day neo-Darwinian molecular biology, providing as it does a much more comprehensive understanding of the way in which the process of evolution may be taking place.

We have, then, the new physics with its understanding of the physical world as a field of energies, an integrated whole, in which the whole is present in every part; we have the theory of morphogenetic fields, within which organisms have been built up continuously and are developing continually into new forms. The principle of formative causation, within specific morphogenetic fields, applies to everything in the cosmos from the organisation of the atom upwards, through the molecule, the cell, the organ, the organism, the plant, the animal and the human. With the advent of the human body that organising power within begins to become conscious. A human being is a form of matter which has reached a very high order of complexity and is so organised as to become conscious. The breakthrough takes place when matter and form, which have been working together, come into consciousness and we can become aware of ourselves as a material organism with cells made up of matter from the first matter of the universe. Each of us, in the cells of our body, are linked with the original matter of the universe because the entire universe, and everything in it, is one integrated whole. We are all linked with all the original cells which began to form on this earth as it reached a state when life could emerge, about four billion years ago. We all have within ourselves the basic structure of the physical universe and of life, but we also have this unique awakening into consciousness. We can begin to control the matter of our bodies.

A great deal of what goes on in our bodies is unconscious; digestion, blood circulation and so on obey the normal laws of biology, but we can also control our bodies to a varying extent. We are discovering today how great that extent can be. Control of the body by the mind can reach high levels. In yoga there are cases where the yogi can completely control his breathing and even the beating of his heart. So we are discovering to what extent the matter of the body can be controlled by the mind. It is becoming clear also that within that material universe there is a latent consciousness. Consciousness was potential from the beginning and it emerges when the organism is sufficiently developed, as in a human body. As consciousness emerges in us we become conscious of ourselves and conscious of the universe around us. Mind is understood to have been present but in a pre-conscious state, in lower levels of the organisation of matter, in stones, metals, plants and animals. In human beings that mind which has been working pre-consciously in the universe begins to emerge into consciousness.

These ideas of how form or field is structuring matter, as I have come to understand it, have some similarity to the position of Teilhard de Chardin (*The Phenomenon of Man*, 1959). The part of Teilhard's great theory which is particularly relevant here concerns the operation of two forces which he calls radial and tangential. The language used is of course metaphorical, but, if we were to think of this visually, the idea would be that there is a centre out of which the world moves. At every moment of time there is as it were a sphere, and the particles on that sphere are governed by a tangential force which corresponds to the forces about which physics speaks, the forces of gravity, electromagnetism and so on. These are the forces which organise and order matter. Then, in Teilhard's understanding, there is also a radial force which encourages the evolutionary movement outward to ever higher levels. At the beginning of the evolutionary process the tangential force dominated, and that is essentially a physical force which is unpredictable. It has no direction and is totally random in terms of the behaviour of the individual particles. Further, it is dominated by the process of entropy as the energy in the system becomes more and more uniformly distributed. As matter gets organised into increasingly complex structure the radial force begins to grow in intensity. So, as the universe continues to evolve, the relative importance of the tangential force decreases while the importance of the radial force increases. The radial force for Teilhard is spirit and he speaks of it as Christ-consciousness. As the universe matures the intensity of this radial force or Christ-consciousness increases exponentially, being continuously contributed to and reinforced by all the centuries of consciousness in the universe.

This is where we move again from physics and biology to psychology. Knowledge of the human psyche has advanced immeasurably beyond Freud. The work of Jung opened it up to much deeper dimensions but Ken Wilber has gone beyond the basic structures as Freud and Jung understood them, linking these up with the highest levels of human awareness. His principal books are *The Spectrum of Consciousness* (1977), *The Atman Project* (1980) and *Up from Eden* (1980), and in these he gives an account of the gradual development of human psychology. This will be examined in chapter two. Here it is sufficient to say that we discover that in us, at the stage of development we are now reaching, the material universe is emerging into consciousness. Our present consciousness is still very imperfect and our control of matter by consciousness is rudimentary, to say the least, but we are beginning to discover that human consciousness can develop far beyond its present level and that, for instance, the ways in which consciousness affects matter are immeasurably more complex than we had previously imagined. This is one of the points at which the link is made between Western understanding and Eastern mysticism, for in the East this whole sphere of psychology has been studied in immense depth for two thousand years at least. Mahayana Buddhism particularly has reached an extraordinarily deep level with regard to the understanding of psychological processes beyond the normal, in other words, of transpersonal, transmental consciousness. Our mental consciousness, which is our normal consciousness, is the level of consciousness emerging from the plant and the animal states but now we are also able to go beyond mental consciousness and experience the transpersonal, transmental or "supramental" consciousness, as Sri Aurobindo called it. So now we begin to see that human evolution has come from the matter of the universe through the plant and the animal levels to our present state of being, and is emerging into a higher state of consciousness. With that development we discover in ourselves the ground of the whole structure of the universe and the whole scope of human consciousness. And that is precisely what took place in India in the fifth century before Christ, when there was a breakthrough beyond mental consciousness to the supramental with the discovery of the Ultimate Reality sustaining the whole universe.

2

The New Psychology and
the Evolution of Consciousness

We saw in chapter one how, in the process of the evolution of both mind and matter, form is constantly ordering and structuring matter/energy and building up the world as we know it until, at the level of the human person, matter becomes conscious. Human knowledge is the knowledge of forms. On the one hand form structures matter and on the other hand, in knowing anything, it is the form of the thing which is received into the mind. That again was the understanding of Aristotle. So, for example, when I look at a tree I receive the form of the tree into my mind. My senses receive an impression which is registered in the brain. The impression results in an image and my mind conceives the form of the tree. The matter/energy, which is in the tree, remains outside; the concept of the tree is the presence of the form within the mind. That is how knowing proceeds. It is, of course, a gradual process. As our science and philosophy develop we get ever deeper understanding and receive an increasingly complete appreciation of the forms.

Beneath the conscious mind there are many levels of the unconscious. Although in human persons the mind of the universe becomes conscious, our present conscious mind is still very limited and beneath the conscious mind are all the manifold levels of what is called the unconscious, or better, the subconscious mind. Here the imagination functions; we form images of the world around us subconsciously rather than consciously. We sense things around us, our feelings and appetites awaken and we form an image of the physical world. All this is the product of the subconscious mind deep within ourselves.

The world as we see it is the world as it is mirrored in our psyche. The psyche, or soul, is a complex organic structure of which the conscious mind is one aspect. All the other levels of the mind exist within the psyche and together they embrace the whole world of consciousness. It is known now that a person can go back through the different levels of consciousness and experience each level. There is no problem about going back to the dream level of consciousness, and we can get back fairly easily to life in childhood and particularly to the emotional aspects of it. Recently it has been discovered in the West that by trance or hypnosis, or using some other technique to induce regression, it is possible to get back to the level of perinatal experience where the whole trauma of the birth process can be relived and worked with. Going even further, it is possible to get back to the experience of intra-uterine life and then to the moment of conception. In working with such experience it has become clear that the whole period from conception to birth is of immense importance for the development of the adult person. If, for instance, a child is conceived with great love and mutual self-giving the developing embryo experiences that unity, but if the child is conceived with feelings of violence and hatred, as for instance in the case of rape, that adverse emotional environment seriously affects the embryo. So the embryo, and later the child, is being affected emotionally from the very beginning. All this is recorded in the subconscious mind and a great deal of insight can be obtained by gaining access to these levels of early personal experience. Where there are deep psychological hurts these can often be healed, even when they were inflicted long before birth.

It is said that it is possible to go behind birth consciousness and conception to an animal consciousness in such a way as to become aware of the animal life within. Further back still an awareness of plant life can be attained and finally it is possible to get back, in principle at least, to the original explosion of matter. The explosion of matter in the universe fifteen billion years ago is present to all of us. Each one of us is part of the effect of that one original explosion such that, in our unconscious, we are linked up with the very beginning of the universe and with the matter of the universe from the earliest stages of its formation. In that sense the universe is within us. We habitually think of the universe as being outside and apart from us but that is because we have become accustomed to projecting it outside.

In connection with this an interesting theory has been advanced by Karl Pribram, the well-known neuro-scientist. Pribram has advanced evidence to show that the brain may function in many ways like a hologram. Holography is a lensless photographic process in which light scattered by an object is recorded on a photographic plate in the form of an interference pattern which looks just like swirls on the plate. When the plate is put in front of a coherent light source, into a laser beam for instance, the original wave field is regenerated and a three-dimensional image of the object appears. What is fascinating about the hologram is that if the photographic plate on which the object is recorded is cut into pieces, each piece when illuminated by coherent light will reconstruct the whole image, perfect in every detail, although less sharply defined. The hologram is a concrete example of the principle that the whole is present in every part. Its discovery confirms the view that in the universe the whole is also present in every part and that this is in fact the structure of the physical world. It is of interest that Pribram is a friend of both Bohm and Krishnamurti, and was a former associate of Einstein. Together with Bohm he generated what is referred to as the holographic theory of reality.

The suggestion is that we receive vibrations of light, sound and matter into our brains simply as vibrations and then, as in the case of the hologram, we project a three-dimensional world around us. On this understanding the world is a projection of our minds; it does not exist as it appears to us. As we shall see in examining the evolution of consciousness, it becomes clear that we do in fact construct the world around us. The world is there of course; the energy and the form exist, but the way in which we apprehend the world depends on our consciousness and the level to which it has evolved. So we project this world around us and think of it as outside, but in reality it is within. The world is of course outside my body; but it is not outside my mind. Aristotle said that the human mind is *quodammmodo omnia*, in a certain sense is all things, because we are capable of receiving the forms of the whole universe into ourselves. We are this little universe, a microcosm, in whom the macrocosm is present as in a hologram.

In Western analytical psychology the person who first opened up the level of the unconscious mind was of course Sigmund Freud, and much credit goes to him for his profound psychological insights. Even though the philosophy in terms of which he explained his psychological discoveries was inadequate, since it was totally materialistic, his work laid the foundations of modern psychology.

Freud did not go much below the level of the personal unconscious. He was essentially concerned with repressed feelings, thoughts, images and desires. These, when repressed into the unconscious, become explosive forces which can break out into a person's life, causing disorder and serious mental illness, not to say madness, if they are too violent. So Freud explored this whole level of the repressed unconscious, in particular repressed sexuality which he termed the libido, and he explained a great deal of the mechanism of the human unconscious. We must be just

31

to Freud in that, by concentrating on this level of the unconscious, he did discover much of which nobody had been aware before. In the same way Karl Marx, by concentrating on the economic level, did reveal how far the economics of life, the getting of one's daily bread, affects the whole structure of society and of course the whole political organisation. These men, Freud and Marx, undoubtedly made fundamental and far-reaching contributions. It was when they tried to explain everything in terms of economics (Marx) or of the personal unconscious mind (Freud) that serious mistakes arose.

Carl Jung, the Swiss psychologist who had originally been a disciple of Freud, went far beyond his pioneering predececessor. Jung realised that beyond the personal unconscious is what he termed the collective unconscious. This is an area which can be contacted, as we have seen, beyond childhood, infancy and perinatal experiences. It is called "collective" because the contents of this level of consciousness are common to the whole human race. The evidence for this is partly in dreams and partly in mythology. Psychoanalysts have discovered that in the dreams of modern people there frequently occur recreations of ancient mythologies. The myths of Greece, Rome and India, for instance, recur in the dreams of twentieth-century people. Jung concluded that the whole mythological world is present in the collective unconscious. We have inherited from the past archetypes which are structured forms or patterns of organic energy, in which the unconscious reflects its experiences. Working with this and related issues Jung opened up knowledge of the unconscious to a far greater depth than Freud. He also made a serious mistake however which Ken Wilber has correctly diagnosed, in that in his interpretation he tended to confuse aspects of the personal subconscious with superconsciousness. Many Jungian analysts still do this, failing to distinguish prepersonal from transpersonal consciousness.

We will see in what follows that there is the level of mental consciousness which is our normal rational consciousness, but below that is a series of subconscious levels, while above it is another whole range of levels of consciousness up to the supreme consciousness to which we are aspiring. The mental consciousness with which we normally identify is in the mid-range of the development of consciousness.

In tracing the process of the evolution of consciousness it is helpful to follow the work of Ken Wilber, particularly in his *Up From Eden*. Wilber distinguishes six levels of consciousness, beginning with what he calls uroboric or oceanic consciousness.

This is the primeval consciousness at which level the human being is totally immersed in nature and is one with the universe. It reflects also the experience of the child in the womb where the child is floating in the amniotic fluid in which it is growing. Floating in that ocean is an experience of a kind of bliss. The child is totally at one with nature without any separation at all. This state corresponds with the garden of Eden; the man and woman of the Genesis narrative were in that state of bliss-consciousness, totally one with nature. At this stage of development however the human persons were not simply animals. Latent in that early human consciousness were all the further levels of consciousness, even the higher levels. The Spirit, in other words, was present in humanity from the beginning. Ken Wilber tends to suggest that what was involved here was only a lower form of consciousness, but we would rather say that in that blissful oneness with nature there was an awareness of the Spirit, the *Atman,* the Supreme. It could not be distinguished or differentiated, but there was an awareness of it in a kind of global experience of bliss. That is the state of Eden, man's original state. There is no separate ego in that state. There is simply an experience of immersion in a cosmic whole, in which the material and the human

33

world are experienced in a global unity with the Spirit which pervades and encompasses them.

The term uroboric which Wilber gives to this level of consciousness comes from mythology, where the uroboros is the serpent with its tail in its mouth and is therefore completely enclosed in itself. This is one of the great ancient symbols. The child in the womb and man in nature are completely uroboric, completely enclosed in the world of nature, without separation having taken place between self and other.

The next stage Wilber terms typhonic. The typhon is a mythological creature, half man and half serpent. While the uroboros is a serpent with its tail in its mouth, the typhon is the serpent which has begun to transcend itself. This indicates the start made by early man to move out of nature, the beginning of separation and the development of consciousness of the body. In the same way the child begins to develop a body consciousness, becoming aware of itself as separate from its mother and siblings. There is self-awareness as body but not yet self-awareness as mind. With this body consciousness the child begins to know itself as an individual but is still very closely bonded with mother and with other children. This oneness of the child with mother and family is an emotional unity, an emotional consciousness. It is the root of all the deep ties we have with mother, family, tribe and race. All these ties develop out of that original, emotional, typhonic consciousness.

Another aspect of the typhonic level of consciousness is that it is a kind of dream state. We go into that dream state at night but ancient humanity lived much more constantly in the dream state. In the dream state things are far less differentiated than in the waking state. Time and space have quite a different character in the dream and so, almost certainly did they have for ancient man. Time and space were not clearly differentiated as they are for us. We all experience the world according to our level of consciousness and early man must have experienced the world much more like a dream. When time and space are not clearly defined things are experienced as flowing into each other, and it is said that at that period personal boundaries were not distinct and there was the sense of flowing into and merging with others. This kind of experience is sometimes referred to as a *participation mystique,* a mystical participation. Having realised that his body is separate in some sense, the person is still part of nature, part of that emotional complex.

The typhonic level of awareness is also the world of magic. In magic no clear distinction is made between the outer and the inner world. Magic is precisely the attempt to affect the outer world through the inner. One example of this is the way in which making an image of a person and sticking pins in it is believed to affect the person imaged. At the time when this was the general level of consciousness, a common practice was what we now know as "sympathetic magic". For example, hunting people made paintings of animals on the walls of their caves and by painting arrows penetrating the image of the bison, or whatever the prey was, it was believed that in a magical way the bison outside was affected. Killing the bison in the hunt then became a matter of actualising outside the event which had been achieved in the cave. So here the inner and outer worlds were not yet differentiated.

At this second stage the notion of time as time has not as yet developed. In the first stage, the uroboric, time did not feature at all; there was simply a unity of being. At the second stage time was beginning to develop as what is now known as a passing present. At that stage there was no awareness of a past or a future. Life was experienced always and only in the present. It is noteworthy that many of the characteristics of these primitive states are much the same as those of the higher mystical states. Ken Wilber makes

35

the very important point, referred to earlier in connection with Jung, that we must not confuse this pre-logical, pre-mental level with the transmental, transpersonal stage, the difference being that in the pre-mental state there is no differentiation; in the transmental state differentiation is transcended. There is, therefore, a profound analogy between these two modes of experience. Thus in mystical experience we rediscover at a fully conscious level our original oneness with nature and sense of the present moment. There is no longer an awareness of either a past or a future; there is only the present, the total reality experienced in its original unity.

At this typhonic level, then, life was lived totally in the present. This was the pre-logical state of consciousness before the development of language. It is uncertain exactly when language began to develop. Many people put it comparatively late. Wilber places this stage at about 200,000 BC. Many think that language did not really develop, apart from very simple words and exclamations, until about 50,000 BC.

The development of language characterises the next stage, which Wilber calls the verbal membership stage. The ability to use words was a remarkable breakthrough in human development because words are signs. Previously, if you wanted for instance to convey to somebody a message about a tree, you had to go up to the tree and touch it to indicate "tree", but once you have a word "tree" that word is accessible wherever you go. So language brings release from bondage to the concrete world and to the present. With words one can distinguish oneself from the body. A word is a symbol which re-presents the object, a tree, a fellow human being, one's own body, and so on. The word for an object makes that object present mentally without that object having to be present in its concrete embodiment. This enables the human mind to span both space and time. Language is the beginning of the first stage of liberation.

The beginning of a sense of time heralded the beginning of the possibility of living in extended time, and there developed remembrance of the past and anticipation of the future. With this came the great change in economic life from hunting to agriculture. As long as people were hunters only they lived in small tribal groups and they lived from day to day, hunting food and eating it as it came their way. This was living in the present indeed. Once agriculture had developed there came the beginning of planning for the future. Crops were sown and plans made for them to be harvested in the future. The early farmers could look back on the past and see for instance that a particular harvest had not been good, and they could begin to fathom the reason for that and act accordingly. At that stage there was the beginning of a clear separation from the world around and there was therefore the possibility of control of the world. While undifferentiated from the world, early man was simply moulded by his environment. But as separation through language began to take place the beginnings of control became possible. Early agriculture was a beginning of the control of the world. The development of agriculture probably took place about 10,000 BC, marking a major turning point in human history.

The next stage of the verbal membership level is that of mythical knowledge, myth being symbolic knowledge made possible through language. Once language developed, awareness of the world around could be expressed in symbols and the great myths are symbolic stories which reflect the world as early man experienced it. It would be incorrect to think that primitive man saw trees, for instance, as we do. . We see trees as outside us because our minds have been accustomed through language to think of trees as objects, and to investigate and use them. Early man by contrast would have seen something much more like a nymph or a dryad. Such entities are images or archetypes of forces which

37

arise in consciousness. All ancient peoples, it seems, had the experience of being surrounded by spirits. Rather than perceiving a three-dimensional world of objects as we do, they lived in a world of "powers" or "presences" to which they had to relate. Through these experiences the whole world of mythology was built up. The ancient world lived the myths as archetypal forms by which they could structure the universe and interpret experience. They formed a total structure of reality in which reality was symbolised in the form of gods and goddesses and spirits of all kinds. In this way the whole order of nature became present through the myths and their symbols to those who participated in them. This stage of evolution was fundamental among all ancient peoples, and it is important to remember that mythology still largely determines the lives of many tribal and other peoples at the present time. It is, in fact, a basic feature of religious consciousness even among educated people today.

The world of myth is the world of the imagination while the earlier stage, the typhonic, is the world of the emotions. The same stages are apparent in the development of the individual. The child has first a body consciousness and later begins to develop an emotional consciousness in relation to the mother, brothers and sisters and others, while later still the imaginative consciousness develops. From about five years onwards the child lives in the imagination. There was a stage in the development of humanity corresponding to this stage in the development of the individual. At this level the characteristic thought process was what is known as concrete operational thinking. This way of thinking applied to man's practical life. He had to farm and to do his work and he did it with imaginative vision within the context of myth. In many people in India today, for instance, a strong element of mythical thinking is still evident and all the rituals that accompany ploughing and sowing and harvesting, birth and marriage and death, are a survival of mythical consciousness. Until as recently as fifty years ago, this was normal throughout the greater part of India. That is why in every village there is the temple and there are the gods, and the whole village lives its life within that mythological world. This type of consciousness is disappearing as modern education becomes the norm.

This world of symbolic imagination is typical of what is known as palaeological thought. This is thought which is not fully logical and which operates largely with images and symbols. In this mythological world people had not learnt to reason accurately or to make clear logical distinctions, and so all sorts of confusions and superstitions easily came to form part of the worldview. But in spite of the problems associated with this stage of consciousness it was also a time of deep insight.

At this stage of palaeological thinking, it has been suggested, language was paratactic and not syntactic. In other words, clauses were merely put together side by side. There were no complex sentences with subordinate and embedded clauses. Today a child of a few years old can learn a language syntactically. The habit has been formed over thousands of years so that it now comes easily and of course, most importantly, the child will be surrounded by adults who use syntax fluently, but it took thousands of years for language to grow in this way. People had to learn, through their experience, to express themselves with the degree of subtlety only possible through fully developed syntax.

In the verbal membership stage the predominant function of the brain was on the right side. It is generally accepted now that the two hemispheres of the brain function rather differently. The right hemisphere is associated with intuitive, imaginative, symbolic, synthetic activity and the left with thought which is rational, analytical and logical. We at our present stage of development are living almost entirely from

39

the left hemisphere and are therefore "one-sided". True human knowledge is that which is balanced between the two hemispheres. Such knowledge arose only gradually in the course of human development.

The next stage was that once agriculture had been established people began to store up food for the future and the point came when there was a surplus. Then, instead of living from day to day or even from week to week, it was possible to live from year to year. This led to the beginning of exchange and barter, and money in some form came to be introduced as the medium of exchange. With this the whole economy changed and it is here that Karl Marx is right, that as the economy changed, the outlook of the people and the whole social structure changed. Surplus food brought money – and cities. Now instead of tribes hunting their prey and living a nomadic life in order to do so, and instead of small groups cultivating a small area, larger communities sprang up and these developed rapidly. In the valleys of the great rivers, the Nile, the Euphrates, the Indus, and the Yellow River in China, there arose the beginnings of the great city civilisations, vast agricultural enterprises producing quantities of surplus food and money. At this point there emerged a caste of people who had leisure; people, that is, who no longer had to be constantly engaged in providing for their daily needs. With such leisure there arose the beginnings of writing, ideograms, the alphabet, the calendar and the observation of the stars. These developments came principally through the temple, since the worship of the gods was the centre of all human life.

At this stage the world of the gods dominated all human concerns. At the beginning of history there was a sense of simply being one with nature, with the world and with the mother. Then, as the separation from body consciousness took place, there was an intensified consciousness of the Great Mother. There was the experience of having come out

40

of the Mother's womb: the whole world of nature was the womb from which humanity came forth, and nature was experienced as nursing and nourishing her growing child. The religion of the Great Mother is the basis of all the great city civilisations. It is interesting that in Tamil Nadu, in South India, the mother goddess is still the main object of worship in the villages and this is no doubt a survival of the primeval culture of India. With the arrival of the Aryans, who were patriarchal, this matriarchal culture largely gave way to patriarchy and to new forms of worship.

When the individual person gets to this point of development there often arises a series of problems. As a person separates from nature and from the body through language and culture it is very easy to suppress the past. There is the tendency to suppress feelings, emotions and contact with the mother. This is where a great conflict begins. As human consciousness develops more and more powers are released, but dangers are increasingly present.

Wilber makes the very important point here that at every stage there is both differentiation and transcendence. As body consciousness is differentiated from oceanic, then verbal consciousness from the body, mental consciousness from the verbal, and so on, at each stage people not only differentiate from themselves but also transcend the previous state. With transcendence there is increased freedom but there is also the necessity to integrate the former consciousness, and it is precisely with the process of integration that the problem arises. All too often the integration fails. We today experience this particularly at our normal level of mental consciousness. We develop mental consciousness from the earliest age. The child of three or four years old begins to develop its mental consciousness and almost simultaneously there begins the repression of emotional consciousness, sexual consciousness and contact with nature. Serious splits are the result. Most people today live with a mind separated from matter, from

41

the body, from sensations and feelings. Modern man is experiencing all these splits and repressions to a tremendous extent, and it is the resultant disorders deep in the psyche which are the cause of the imbalance of modern society.

Another risk is that as the person separates and gains mental consciousness there is the danger of going back to the mother. This is experienced again and again. Instead of separating from mother and then uniting properly with her in an adult way, people allow themselves to be dragged back to the mother. The child wants to cling to the mother and refuses to become free and separate; and the mother clings to the child, refusing to allow it to grow up and become free. This produced a terrible crisis when the mother was conceived as devouring the child. Mother Nature was always seeking to devour her children, to drag them back into the emotional world, into the world of sex and nature. One of the great struggles that the Hebrew prophets had to engage in was precisely that. All the surrounding peoples were experiencing this attraction of the power of goddesses, which were representations of the Great Mother. So there arose many myths in which the mother is the devourer of the people and the hero is one who is trying to escape and to rescue them from the mother.

It is at this point that the rites of sacrifice underwent a new development. Sacrifice probably began in the typhonic stage and was certainly established in the verbal stage. The meaning of sacrifice is this. Human beings were from the beginning aware of themselves as parts of a cosmic whole. At every level there was spiritual awareness. Even at the very first stage there was a global awareness of the Spirit in all nature. In the typhonic stage there was awareness of the Spirit within the body, in all bodies and in the whole emotional world. Then, as development took place into the imaginative and symbolic world, there was awareness of the

Spirit as expressing itself through those images and symbols which are the origin of the forms of the gods. The gods, in other words, are manifestations of the Spirit in symbolic forms. Then there followed the need to express dependence on that Spirit. Sacrifice, in its proper form, was an expression of dependence on the great Spirit. It may be dependence on the Great Mother, accompanied by the sense that thanks must be expressed to her when she granted a good harvest, or that there was the necessity to pray that she would make it successful. And so at first things are offered. The first fruits of the harvest, for instance, might have been brought and offered to the Mother, to the great goddess. That was genuine sacrifice. But then the danger was that people began to think that it was the thing offered that mattered, rather than their own prayer and thanksgiving.

Then began the terrible phenomenon of human sacrifice. Things went wrong, there was no harvest and starvation abounded. This was interpreted in terms of the Mother being offended, and something had to be done to propitiate her. Goats might have been offered, for instance, but this did not satisfy her. There was still no harvest; the situation is critical. So, the logic ran, a person must offer his own sons and daughters for they are most precious of all. With this reasoning human sacrifice had arrived. An orgy of human sacrifice took place at this time in many cultures. That again was part of the situation against which the Hebrew prophets were protesting. The perceptive could see that when this reasoning was being followed all sacrifices were substitute sacrifices; instead of making the real sacrifice of one's own worship, praise and thanksgiving, substitute gifts were being offered. The story of Abraham is interesting here, for it marks the precise point when humanity discovered that God did not want that kind of sacrifice. Abraham was taught at that point not to sacrifice his son but to offer the ram instead, as a sign. That was the exact point at which human sacrifice

43

was surpassed in Israel, while up to that time it was part of the cult.

At this stage came war. Previously, war was unknown. In the earlier uroboric state war was inconceivable, and at the typhonic stage there was general harmony between the tribes punctuated only by occasional incidences of tribal conflict. It is very interesting that among animals, as well as among primitive human beings, although there is often conflict and they may fight they never totally destroy one another. Animals will fight for territory, for instance, but they do not annihilate one another in the process. It is only human beings, and advanced ones at that, who deliberately annihilate one another. The tragedy is that as higher powers develop the possibilities of misusing them more effectively increase. At this stage of development there took place the most terrible wars.

Assyrian kings, for instance, boasted of how many cities they had sacked and of how many men, women and children they had killed, or conquered and made slaves. A terrible power began to grow up when man had separated from nature and had begun to discover his own power; it is this that marked the development of the ego mentality.

Returning to the stages in the development of consciousness, it must be appreciated that these cannot be sharply differentiated from one another, though it is helpful to see them as successive stages in a gradual evolutionary process. The next major stage was that of mental consciousness when, through language, it became possible to go beyond mere words to logical thought. The ability to think logically was a great breakthrough. It took place at a very late date, beginning probably not earlier than 1000 BC becoming established in about 500 or 600 BC. The rise of the Upanishads and the Buddha in India and the beginning of Greek and Chinese philosophy are dated around 600 BC. At that stage people began to think rationally, whereas previously symbolic thought had predominated.

The development of logical thought is correlated with the development of the brain. The human brain has three levels: the reptilian level, the limbic brain and the neo-cortex. The reptilian level corresponds with our most basic consciousness, our unity with nature, with matter, with life and the emotional world. With the limbic brain, which developed later, the faculties of imagination and symbolic thought emerged. The most recent level, the neo-cortex, although present in human beings from the beginning, now developed prodigiously, covering the two earlier layers. This is where the rational functions take place and it is at that point in evolution that the ego began to develop. Until that time there was no consciousness of oneself as a separate individual; one belonged to one's family, to one's tribe, to the world around. This was beautiful in its way but it could only be a passing stage. In growing out of and beyond it there had to be the development of an ego. The ego, however, as we shall see, is the great obstacle as well as the great means of progress.

With the development of the ego came the discovery of the power to control oneself and the world around. With the discovery of control the whole structure of sacrifice became distorted. Instead of sacrificing oneself, one's ego, to God, the Supreme, and receiving gifts, substitute sacrifices were made. The aim became the strengthening of the ego and the more people and things that could be sacrificed, the more people who could be killed in war, the greater the build-up of power and the stronger the ego.

It is at this point that the myth of the hero arises. The hero was the one who fought many battles, overcame enemies and achieved some great work. This heroic stage is also the point at which patriarchy began to dominate. Up to now societies had been mainly matriarchal. In agriculture the mother was certainly central. It was she who did the work in the fields, sowing, planting and harvesting. And it was Mother Earth who in the same process was giving of her gifts. But now the father came to the fore, developing this great ego and becoming associated with authority and power.

This is also the stage of the human person's separation from nature. The man, as male and as father, is essentially separate. In man-woman relationships the man inseminates the woman but it is significant that after that initial act the man is quite free of the child. It is the woman who has to bear the child and she is responsible for it. And so the child is bound up with the mother and only later begins to relate to the father who is always, as it were, outside. The mother relates within, supporting the child; the father is separate and outside, challenging and drawing the child out. That then was the beginning of the patriarchal age, the age of the heroes, and in many ways we are still in this stage. It began about 2000 BC so for around four thousand years we have been living in a patriarchal culture. This has profoundly affected all our religion as well as everything else. Why in Christianity do we have only a male deity? It is because we belong to a patriarchal culture. Only now are we beginning to see that there are feminine aspects in God which are just as important as masculine. God is neither male nor female and can just as easily be called mother as father. Although we are still deeply involved in patriarchal structures, many people today feel that we are moving into an age where the patriarchal and the matriarchal, the masculine and the feminine, will once more come together in balance and harmony.

During this patriarchal stage there emerged consciousness of self, whereas previously people had not been self-conscious at all. Self-consciousness is correlated with the development of ego and it marks a considerable advance. Self-consciousness had to arise in order that people could know themselves apart from others and be themselves. It is there-

46

fore quite appropriate for children at a certain stage of development to become somewhat aggressive and to try out their powers and explore their world, relating everything to themselves. It becomes disastrous after childhood, however, if the person goes on and on building up the ego and exploiting other people. So the growth of the ego is necessary but is highly dangerous when pursued into the later stages of life.

At this stage of mental consciousness there arises the concept of linear time as distinguished from cyclic time. We have seen how the sense of time gradually grew, but in all ancient culture time was experienced as cyclic because it was connected with the course of nature where everything goes in cycles, the sun rising and setting, the moon waxing and waning, the seasons following one another. All ancient cultures, including the whole Indian culture up to practically the present time, had a cyclic view of life. But at this stage begins the linear view of time with the idea that the past is moving into the present and the present into the future. The linear view was developed particularly by the Hebrews. Along with the linear view of time there arose a particular historical consciousness. Prior to this there was no history. Herodotus, the Greek historian par excellence, lived in the sixth century BC. India had very little history at all at this time. It was the Hebrews particularly who developed a sense of history; though the patriarchs and even Moses belong to a large extent to a legendary time, with Samuel, David and Solomon we are well into the period of historic time.

At this level of mental consciousness when the mind experiences itself as separate from the body, there is a great danger of repression and this is where the so-called demonic forces come into play. What happens is that natural energies like sex and anger, for instance, are repressed. Having been relegated to the unconscious, they may be experienced as demons or devils. The concept of demons and devils arises

47

when the ego is trying to repress unacceptable parts of the self. A hostile force is experienced within, and when repression continues that may be projected outside and experienced as coming from outside. To that experience the name demon or devil is given. But these experiences occur not merely in the individual soul but in the collective unconscious, so that they are experienced as cosmic forces.

We are still in the period of the development of mental consciousness. Normal people today have all, from childhood, developed first from the uroboric stage through the typhonic, through the verbal, to the discovery of the ego. The danger is in stopping at the level of the ego and the mental consciousness. Most people at the present stage of development do stop at this point, not envisioning that there is anything beyond. Stopping at the mental, rational consciousness, with science and technology seen as the highest achievement, the ego is exalted as the centre. Everything is referred to the ego, the centre of the individual self, and life is lived as if there is nothing beyond that. Western materialist philosophy has contributed largely to this arrested development and most of Western science and philosophy is being kept down at that level. But this is precisely where the East has gone far beyond the West and has developed the understanding and experience of transpersonal consciousness. In the next chapter we shall be considering how this developed in India, in Hinduism in particular. In the fifth and sixth centuries before Christ there took place in the East the breakthrough beyond the mental consciousness and beyond the ego to the the transegoic, transmental consciousness. That is the supreme achievement of the human race, when, beyond the ego, we opened ourselves to the transcendent.

There is, however, an intermediate stage which needs to be examined here. It is not simply a matter of immediate transcendence to the Ultimate. Between the mental con-

48

sciousness and the supramental there is what can be called the psychic or subtle world. The Hindu speaks of the gross world, which includes everything which can be known through the gross or ordinary senses, and of the subtle world which is beyond the ordinary senses. In this subtle realm there operate the subtle senses, clairvoyance and clairaudience for example. These are definite faculties, transmental, psychic faculties, which in the ancient world were in fact quite normal. It was not at all unusual to see visions of angels or gods, and to experience fairies, elves and goblins. These are visionary experiences of the psychic faculty. We need to understand that the psychic world is interwoven with the physical world. There is a complete physical world with the whole range of physical causality and structure which science explores, but interwoven with that is the psychic world which is perceived through our psychic, rather than physical, faculties. Westerners today have largely lost these psychic powers whereas all ancient peoples, in India and elsewhere, lived to a large extent in that psychic world. But we are beginning to recover it. All over the world today people are discovering this realm of psychic experience. There needs to be a warning here that entering the subtle realm has its own particular dangers. Every advance is accompanied by dangers which have to be faced, and at this level there is still both good and evil.

The phenomena indicative of the subtle level of consciousness are well-established and parapsychology, which is concerned with these phenomena, is now a recognised science. Associated with this level, apart from the subtle senses themselves, there are, for example, telepathy, experiencing events at a distance, and knowledge of the past and future. The latter is very common in India where, for instance, palmistry and astrology may be the means by which such knowledge is concretised. The phenomenon referred to as astral travel is also well-known in India. There are many

49

reports of yogis appearing to their followers at a distance and talking with them. Sai Baba is a contemporary example of this and many people report how he has appeared to them and spoken with them or helped them in some way, when all the time he is physically in his ashram at Puttaparthi.

Another series of phenomena at the subtle level are the *siddhis*, which are all based on the control of matter by the mind. These have been developed by Sai Baba to an extraordinary extent and have been observed by multitudes of peoples, many of whom are qualified scientists and psychologists. These powers are latent in all of us. They are not properly supernatural but are present, at least latently, in human nature as such.

Powers of this kind were common in the earlier stages of human development and are seen in the phenomenon of shamanism. Shamanism has recently been studied extensively and has been found to occur all over the world, among the Arctic people, the American Indians and in India. A shaman is a person who develops psychic powers for the good of his community and he is usually an odd person who does not fit in with the ordinary way of life. He or she begins to have dreams and visions and he cultivates these. Among the American Indians a boy who is developing shamanistic powers has to go through an initiatory ceremony. He might, for instance, be taken out alone to a hill where a pit would be dug and he would have to stay three days and three nights in that pit without food or water or any companionship at all. Through that experience he is expected to receive a vision of the gods, of the powers which are thought to control the world. Once the shaman's psychic powers are developed he becomes a healer and a guide to the community. The same kind of thing happens in India in the villages, where there is usually someone who has psychic powers to whom the villagers go for help. Sometimes those shamanic people are frauds and they may be dangerous, but they may also be quite genuine. This then is the realm of the psychic powers and is the level where extraordinary control over the body can be achieved. In yoga, in particular Tantric yoga, these powers have been systematically developed, and not only the breathing but even the circulation of the blood and the beating of the heart can be controlled.

The subtle level is also the world of the elemental spirits. The ancient peoples were aware of the world around them as inhabited by spirits; in other words, they were as much aware of the psychic world as of the physical. Their knowledge of the physical world was of a limited kind compared with ours today, but they had a vast knowledge and experience of the psychic world and they communicated this in the form of images. We must not be misled by the idea of angels with wings and devils with horns and hoofs; these are only images which the psyche calls up in different forms in different people. The Hindu people, for instance, represent gods with many arms. These, and all the other representations of the gods, are simply images but behind the images are the powers, the elemental powers of the universe, which St Paul calls the *stoicheia*. These are, first, the ever-present elemental powers of earth, water, fire and air. Then there are the powers of plant and animal life, of ghosts and ancestors. At a higher level the powers of heaven, the angels and the gods, and finally the supreme God, the supreme Person beyond. In this way the whole religious world was built up through psychic experience. In the Bible this psychic element is always present; for instance in Exodus, when Moses saw the burning bush, it was a psychic experience. The column of fire and of light which followed the Israelites through the wilderness was a psychic or subtle phenomenon. Again when Elijah went up into the mountain and there was thunder and lightning, and an earthquake and finally "a still, small voice", the experience he had there of Yahweh was in this higher, subtle level of consciousness. There is evidence of this kind of experience right through the Old Testament and the figure of Yahweh was a development from experiences at this level. We must distinguish between the subtle, or psychic, and the spiritual, and we shall see how the subtle level of consciousness is the basis for, and is followed by, the spiritual level.

But we must always remember that on the psychic level there are both good and evil forces. Just as there is violence and destruction on the physical plane, so there are forces of violence and destruction on the psychic plane. The gods and angels are symbols of cosmic powers, which work through the whole universe and through human history. These are the "principalities and powers in high places" of which St Paul speaks. When these forces are subject to the Supreme Power, they act as creative forces in nature and in history. But when they become separated from the Supreme and act independently, they become demonic and destructive. A beautiful illustration of this is given in the Kena Upanishad, where it is said that once the gods won a victory over other powers and attributed the victory to themselves. But Brahman, the Supreme Power, then appeared to them and revealed that it was through him alone that they had gained the victory. In the Hebrew tradition also the "gods of the nations" are seen as fallen angels, daemonic powers which have rebelled against the Supreme God. It is always by rejection of the Supreme Being, the ultimate Truth, that human beings become subject to daemonic forces. In modern times Hitler and Stalin can be seen as instruments of these daemonic powers.

This then, was the world of the gods and the angels, leading up to the Supreme God and the function of all the prophets was to assert the authority of the Supreme Being over all other gods. In Israel Yahweh was realised by Moses to be the Supreme God. In Greece Zeus was understood as the Supreme God who was seen by Aeschylus as essentially a moral being, though Zeus could never attain to the level of a fully transcendent god. In Islam the Supreme Being was revealed as Allah and Islam has borne witness to the One God ever since. But in our understanding and interpretation of the Bible it is important to be aware of the development of this psychic dimension and of the images to which it gave rise in the unfolding of ancient religion.

This whole stage of psychic development belongs to what Wilber, using Buddhist terminology, calls the *sambhogakaya*. In this system there are three levels corresponding to the three bodies of the Buddha, the *nirmanakaya*, the *sambhogakaya* and the *dharmakaya*. The *nirmanakaya* was the body of the Buddha's manifestation in this world and is what is called the gross body. Then the Buddha had the subtle body of the *sambhogakaya* level. The *bodhisattvas* and the *dhyani buddhas* also belong here to the *sambhogakaya*. In philosophical terms, these psychic powers were conceived as the world of ideas. Plato, for instance, held that while matter and forms together structure the physical world the source of form is what he termed the ideas, and they are eternal. Eternal ideas of all things exist in the eternal world and are reflected in this world, in our human experience and in the physical world around us. Plotinus, in the Neoplatonism of the third century AD, developed Plato's philosophical understanding and speaks of two levels here, the world soul and the *nous*. The world soul is the power which brings into being and sustains the universe and it is intermediate between the *nous* and the physical world. In the *nous* the forms of all things exist eternally, prior to being manifested in the temporal world through the world soul, in the forms of nature and of man. In Hinduism the psychic world, the world of the gods, is known as the Mahat, the Great World, and the world soul is conceived as Hiranyagarbha, the Golden Seed. A similar understanding with variations is more or less universal.

Thus in the perennial philosophy there is the concept of

a physical world based on matter and of a mental world of forms and concepts comprising the whole realm of human understanding, and then beyond that the world of ideas, the transcendent reality. At this level there is still duality; it is still a matter of this world and the world of "ideas", for the *sambhogakaya* is not the final stage of consciousness. We can go into that state of consciousness, and initially in meditation the aim is to go beyond the *nirmanakaya* to the *sambhogakaya*, beyond gross experience to the subtle. We can go through various levels of the subtle to experience the presence of God and the angels and saints; all this belongs to the *sambhogakaya*. But beyond the *sambhogakaya* is the *dharmakaya*, the body of reality. The Buddha's supreme being is the *dharmakaya* and this is the supreme consciousness.

It is the view of Wilber and others that there is, as it were, a spectrum of levels of consciousness, from the basic oceanic consciousness, through all the levels right up to the supreme consciousness. The levels are hierarchically structured in such a way that the lower levels are integrated with the higher. At every point of transcendence there has to be differentiation from the previous level and integration of it. So at the level of mental consciousness one differentiates from the level of the imagination and one opens oneself to the world of concepts, logic, reason, science and philosophy, then one has to integrate the previous level of the imagination, and the senses. There should be no rejection of the other levels nor should they be left behind. Particularly, in going beyond the mental consciousness into the *sambhogakaya*, there must be integration of the mental consciousness. If the mental consciousness is not integrated, the result can be madness. Exploration of this psychic world of angels, spirits, demons and other entities, without retaining and integrating mental consciousness, can result literally in losing one's reason. Because of this it is very dangerous to enter into the *sambhogakaya* without proper guidance.

54

That is why in meditation when one goes into that subtle world it is important to have a teacher, a guru who will guide and direct progress. But in meditation the aim is always to go beyond this subtle psychic world, the world of ideas, of gods and angels, and to enter the *dharmakaya*, the realm of ultimate reality, which is beyond duality. In the ultimate reality all levels of previous experience are integrated. This means that, just as mental consciousness has to be transcended and integrated in experience of the *sambhogakaya*, so when one goes beyond the *sambhogakaya*, that level also has to be integrated into the experience of the transcendent. The importance of integration is often misunderstood, and it is frequently thought that on reaching the level of non-dual awareness everything disappears and there is simply pure identity of being, *saccidananda*, being, knowledge and bliss, without any differentiation. But the truth is that all the lower levels of consciousness have to be taken up into the Supreme and that is what constitutes total realisation, that is, realisation of the total reality. Boethius, the great sixth-century Christian philosopher, said that eternity is *tota et simul possessio interminabilis vitae*, the total simultaneous possession of unending life. The total reality is present simultaneously. On reaching that final state a person "realises" the whole creation. At the lower stages we know the forms of things but our knowledge through science, philosophy and ordinary experience is always of objects and persons separated in space and time. When we enter into the *sambhogakaya*, to a higher, more subtle level of consciousness, we get a deeper awareness of the reality of these forms and their ideas; we discover the eternal realities behind the forms. But now we can go beyond the ideas into the Godhead itself, the Ultimate, and there all is gathered together in the One. The Godhead is the Supreme Reality in which the whole creation and every human being in the creation and every experience in the whole universe is gathered into total unity. This is what Nicholas of Cusa called the *coincidentia oppositorium*, the "co-incidence of opposites" in ultimate truth. And that is the ultimate goal of life, to reach that total unity where we experience the whole creation and the whole of humanity reintegrated in the supreme consciousness, in the One, which is pure being, pure knowledge and pure bliss, *saccidananda*.

3

The Eastern Vision of the Universe

Having considered the nature of the physical world and the psychological universe according to Western science and Western psychology, the next stage is to examine the oriental vision of the universe. I take the Hindu vision because it is best known to me, although the Buddhist or Islamic understanding would be equally revealing.

We begin with the pre-Vedic period, before the Aryan invasion which is believed to have taken place in the second millennium BC. In India from about 4000 BC there was a culture akin to that of Egypt and Mesopotamia, which were both matriarchal and worshipped the Mother Goddess. At Mohenjo-Daro there are relics of that culture amongst which is an interesting figure generally believed to be a representation of Shiva, or of the god who was later to become Shiva in the Hindu tradition. He is called Pasupati, the Lord of animals, and he is seated in the lotus posture with animals in front of him and with some sign of a *lingam*, the symbol of Shiva in later times. So the probability is that Shaivism, the worship of Shiva, which is one of the main schools of Hinduism, derived from the pre-Aryan culture. This is supported by the fact that Shiva is a dark god; he dwells in the mountains and deserts and graveyards. At first outside the civilised world of the Aryans, he was later taken in and became one of the principal forms of God.

With the Aryan invasion in the second millennium, there arose the beginnings of a patriarchal culture. It is believed that the Aryan invasion started from what is now South Russia and spread both East and West, involving in the

West the Greek, Latin, Germanic and Celtic peoples, and in the East, the people of Persia and India. This was historically the beginning of the new mental culture which was considered in the last chapter. Signifying as it did the awakening of the mind, this was one of the supreme moments in human history. From the world of the imagination and of myth there began the great passage into the world of reason and understanding, the world of the mind. In the Vedas this transition is evident; both stages are represented and the new development is seen to emerge out of its mythological background.

The Vedas are generally considered to be the most ancient form of poetry in the world, and are concerned with the whole range of the gods and their worship. These gods are the cosmic powers of St Paul referred to in the previous chapter. It is important to notice, however, that although there were many gods, representing all the powers present in the cosmos, there was always the tendency to relate these powers to one another and to see them as one. The human mind has always this urge to unify, to see the one behind the many. In the first book of the Rig Veda in fact the gods are recognised to be the names and forms of the one Being (*ekam sat*), who has no name and no form. That is basic Hindu doctrine.

In the Vedic vision there is the understanding that there are three worlds, the physical, the psychological and the spiritual. It is very significant that the people of the ancient world of the Vedas never separated these aspects. The whole universe was seen to be one, but manifesting at three levels. Nothing, therefore, in the physical world was considered to be merely material. As was shown in chapter one, a major outcome of the development of Western science was the separation of the material from the psychological and the spiritual. Material phenomena came to be observed in isolation and apart from the psychological world, so that science came to concentrate on the merely quantitative aspects of matter. This was valid in its way but it limited the investigator to a very narrow sphere of reality, and when that narrow sphere was taken for the whole of reality the result was a tragic illusion. This is what is known in Hindu tradition as *avidya* (ignorance) and *maya*. This is exactly what took place in the Western world.

In the thinking of the ancients the three worlds of the Vedas were always seen to be interwoven. A good example of this, in terms of which it can be explained, is the god Agni, the god of fire. Fire, of course, is physical. In the Vedas it is quite clear that Agni at one level is the physical fire, the fire which was lit at the sacrifice. This fire also has a wider physical aspect, for it is the energy which works through the universe and manifests as fire. But at the same time it has a psychological aspect, being the fire of life and the fire of the mind. Agni is said to know everything. We would never think of fire as "knowing", but to these ancients the fire had a psychological aspect; it is the all-knower. As the fire of the mind, it is the energy which rises up within us and manifests itself in thought. Thirdly, as there was the physical aspect of Agni and the psychological aspect, so there was also a spiritual aspect. Both the physical and the psychological were understood as manifestations of the one supreme Spirit, which is manifesting at all levels of the universe.

The Vedic understanding of the three integrated worlds, physical, psychological and spiritual, is typical of the whole ancient world which had emerged out of the mythological world of more ancient times. The vision of an integrated universe was lost at the Renaissance; today we are trying to recover it. In our Western style of thinking we have separated matter from mind, and have separated both matter and mind from the Supreme Reality, from God, or whatever name is given to it. In the ancient vision there could be no separation of matter from mind or of matter and mind from the Supreme Spirit, which in India came to be known as Brahman, that which holds everything together.

The Vedic concept that fire is the origin of the universe is particularly interesting because first of all, from the point of view of modern science, it is held that when the universe originally exploded into being it was as a burst of energy at an extremely high temperature in which nothing separate could exist; it was pure fire. Only gradually did the heat diminish, allowing matter to be formed out of that fire. The ancient Eastern world had this view that fire was the origin of all things. In the same way the Greek philosopher Heraclitus said that fire is the origin of all things and is working through all things. Fire is obviously a form of energy, and thus the ancient world arrived at the concept of energy working through both the physical and the psychological world and having its source in the transcendent world beyond. So fire is the source of all. There is a beautiful verse in the Vedas which says, "The fire which is the sun, the fire which is the earth, that fire is in my own heart".[1] There we have the precise doctrine: the fire in the sun above, the fire in the earth beneath and the fire in our own heart constitute the three worlds. It is expressed in terms of images where heaven is the spiritual world, earth is the material world and the human being is the psychological world which stands between the two.

The Vedic religion centered on the fire of sacrifice, the *yajna*. A very elaborate altar was built according to specific rules. Fuel was put on the altar and lit and then sacrifices were offered in the fire. The idea behind the ritual was that fire comes down from heaven; fire is in heaven above and it is centred in the sun. Coming down from heaven, the fire is buried in the earth. It is underneath the earth, as we know today it is, within the earth's crust. When the sticks or stones were rubbed together or struck, the fire burst forth and Agni carried these gifts back to heaven. Because of this Agni was known as the mediator between heaven and earth, the priest who took the sacrifice and offered it to the gods above. This, then, is the eternal living fire which exists in heaven and comes down to earth, and the sacrifice is the returning of all things on earth to their source in heaven. This returning of all things to their source is called turning the wheel of the law, the *dharma chakra*.

In the Vedic view, if we live constantly returning things to their source, then we are living in the harmony of the universe, the rhythm, *rita*, of the universe. Conversely, if we do not turn the wheel of the law, if we appropriate things to ourselves, then we are committing sin. Sin is separating oneself from the order of the universe, making oneself an isolated person. To separate oneself in isolation is to go against the law of the universe, while sacrifice puts one in harmony with the universe and with the sacred fire, or energy, which is working in the heaven above and in the earth beneath, and which is working in one's own body. There is a familiar verse in the *Bhagavad Gita* which says, "I, the Lord, become the fire of life and seated in the body I consume the four kinds of food."[2] That fire, which is in the heaven above and in the earth beneath, is in our own bodies; we offer our food in sacrifice in that inner fire and it is consumed in the fire and surrendered to God again. So a meal is a sacrifice. The *Bhagavad Gita* says that anyone taking a meal without sacrificing is a thief; this is to take the gifts of God and appropriate them to oneself instead of receiving them as gifts and returning thanks.[3]

The name given to the transcendent reality which is manifesting through the whole universe was *brahman*. The root of the word *brahman* means to swell, to grow, and it is thought today that the original meaning was that it was the word which grew or swelled up in one. When offering the sacrifice one felt something welling up within, and when one

61

uttered the word it was something very powerful. Language was seen as the means by which human beings related themselves to the universe and words were sacred. To utter a word was to put forth power. Even to name somebody was to have power over him. People did not like one to know their name, for knowing a person's name gave one power over him. That is also why, in the book of Exodus, when Moses asks, "What is your name?" the response of God is, "Why do you ask me what is my name?" The name is power. So the word uttered in the sacrifice, expressing the meaning of the sacrifice, was *brahman*. This was probably the original meaning of the term. Then, because that word and the accompanying sacrifice sustains the universe the word *brahman* came to mean that power which sustains the universe. In this way there began the development of the concept of the universal power or energy, originally conceived as fire, which pervades the whole universe, the heaven above, the earth beneath and our own bodies and minds, and expresses itself in the word (*vac*) which contains within itself the power of life. In this way OM came to be conceived as the great word, the *pranava*, which expresses the whole meaning of reality.

After the *Rig Veda* came the *Brahmanas*, treatises on the sacrifice. The *Rig Veda* is generally dated at about 1500 BC and the *Brahmanas* about 1200 BC. The sacrifice was the most sacred act and the ritual came to be very elaborate. Eventually it became almost a kind of magic. Magic is typical of an early stage of religion in the ancient world and always tends to survive in later stages of religion. Something is magical when the people using it feel that it has power in itself. And so with sacrifice, instead of being conceived as something coming from above and being the means of a person's surrendering to that which is above, it came to be regarded as having power in itself such that if the right ritual was performed then the right effect would be achieved.

Magic always depends on doing certain rituals and believing that those rituals will have an inevitable effect. There is then a certain magical character in the *Brahmanas*.

The third stage was that of the *Aranyakas*, the Forest Books, perhaps about 800 BC. This was the turning point, certainly in the history of India and to some extent in the history of the world. Here there took place the great breakthrough from the ancient, mythological, ritualistic religion to the discovery of the inner self. This happened when the *rishis*, or seers, instead of offering sacrifices in an external fire retired to the forest to meditate and began to build up the fire within. The idea grew that instead of building a fire outside and offering objects symbolically outside the body, they could build the fire within, offering sacrifice in the inner fire of the body. Now everything had to be offered in that inner fire, sins, thoughts, fears, desires, life itself. This was the point where, out of the external religion, the interior religion which had always been there began to be realised. For this reason it was a crucial period for it was here that a new psychology emerged, along with a new understanding of man and the universe. This emergence occurred in the *Upanishads* but it took place also at almost the same time in Sakyamuni Buddha, who made the same breakthrough beyond the physical world and beyond the psychological world to the reality beyond.

At the same time Greek philosophers, Heraclitus and others, were discovering the mind or *logos* as the basis of the universe, and the Hebrew prophets, Isaiah, Jeremiah and Ezekiel, were simultaneously discovering the reality of the transcendent God. This was a key period in human history, and practically all religion today stems from this great experience of the fifth and sixth centuries before Christ.

In this way then the seers of the Upanishads began to meditate and they made the great discovery that this *brahman*, this power in the universe, this power which was

63

believed to be in the sacrifice which sustained the universe, this power is within each person. The *mahavakya*, the great saying of the Upanishads, is *prajnanam brahman*, "Brahman is consciousness". That was a tremendous step, for it was a movement beyond the physical world. *Brahman* was understood previously to be manifesting in all the universe, in the heaven and the earth, and in man; *brahman* is everywhere. But now came the discovery that *brahman*, that reality without, is one with one's own inner consciousness. This is the awakening of the inner self for the first time. Previously man had been living in the outer universe and experiencing God, *brahman*, the reality, in that outside universe but not in himself. Now man discovered himself. The word for self is *atman*, so now it is said, *ayam atman brahmanasti*, "That self is Brahman", meaning that this self which I discern within me, is one with *brahman*, one with the reality of the universe outside me. The third great saying or *mahavakya* is, *aham brahmasmi*, "I am Brahman". This means that if I go to the depths of my being, beyond my body, beyond my thoughts and my feelings, I discover the "I", the *atman*, and come to know that *brahman* in myself, as my true being. The fourth *mahavakya* is, *Tat Tvam asi*, "Thou art that". It occurs in the *Chandogya Upanishad* where the guru tells the disciple to take a fruit from a tree, break it open and then take a seed and break it open, and he asks the disciple what he can see. The disciple says, "I see nothing," to which the guru replies, "In that nothing, that hidden essence which you cannot see, the power of the growth of the whole tree consists." So also there is a secret essence in all creation, in everything which exists, which is the source of all being; and "Thou, Svetaketu, art that."[4] In other words, the source of the universe around us is the source of our own being. This was the great breakthrough of the Upanishads, and still today in India these four *mahavakyas* are considered the supreme wisdom of the Vedas.

64

It was in the sixth century that the *Aranyakas* gave way to the Upanishads, the last stage of the Vedas, or Vedanta, as it is called. The Upanishads are the discourses of the *rishis* to their disciples, revealing the great discovery that had been made. The *Brihadaranyaka Upanishad*, which is the earliest we have, gives the greatest insight into this understanding of the universe in terms of *brahman*. There are two particularly important sayings. The first is, "Verily in the beginning this was Brahman, one only".[5] This is a very important insight, for what it means is that behind the phenomena of the universe, behind all the phenomena of human existence, the *rishis* had discovered the *brahman*. They had found the source of the universe and the source of humanity. In the beginning was that *brahman*, one only, and the whole physical and psychological universe comes forth from the one. That was the profound insight that was reached at this time.

The second saying is, "In the beginning this was atman alone in the form of Purusha", or, "This was the Self, the Spirit alone, in the form of a Person".[6] So there were three words now to describe this ultimate Reality. The first was *brahman*. When you look at the world around you, you see the source of all in *brahman*. The second word is *atman*. You look within yourself and you see that the source of your own being and consciousness is the *atman*, and that the *atman* is one with *brahman*. Thirdly, there is the conception of the whole universe as being a great person, a *purusha*, who contains the whole universe in himself. The *purusha* occurs in the *Purusha Shukta* of the *Rig Veda*, where it says, "A thousand heads has Purusha, a thousand eyes, a thousand feet, on every side, pervading the earth."[7] This *purusha* is the supreme Person who fills the whole creation. A thousand is the sign of completeness, perfection. All the creation is filled with this *purusha*. It goes on, "This Purusha is all that has been and all that will be, the Lord of immortality." Then it

65

says, "With three fourths Purusha is in heaven; one fourth is here on earth." This means that this *purusha* transcends the whole creation with regard to three fourths of his being and he is immanent in creation with one fourth. There is here the concept of a unified creation which has the character of a person who embraces the whole universe and at the same time transcends it. So *brahman*, *atman* and *purusha* are the three terms for ultimate Reality.

Brahman is the ground, the source, of everything. There is a beautiful illustration of this in the *Brihadaranyaka Upanishad* where Yagnavalkya, one of the great sages, is talking with Gargi, his wife. Women at this stage took part in discussions on equal terms with men although later they were not even allowed to read the Vedas. Here Gargi asks Yajnavalkya, "Everthing here is woven like warp and woof in water, then what is that in which the water is woven like warp and woof?" The point of this question was the attempt to discover the source of the universe. A very common view was to say that it all came from water. In the Greek philosophers there was the same questioning as to the origin of the universe, and often the same answers. Thales, for instance, in the seventh century, said that everything comes from water. It is a simple idea because water is liquid, but when heated it becomes vapour and when frozen it is solid, so water embraces the three states of matter. Later, Anaximines asserted that everything comes from air. Later still Heraclitus said that everything comes from fire and finally Empedocles held that everything comes from the four elements, the earth, the air, the fire and the water. In this way the Greeks built up their understanding of the universe. The same kind of process is taking place here. Gargi said, "Everything here is woven like warp and woof in water. In what is the water woven?" And Yajnavalkya replied, "In the air, O Gargi." She continued, "Then in what is the air woven like warp and woof?" and he replied, "In the sky, Gargi." Then she

66

said, "In what is the sky woven?" to which he replied, "In the *gandharvas*," which means the spirits.

This is going beyond the physical to the psychological world, the world of the spirits and angels. Gargi then asked, "In what is the world of the *gandharvas* woven?" and he replied, "In the world of the gods, O Gargi". Then she asked, "In what is the world of the gods woven?" "In the worlds of Indra," he replied. Indra is the supreme god, so there is an upward progression from the spirits, to the gods, to the Supreme. Gargi then asked, "In what are the worlds of Indra woven?" and Yajnavalkya replied, "In the world of Prajapati, O Gargi." Prajapati is the lord of creation. Gargi asked again, "In what are the worlds of Prajapati woven, O Yajnavalkya?" and he replied, "In the worlds of Brahman." She then asked, "In what are the worlds of Brahman woven like warp and woof?" to which he responded, "O Gargi, do not ask too much lest thy head should fall off."[8] That means that there is no going beyond *brahman*; *brahman* is the limit.

This is a beautiful example of how at this stage the ancients were investigating the universe, asking, "What does it all come from?" "How is it built up?" "What is the source?" It is very elementary in a way, but to see here the human mind first asking these questions makes it fascinating.

Brahman, then is the ground in which the whole creation is woven. Everything comes out from *brahman*, emerging as from a source. The text says, "As the spider comes out with its thread or as small sparks come forth from fire, thus do all the senses, all the world, all gods and all being come forth from that Spirit." It is the source. The text goes on to say, "That Atman is the *satyasya satya*", which means "the truth of the truth", "the real of the real."[9] The world of the senses is real, but the *atman* is the reality behind the senses. It is the source behind the sense world. In this context the terms *brahman* and *atman* are interchangeable.

So *brahman* is the source, *brahman* is the ground in which everything is woven, but *brahman* is also the end towards which everything is moving. This truth appears again in connection with Yajnavalkya, who had another wife called Maitreyi. This is interesting because Yajnavalkya was going into the forest to become a *vanaprastha*. After an appropriate time of married life the practice was to retire to the forest to meditate. Yajnavalkya wants to make a settlement with Maitreyi so he says to her, "I am going away into the forest, therefore let me make a settlement with thee." And she said, "My Lord, if this whole earth full of wealth belonged to me, should I be immortal by it"? "No," replied Yajnavalkya, "like the life of rich people will be thy life." In other words, there is no hope of gaining immortality by wealth. Maitreyi responded, "What should I do with that by which I do not become immortal? What my Lord knows, tell me that." Here they have gone beyond the desire for wealth, awakening to the desire for immortality. So he accepts her, and this is what he says, "Verily a husband is not dear that you should love the husband but that you may love the Atman, the Spirit, the Self; therefore a husband is dear. Not for the sake of the wife is the wife dear but for the sake of the Spirit, the Self; therefore a wife is dear. Not for the sake of sons are sons dear, but for the sake of the Self."[10] This means that everything that is loved in this world has to be loved not for itself alone but for the sake of that eternal Spirit which is manifesting in it. *Brahman*, or *atman*, is the source, the ground and the end of all human endeavour. It is the Supreme Reality, which embraces everything. The whole creation is pervaded by *brahman* and contained within it.

The *Brihadaranyaka Upanishad* goes on to say that it is impossible to speak properly of this *brahman*, this *atman*, this *purusha*, for it is beyond words. This *brahman* or *atman* is *neti neti*, "not this, not this." No created thing can express *brahman*. It, or he, is always beyond words and beyond thought: it is the one reality. So this is the breakthrough beyond the physical and beyond the psychological, to the transcendent reality which embraces both the physical and the psychological and which fills the whole creation. That is the concept of the *brahman* in the Upanishads.

In the *Chandogya Upanishad* there is a description of the city of Brahman, conceived as the human body. The *brahman*, and in a sense the whole creation, is present in everybody and everything. So, "Within the city of Brahman, the human body, there is a small shrine. And in that shrine there is a lotus and in that lotus there is a small space. What exists in that small space in the heart of the lotus, that is to be understood." It goes on to say, "As large as is the space which contains the whole universe, so large is that space within the heart. Both heaven and earth are contained within it, fire and air, sun and moon, and lightning and stars; whatever there is here in the world, and whatever is not, all that is contained within it."[11] So the whole universe is within each of us, as we saw in the last chapter. The whole universe is contained within consciousness. When one goes beyond the outer world of the senses where one is just part of the external universe, one discovers the inner reality and experiences that the whole universe is within. That is the profound insight which was reached in India at this period.

In a later Upanishad, the *Katha Upanishad*, dated at about 500 BC there is a further understanding of this hierarchy of being. The text reads, "Beyond the senses there are the objects, beyond the objects there is the mind, beyond the mind there is the intellect, beyond the intellect is the great self, beyond the great self is the Unmanifest, beyond the Unmanifest there is Purusha, the Person."[12] This maps out the structure of the universe as it was conceived at this time. First of all there are the objects of the senses, then the senses themselves which observe the world around. Beyond the

69

senses there is the *manas*, the mind, which works through the senses. When anything is observed, the senses register the impressions, the sense data, but the mind interprets what the senses register. Beyond the *manas* is the *buddhi*, which is the intellect as distinguished from the reason. Thomas Aquinas speaks of the *intellectus* and the *ratio*, and in Greek thinking there is a similar distinction between *nous*, the intellect, and *dianoia*, the reason. In Sanskrit there is the *buddhi*, the intellect or intelligence, and the *manas*, the active reason. The *buddhi* is the pure intelligence which opens us to the source of reality. The *manas* works through the senses and is the logical, scientific mind, but the *buddhi* is the higher aspect of the mind which goes not only beyond the senses but beyond the ordinary functioning of the mind and is open to transcendence.

Beyond the *buddhi* is the *mahat*, or great world, the world of the gods and the cosmic powers. Going beyond the higher self we become aware of the world of spirits, the psychic world, to which we belong. Beyond the physical is the psychic and each of us is a member of that vast world, the great world or the Great Self.

Beyond the *mahat* is the *avyakta*, the unmanifest. The gods, angels and powers are all manifestations of an unmanifest which is the source from which they come. And again, beyond the unmanifest is *purusha*, the Person, the Supreme, and from him everything comes. The text says, "Beyond the unmanifest there is Purusha; beyond Purusha there is nothing. That is the goal. That is the highest road." At that stage we have reached the Ultimate.

There is a progression from the senses, through the mind, through the intellect, and through the cosmic mind or cosmic order, to the Unmanifest. Before anything comes to be manifest, whether physically or psychologically, it has an unmanifest source which is rooted in the Person, the supreme cosmic Being, from whom the whole creation comes. That is the structure of the universe as it emerged in the Upanishads in the fifth century before Christ.

Now we take a step further to the *Svetasvatara Upanishad*, about 300 BC, where we see the figure of *purusha* emerging more clearly. In the early Upanishads the interest was primarily in *brahman*, the reality behind everything, and in the *atman*, the Spirit within everything. Now the interest moves to the personal God and their understanding of the universe was expressed in terms of the *purusha*, the cosmic person, who embraces the universe and yet goes beyond it; three parts are in heaven and one part is here on earth. The text says, "What is praised in the Upanishad is the highest *brahman* and in it there is a triad."[13] The highest *brahman* is the sole support, the imperishable, but within that *brahman* there is first of all the *isha*, the Lord. This shows how the personal God comes to be related to *brahman*. *Brahman* is the ultimate Reality and the Lord, the *ishvara*, the personal God, is a manifestation of *brahman*. Beneath *isha*, or Hara, which is another name for him, is *jivatman*, the individual soul. Beneath that is the *pradhana*, the material universe. So here are the three worlds again, the *pradhana*, the material universe, the *jivatman*, the psychological world of the soul, and beyond that, Hara, or *ishvara*, the Lord, and all are embraced in Brahman. Brahman embraces the whole, the material, the psychological and the spiritual. All are contained in him. This is an insight of great profundity.

The *Svetasvatara Upanishad* is also important because in it for the first time the god Shiva comes to be recognised as the Supreme Reality. Shiva was a god from outside the Aryan culture and only here is he being brought into the main tradition of the Vedas and the Upanishads, and recognised as the Supreme. The word Shiva means the Blessed, the Kindly One. Having originally been considered as very fierce, he was given this beautiful name and gradually a most beautiful character was built up around him. Eventually he was considered as the God of love and recognised more and more to be the source of all.

The *Svetasvatara Upanishad* describes the work of *purusha* when it refers to him as the creator and supporter of the gods. The Supreme is above the gods. The gods are on the level of the angels and are the cosmic powers but he, the Lord, is beyond them all. Earlier he had been known as Rudra, the great seer, the *maharishi*, but now he comes to be understood as the Lord of all, the sovereign of the gods, the one in whom all the worlds rest, who rules over all beings. The text goes on to speak of him "who is more subtle than the subtle, in the midst of chaos creating all things." Matter is chaos, as we saw in chapter one. It is potentiality of being, indeterminate, unpredictable, the base from which everything comes. The idea here is that Shiva, the Lord, is creating continuously in the midst of chaos. "In the midst of chaos, creating all things, having many forms and alone enveloping everything."[14] Creating the worlds from chaos, he takes the form of all the universe. He is in the earth and in the plants and in the trees, and in animals and in men. He is manifesting in the earth and the sky and the stars and the sun and the moon, manifesting in all creation. Enveloping all things, he is within all things. Embracing all things, he transcends all things. That is the cosmic Lord, Shiva.

We come now to a very important development. The Vedic period, the time of the Vedas, the Brahmanas, the Aranyakas and the Upanishads came to an end about 500 BC, although many of the Upanishads like the *Svetasvatara Upanishad*, to which we have just alluded, date from later times. Contemporary with the *Svetasvatara Upanishad* is the *Bhagavad Gita*. Whereas in the *Svetasvatara Upanishad* Shiva is the form of the Supreme God, the Supreme Reality, in the *Bhagavad Gita* the Supreme Reality is *Vishnu*. The majority of Hindus are either Shaivites or Vaishnavites. Vishnu belongs

72

more to the Aryan world. He is the god of heaven, a gracious god, the pervader of all things. Vishnu manifests himself through a series of incarnations, *avataras*, and the great *avatara* of Vishnu was Krishna. The *Bhagavad Gita* was written to celebrate the *avatara* of Vishnu as Krishna. In the *Bhagavad Gita* Krishna is revealed as the supreme Lord of creation, the creator God. This is a development along the same lines as the *Svetasvatara Upanishad*.

The *Bhagavad Gita* marks an advance even on the *Svetasvatara Upanishad* in that Krishna is revealed as both totally transcendent and totally immanent. In the *Bhagavad Gita* Krishna says, "All this visible universe comes from my invisible being. All beings have their rest in me but I have not my rest in them."[15] The whole creation comes from him; all rest in him and depend on him, but he does not depend on them. Then he says, "In truth they rest not in me. Consider my sacred mystery, my *maya*. I am the source of all beings, I support them all but I rest not in them."[16] There is here the concept of a totally transcendent God. Krishna transcends the whole universe. It comes forth from him and he supports it, but he does not rest in it and in a real sense it does not rest in him. He is transcendent over it all. This is a profound insight which was reached at that point.

Later, in the tenth book of the *Bhagavad Gita*, Krishna speaks of the whole universe being in himself. "I shall reveal to thee some manifestations of my divine glory. For there is no end to my infinite greatness. I am the beginning, the middle and end of all that lives."[17] Krishna is the source, the middle and the goal to which all is tending, the all-pervading Lord. He then gives various mythological accounts of all these forms which are in him. Then in the eleventh book, the book of the great theophany, Krishna reveals himself to Arjuna as the Lord in whom the whole creation exists. The text says, "Then Krishna appeared to Arjuna in his supreme

73

divine form ... and Arjuna saw in that form countless visions of wonder. He saw in that radiance the whole universe, in all its variety, standing in a vast unity, in the body of the God of Gods."[18] The whole creation in all its variety and yet in its unity was revealed within the body of the Lord, the Lord who sustains the whole universe and carries it in himself. But he has made it clear that, while he is immanent and sustains all, he is also transcendent and beyond all. The vision of Krishna as the Lord is a wonderful theophany. Arjuna bows in adoration before him and says, "I have seen what no man has seen before. I rejoice in exaltation and yet my heart trembles with fear."[19]

A further stage in the development of the idea of God is found in the Tantras. This was a very important movement. So far we have been considering the Vedic religion in its original form, but now it seems quite clear that as the Aryans came down through India from the North to the South more and more of the indigenous people, basically Dravidians, were drawn in to this religion. The history of Hinduism is the history of the gradual assimilation of the different peoples of India into the Vedic world. It seems clear that Shaivism as a whole derives from the indigenous Dravidian religion. Shiva is still the great God in the South, while Vishnu is more popular in the North. There has been mixing, but it is clear that the former derives from the ancient matriarchal religion.

The earliest Tantric texts date from the third century AD but Tantrism goes back beyond that. At first Tantra was an undercurrent and is not documented among the Dravidian peoples much earlier than the third century. It belongs essentially to the world of magic and of myth. At this stage the Tantra begins to enter the main stream of Hinduism and a new development takes place. So far the aim had always been to go beyond the physical and beyond the psychological to the Supreme Reality, and to see everything in that light. In practice that entailed a strong tendency towards asceticism, which prevailed in Hinduism as a whole. Leaving behind the body, the soul, the mind and all its activities, the aim was to unite oneself with the supreme *brahman*, the supreme *atman*. That is the basic movement of *sannyasa*, renunciation. The Tantra arose in opposition to that, to assert the values of nature and of the body, of the senses and of sex. All that world which tended to be suppressed in the other tradition now comes to life. This is why Tantra is particularly important today. There is a great revival of Tantrism taking place at the moment. The late Swami Muktananda of Ganeshpuri in Maharashtra, for instance, was one of the great exponents of it. People are discovering this other side of nature, the side represented by the mother, and are coming to appreciate the Great Mother, the earth mother, who nourishes us all, from whom we all come and from whom we all receive our bodily existence and the power of the senses.

A key doctrine of the Tantras is, "that by which we fall is that by which we rise." In other words, as we fall through the attraction of the senses, through sex, passion and desire, so we have to rise through them, using them as the means of going beyond. The Tantra has the marvellous vision of the whole cosmos in terms of *shakti*. *Shakti* is energy. This is where the link with the contemporary world is so fascinating because, in the tradition of the Tantra, Shakti is the source of the universe and she is the mother, she is feminine. Whereas the other religions are patriarchal, Shaivism stems from the matriarchal religion where the mother is the source of all. The mother goddess (*devi*), is *shakti*, energy. In Shaivism Shiva is normally considered to be consciousness or spirit, and Shakti is his energy, his power. The world comes into being through *shakti*, through energy. Iconographically Shiva is portrayed in deep contemplation, surveying the creation, while Shakti, his consort, moves the whole universe. With this there is the beginning of a new understanding of the universe as a form of energy. Tantra was explored deeply and its teaching brought to light by Sir John Woodruffe, a British judge in Calcutta in the last century.

Of particular interest is the tantric conception of *bindu*. *Bindu* is a point, but a point in which all the energy of the universe is concentrated. *Bindu* is said to be the origin of the universe, the whole energy of the universe concentrated in a single point. From that highly concentrated point energy expands outwards. That is very near to how we today conceive the origin of the universe. All the energy seems to have come out from a point, from nothing, in a sense. It is interesting that in the Tantra the energy is understood to come out of the *bindu* in mathematical form, in triangles and squares, for instance. Galileo also had this idea that the geometrical forms come out from the original matter. So there is this concept of original matter exploding, as it were, into the forms of the universe. The universe was considered to be in the form of a *yantra*. A *yantra* is a structure, a kind of diagram or picture, composed of triangles and squares. In that *yantra* all the powers of the universe are concentrated. Again the practice associated with this comes very near to magic at times. If one constructs a *yantra* it is accorded tremendous power. Still today in a Hindu temple, in the inner sanctuary there is often a *yantra* which is held to have this magical power in it. There can be real power in those *yantras* because they are designs in which, as it were, the power of the universe is concentrated.

In Tantra it is understood that everything comes forth from the *bindu* and it structures itself in the physical universe in a mathematical form. The *yantra*, is a representation of the structure of the universe. By meditating on the *yantra* one unites oneself with the whole universe.

The universe is composed of centres of energy known as *chakras*. Out of the *bindu* come all the *chakras*, each of which is a centre of energy – we would speak in terms of atoms, molecules, cells, organisms. The whole universe comes forth in these centres of energy, culminating in the highest human centre of energy, the human consciousness. The important point here is that, as the universe comes forth from the *bindu* and structures itself around the person, so the same power is present in one's own body. One's own body is a micro-cosm: the whole universe is within.

This idea is particularly worked out in Kundalini yoga, where the understanding is that Kundalini is the serpent power. The serpent was always the symbol of this earth power. That power is supposed to be coiled up like a serpent at the base of the spine and is understood to be the source of all psychic energy. That energy, *kundalini*, rises up through seven *chakras*, or energy centres, from the base of the spine to the crown of the head. As the Kundalini, which is really the goddess Shakti herself, rises up through the body the whole being is gradually transformed, from the physical, through the psychological, until finally spiritual evolution is attained. It all takes place within, and what takes place within is reflecting and resonating with what is taking place in the universe outside. The whole process is conceived as the marriage of Shiva (consciousness) with Shakti (energy).

That is the vision of the universe in the Hindu tradition, in which there are many similarities with the vision of the Western scientist and philosopher today. Western science, having lost itself in materialism, is discovering its mistake and is opening itself now to the ancient wisdom, and East and West are beginning to come together.

The Christian Vision of the New Creation

In the previous chapter we examined the vision of the universe in the ancient world and saw that, particularly in the Hindu tradition, the universe was understood to be an integrated whole. The three worlds, the physical, psychological and spiritual, were seen to be interrelated and integrated, so as to form a unity. This corresponds very closely with the vision of the universe which is emerging now in Western physics and psychology, where the universe is seen as a unity of interdependent relationships. Looking at religious experience as a whole, it can be seen to follow a certain pattern. In the earlier stages humanity was immersed in the world of the senses but was aware, with a kind of global awareness, of a Spirit which pervaded the whole universe. This was at first latent and only emerged clearly with the appearance of myth, the symbolic language by which these early experiences were interpreted. At this point it becomes clear that the people of the ancient world recognised three distinct worlds. They were aware of the physical world around them and their own physical bodies, but they were also aware of a psychic world penetrating the physical world and their own psyche. In this psychic world were encountered all kinds of spirits and powers, in the earth and the atmosphere, in rocks and trees, plants and animals, in human beings and in the ancestors of the race. In the course of time these spirits and powers were conceived to be manifestations of one supreme Spirit and Power. We can see this process taking place among the American Indians and African tribal people and among the Australian aborigines.

In the Hebrew revelation contained in the Bible we can detect something of the same stages. The Hebrew word for God is *elohim*, and this is a plural form of the word *eloha*. This clearly points to a time when many gods were recognised. It can even be used of a ghost, as when the witch of Endor called up the ghost of Samuel and said, "I see Elohim coming up out of the earth".[1] The word Elohim must at one time have signified the whole world of the sacred, the psychic world. A simpler form still of the word for a god is El. This appears frequently in the book of Genesis and seems to have been a common name for a god among the Semitic peoples, which points to a time when there was a kind of "henotheism", one God, an El, manifesting in different forms on different occasions – much like the *deva* in Vedic religion. When Jacob was journeying, he had a vision while he was asleep of a ladder going up to heaven on which the "angels of God" were ascending and descending, and when he awoke he said, "Surely the Lord is in this place" and he called it Bethel, the house of El, because El had appeared to him there.[2] Later when Jacob wrestled with a man all night, on waking up and considering what had happened, he called the place Peniel, which means the "face of El".[3] Thus El at this stage might be encountered in the form of a man.

On other occasions El is given a particular name, El Roi,[4] the God who sees, or El Olam,[5] the everlasting God. Perhaps the most significant of all is the name El Elyon,[6] the "most-high God", which may be an indication that a supreme El was recognised at this stage, which has its counterpart among the Phoenicians and other neighbouring nations. In later times the name El Shaddai, which is usually translated God Almighty, but may mean God of the Mountain, was considered the proper name of God at this period,[7] which again may indicate that a supreme form of God was emerging at this time. But the decisive moment came with Moses when the name Yahweh was revealed as the proper name of the God of Israel[8] and the unity of the divine being was clearly established. From this time Elohim came to be used as a singular, identified with the one supreme god of Israel. It seems clear, though, that Yahweh was originally a thunder god. This is indicated by the way he is associated with thunder and lightning on Mount Sinai. In any case, Yahweh at an early stage was clearly a tribal God, who was called the Lord of the armies of Israel, driving out their enemies before them. Later the same name, Lord of armies or of "hosts", was given to Yahweh as the Lord of the "hosts of heaven", so that from being a local tribal god, he came to be recognised as a Cosmic Lord.

In the great prophetic movement of the eighth century Yahweh finally passes from being the mythical god of thunder and the tribe to the status of the one transcendent God of all creation. At first Yahweh was conceived as above the other gods but still one among many; only later was he recognised as the one God compared with whom the other gods were nothing, and eventually these gods came to be regarded as "demons", that is, as powers opposed to the one God like the *asuras* in Hindu tradition. Perhaps the greatest significance is to be found in the interpretation of the name of Yahweh as "I am". This was the profound insight that the supreme Person is essentially supreme Being. It may be that the name was first of all taken to mean "I will be", signifying the relationship of the God of Israel to his chosen people, but the deeper insight that God is absolute Being must have been reached in time. This is the same insight which is found in the *Katha Upanishad*, where it is said: "How shall we speak of him except by saying, 'He is' (*asti*)?"[9] Thus one can trace the slow stages by which the idea of God evolved in Israel as in the *Vedas*, the *Upanishads* and the *Bhagavad Gita*. Each appears as a unique revelation

80

by which the true nature of absolute Truth and Reality came to be known.

When we come to consider the relation of humanity and the world to this God of Israel, we find that in Israel God was commonly conceived in a dualistic manner as totally separated from the world. The very word "holiness", which is the essential attribute of the God of Israel, means literally "separate". He was often conceived on the analogy of a potter making a pot, as though the universe existed apart from God. But there are indications also of a deeper understanding. In the creation story of Genesis the world is said to have been created by a word. God said, "Let there be light, and there was light". This suggests that the universe comes forth from the mind of God, as a word expresses the mind of a person. In the New Testament this was developed into the concept of the Logos, the Word or Mind of God, through whom and in whom the world was created. There is also in the Genesis story the conception of the Spirit or Breath of God brooding over the waters. This suggests something of an immanent presence, which will develop later into the profound understanding that "the Spirit of the Lord has filled the whole creation"[10] and to the conception of the Wisdom of God, which "pervades and penetrates all things".[11]

But it is in the story of the Garden of Eden that one can find the most significant symbol of original unity of creation. In the Garden of Eden humanity is represented as being in harmony with nature, with itself and with God. The earth brought forth every tree, "which is pleasant to the sight and good to eat",[12] and the man and the woman "were naked and were not ashamed".[13] This is a symbolic picture of the original harmony of humanity with nature, and at the same time the Lord God was seen to "walk in the garden in the cool of the day".[14] In other words, human beings were at peace with the world around them, with themselves, and

81

with the indwelling Spirit who "walked" with them. But there was already a power of evil, of disharmony there. The serpent was "more subtle than all the beasts of the field"[15] and proceeded to tempt the human couple. There are two things to be observed about this. The first is that in the ancient world, as among the American Indians today, animals were conceived as parts of the cosmic whole, in which trees and animals and human beings were all subject to the cosmic powers, the gods and angels, and to the supreme Spirit who pervaded all things. The second is that what we would consider to be subjective phenomena, experiences of the inner self, were then experienced as objective realities. Gods and angels and all kinds of spirits and the Lord God himself, were all conceived as objective beings. Paradoxically, what we take to be objective, the phenomenal world "outside" us, they conceived as a spiritual phenomenon, a psychic event, and what we take to be subjective, our thoughts and feelings, they conceived as objective realities. This, of course, is simply due to the difference in the functioning of the human mind, the reality itself being always beyond the sphere of the dualities.

The serpent was a symbol of cosmic evil, the disintegrating force in the universe, the source of all dualities. This was understood in Israel as the result of the "fall of the angels". An angel or a god is a reflection in the sphere of multiplicity of the one supreme Spirit and when the angel or the god remains in the harmony of the Spirit, it becomes a creative force in the universe. But when the god or angel centres on itself and becomes a separate force and is worshipped as such, it becomes a power of destruction, of disintegration. This "fall of the angels" was considered the original source of conflict in the universe, of all these forces of disintegration which disturb the order of creation. But for this to become effective in human beings there had to be a consent of the will. The "fall of man" follows on the fall of the angels, when the human being falls away from the guidance of the inner Spirit and allows itself to be seduced by lower spirits and comes to centre on itself. This is the essence of sin and of evil, the fall from the unity of the Spirit, the all-pervading Word and Light and Life, which is the Ground of the universe, and the centring on the separate self, the ego-mind, or *ahankara* – the I-Maker – which sets humanity in conflict with nature, with itself and with the Ground and Source of all.

This, then, is the fallen universe into which we are all born, and which we see today threatening the destruction of the planet on which we live through human co-operation with the forces of destruction in the universe. But at the same time we see in the story of Genesis the promise of restoration. The main theme of the Bible is the restoration of humanity and, through humanity, of the whole creation to its original harmony. The Bible begins with the creation of "heaven and earth"[16] and it ends with the new creation, of a "new heaven and a new earth".[17] This is the theme which we have to follow out, if we want to understand the biblical vision of human destiny. The effects of sin are seen first of all in the murder of Cain by Abel. This reflects a conflict between the agricultural and the pastoral people, for "Cain was a tiller of the earth and Abel was a keeper of sheep."[18] The significance of this is that the agricultural people, typified by the Canaanites (the supposed descendants of Cain), the Babylonians and the Egyptians, were responsible for the building of the great civilisations of the ancient world and were seen by the Israelites, who were a pastoral people, as nations who made their home in this world of sin and duality and gradually lost sight of the transcendent reality of the Spirit, in which human happiness is to be found. They correspond with the great powers of the modern world, which have built up the present industrial civilisation.

83

The story of the Flood, which almost certainly reflects the memory of the flood in the Mesopotamian valley, was seen as a judgement on this civilisation, while the building of the "tower of Babel", the memory of the Babylonian *ziggurat*, was seen as typical of the ambition of such civilisations to "build a tower up to heaven",[19] that is, to dominate the world and make the spiritual world (heaven) subject to the material world. This again exactly reflects the present state of the world, where western science and technology, based on a mechanistic view of the universe, seek to control the world and subject nature to the machine. The ecological disaster which is now overtaking the civilised world and the threat of planetary destruction are the inevitable result of this type of civilisation.

In the Hebrew tradition the restoration of the world to its original unity begins with the call of Abraham. Abraham is told to leave his "country and his kindred and his father's house",[20] in other words to leave the Babylonian world into which he had been born, and to go to the land which will be shown him. There are three things to be noted in the call of Abraham. The first is that he has to follow the call of God and to venture out into the unknown. The second is that he is called to become a great nation and to be a blessing to all the earth. The third is that he is promised a "land", a place in which to dwell. These three callings represent the call of humanity to return to its origin and to rediscover its ultimate destiny. Humanity is to be reconciled with God by going out from its present state of civilisation and venturing into the unknown. To bring this about it has to be formed into a new people, a community which will bring a blessing and reconciliation to the whole world. And finally this new people will be reconciled with the earth, with the world of nature by being given a land in which to dwell.

These three themes, the reconciliation of humanity with God, the supreme Reality, by the venture of faith in the unknown; the reconciliation of humanity with itself by the formation of a new people, a new humanity; and the reconciliation of humanity with the earth, that is, with the whole world of nature, by the promise of a land, can be traced through the whole biblical revelation. This promise is given to Abraham, to Isaac and to Jacob, the founders of the people of Israel, and in each case the future of the people is seen to be bound up with their settlement in the land. When Israel goes down into Egypt, symbolising the subjection of the people of God to the powers of this world, the promise is renewed to Moses, "I have heard the cry of my people and I have come to deliver them and to restore them to the land which I have promised them".[21] Again, when Israel is taken into captivity in Babylon – the people of God made captive to the other great civilisation of the ancient world – the theme is taken up by the prophets, "You shall dwell in the land that I gave to your fathers and you shall be my people and I will be your God".[22] Human liberation is always seen as reconciliation with God and with nature in a renewed humanity.

A beautiful example of this is given in the famous prophecy of Isaiah where the destiny of humanity is seen as a return to Paradise. First of all it is said that the Spirit will be given, "the Spirit of wisdom and understanding, the Spirit of counsel and might, the Spirit of knowledge and the fear of the Lord". The fall of humanity came from turning away from the Spirit and centring on the separate self, and restoration can only come by the gift of the Spirit reconciling humanity with God. Then it is said, "the wolf shall lie down with the lamb and the leopard shall lie down with the kid, and the calf and the young lion and the fatling together and a little child shall lead them". This is the restoration to Paradise, a state which can only be found when we have passed through death into the new world, as Jesus promised the thief on the cross, "This day you shall be with me in

85

Paradise". Then the whole creation will pass from its present state of extension in time and space with all the divisions and conflicts which mark this state, and the animal world will be reconciled with itself and with the human world. Finally it is said, "They shall not hurt or destroy in all my holy mountain, for the earth shall be full of the knowledge of God as the waters cover the sea".[23] This state of Paradise comes when humanity emerges into a new state of consciousness, a state described as the "knowledge of the Lord", that is the higher knowledge or *gnosis*, known in India as *jnana*, the direct experience of the indwelling Spirit of God.

Another interesting example of this vision of a restored humanity is found in the prophet Hosea, where it is said, "I will betroth you to me in faithfulness and you shall know the Lord". Again it is the "knowledge" of God which comes through faith which brings about the transformation, and it is said, "I will answer the heavens and they shall answer the earth and the earth shall answer the corn and the wine and the oil and they shall answer Jezreel (that is, God sows) and I will sow her unto me in the earth".[24] This passage reflects that deep sense of the solidarity of humanity with the earth, which is found in all ancient peoples and which we are seeking to recover today, lest we should destroy the earth by the violence of our assault on it.

But while we recognise this sense of the solidarity of God and humanity with the earth and the animal world among the prophets of Israel, we must also recognise that the opposite tendency was always there. Already in the story of Genesis the human pair were instructed "to fill the earth and subdue it" and there is throughout the history of Israel an element of violence and domination which has left a terrible legacy to mankind. The Israelites were a patriarchal people and their God was always conceived in masculine terms, while the gods of the surrounding people with their worship of the Earth Mother were totally rejected. Of course, it is true that there were daemonic elements in the religion of the people of the Middle East as in all religion, but by totally rejecting the religion of the Great Mother with all its feminine characteristics, Israel became subject to daemonic forces in its own religion. Even at the time of the Exodus, the foundational event in Israel's history, the God of Israel is represented as massacring all the first-born children of the Egyptians and drowning the armies of Egyptians in the sea without the slightest sense that the Egyptians as human beings have any rights before God.[25] Again when the Israelites were about to enter the land which had been promised them, they were told to destroy all the people of the land, "You shall smite them and utterly destroy them!"[26] Again in the book of Samuel, Saul is commanded, "Go and smite Amalek and utterly destroy all that they have and spare them not; but slay both man and woman, infant and suckling, ox and camel and ass".[27] Of course, we must remember the context of the civilisation in which this took place, yet what is shocking is that it is presented as the command of a God who is supposed to be "righteous" and this attitude of hatred for one's enemies became a permanent feature of the religion of Israel. The Psalmist never ceases to proclaim his hatred for his enemies and to ask God to destroy them. When personal or racial enemies are seen as enemies of God there is no limit to the violence and hatred which they evoke. Unfortunately this spirit has entered into all the Semitic religions and has left a terrible record of war and violence behind.

This is the dark side of the Semitic religions which has so disfigured their history. It was this that led to the Inquisition, the crusades and the wars of religion, and it would be difficult to say how much of the violence of the Western world today with its desecration of the earth and its threat of nuclear war does not stem from this original tradition of the biblical religion. Yet, when we have said this, we must

87

always remember that there is another side to the religion
of Israel. Together with its exclusive character, which rejected all other religions, there was also a complementary
trend. The people of Israel were a "holy" people chosen
apart from all other peoples to witness to the holiness of
God. But from the beginning there was the belief that the
election of Israel was for the benefit of the whole world. This
note of universalism runs through the whole Bible together
with the opposite note of exclusiveness. But there are occasions when it becomes unusually clear. One of the most
remarkable is the prophecy of Isaiah, "In that day shall
Israel be a third with Egypt and Assyria, a blessing in the
midst of the earth". Here we have Egypt and Assyria, the two
great world powers, Assyria being simply the predecessor of
Babylon as a world power, associated with Israel as a third,
and the text goes on to say, "Blessed be Egypt my people
and Assyria the work of my hands and Israel my inheritance".[28] It would be difficult to overemphasise the importance of this text. It does away with any suggestion that the
world powers are essentially evil. They are also "work of
God's hands"; it is only the elevation of science and technology to a place of supreme importance, instead of making
them subordinate to the real needs of humanity and the life
of the Spirit, that makes them evil and oppressive.

The reconciliation of humanity with nature and with God
is represented in a later chapter of Isaiah in terms of a
marriage, where it is said, "You shall no longer be forsaken
nor shall your land be called Desolate; but you shall be
called My Delight and your land Married, for the Lord
delights in you and your land shall be married".[29] This
brings out again the sense of the solidarity of the people and
the land, of humanity with the earth to which it belongs.
But the climax of this theme of the reconciliation of heaven
and earth is found in the last chapters of Isaiah where it is
said, "Behold, I create new heavens and a new earth; and

the former things shall not be remembered or come into mind". This reveals the final destiny of humanity and creation. The heaven and the earth which we experience through our limited mental consciousness is only a passing phenomenon. We are destined to pass beyond our present level of consciousness, where we see everything in terms of dualities, of subject and object, time and space, heaven and earth, and to enter into the unifying consciousness beyond the dualities of the mind. Then alone will humanity find its fulfilment. As the text goes on to say, "I create Jerusalem a rejoicing, and her people a joy".[30] With the coming of the new consciousness humanity, typified by Jerusalem, the city of God, enters into the joy, the *ananda* of Hindu tradition, the blissful state of pure consciousness where all the dualities of sin and evil have been transcended and humanity is at peace with God and creation.

When we turn to the New Testament, we can see how this concept of the relationship of the people to the land, of humanity to this world, undergoes a profound transformation. The key text is that of the letter to the Hebrews, where it is said, "People who speak thus make it clear that they are seeking a homeland. If they had been thinking of the land from which they had gone out, they would have had the opportunity to return. But as it is they desire a better country, that is, a heavenly one".[31] The land of Palestine to which Israel was so attached – and remains so to this day – here undergoes a radical transformation. It becomes a symbol of something much more profound. Human beings desire fulfilment in a concrete manner and seek for fulfilment in this world by the possession of a land, by contact with the earth. But they have to learn that there is no fulfilment in this world of space and time. The real object of human search is not for a dwelling in this world; it is not for an earthly city but for the city of God, the state of transformed humanity. This is what is meant by a "heavenly country".

This earth and all that is in it, and the whole cosmic order to which it belongs, has to undergo a transformation; it has to become a "new heaven and a new earth". Modern physics helps us to realise that this whole material universe is a vast "field of energies" which is in a continuous process of transformation. Matter is passing into life and life into consciousness, and we are waiting for the time when our present mode of consciousness will be transformed and we shall transcend the limits of space and time, and enter "the new creation".

There is a remarkable anticipation of this view in the Letter to the Romans, where St Paul speaks of the whole creation "groaning in travail". For the creation, he says, "waits with eager longing for the revealing of the sons of God". The "revealing of the sons of God" is of course, the passage of humanity into the new state of consciousness. For "we ourselves", he says "groan inwardly as we wait for the adoption of sons, the redemption of our bodies".[32] Our adoption as sons is our passing from human to divine consciousness, which is the destiny of all humanity. And this will come through "the redemption of our bodies". The new consciousness is not a bodiless state; it is the transformation of our present body consciousness, which is limited by time and space, into a state of transformed body consciousness which is that of resurrection. In the resurrection Jesus passed from our present state of material being and consciousness into the final state when matter itself, and with it the human body, passes into the state of the divine being and consciousness, which is the destiny of all humanity.

This is the "new creation" of which St Paul speaks and which is revealed more explicitly in the second Letter of Peter, where it is said, "According to his promise we await a new heavens and a new earth in which righteousness dwells".[33] This is the ultimate goal of human history and of the created universe. Many people today imagine some kind of Utopia, in which humanity will be set free and enjoy peace and prosperity in this world. But this is a pure illusion, as can be seen as each revolution which is to usher in the new age ends in frustration and disillusionment. It is not only that humanity has within itself so much violence and division that in its present state it can never reach a state of equilibrium. The problem is that the very universe to which we belong is threatened with entropy in which all stable order and harmony will be lost. The vision of the New Testament is much more profound. It was recognised that this whole universe has to undergo a radical transformation, in which the present time-space will pass away and a "new heaven and a new earth" will be revealed. It is then only that humanity will find the state of "righteousness" for which it longs. There is no final liberation in this world. Every serious religious tradition has recognised the need to transcend the present condition of this world, if humanity is to attain fulfilment. This goal was commonly expressed in mythological terms, but we recognise today that myth is the most adequate way of expressing what cannot be properly expressed in human language. The ultimate state of humanity and the universe cannot be properly conceived, since it must transcend our present mode of consciousness. Myth or symbolic language is the only way in which the ultimate truth can be presented. Even the language of science is essentially symbolic. Modern science in particular, is ultimately based on mathematical symbolism which expresses one aspect of reality, that is, its quantitive aspect, but ignores all other aspects.

The final statement of the myth of the new creation is to be found in the last book of the Bible, the Revelation of St John, where it is said, "I saw a new heaven and new earth; for the first heaven and the first earth had passed away, and the sea was no more". Thus the biblical revelation which

91

began with the creation of heaven and earth is brought to a climax with the coming of new heaven and a new earth. Then it is said, "I saw the holy city, the new Jerusalem, coming down out of heaven from God, prepared as a bride adorned for her husband".[34] The "new Jerusalem" is a symbol of redeemed humanity, which "comes down out of heaven" because it emerges out of a new consciousness. Our present world is conditioned by our present mode of consciousness; only when that consciousness passes from its present dualistic mode conditioned by time and space will the new creation appear, which is the eternal reality of which our world is a mirror.

The myth of the new creation has been given a new expression in recent times by Teilhard de Chardin who, writing from a scientific point of view, was able to give it a meaning for modern man. Teilhard presented an evolutionary view of matter evolving into life and into consciousness, as matter developed ever greater complexity and concentration. The point at which all matter and life and consciousness finds its ultimate meaning and purpose he called the "Omega point". He saw the whole universe converging on this ultimate point, where it is totally unified and centred. It is towards that supreme point of unity that the whole creation is moving.

The other person in modern times who had the deepest insight into this mystery is Sri Aurobindo, the sage of Pondicherry in India. What Teilhard de Chardin did for Christianity, Aurobindo did for Hinduism. He developed a system of Vedanta which incorporates the concept of evolution into the Hindu vision of the universe. He starts from the concept of the supreme Reality as *saccidananda*, pure being in perfect consciousness of absolute bliss. This is the one absolute Reality. This supreme reality proceeds to "involve" itself in matter, where it appears as unconscious being, but always behind the unconscious state of matter is the full consciousness of the eternal Spirit, which is manifesting itself in it. This is similar to David Bohm's concept of the implicate order, which is always present behind the explicate order of the world as we know it. In the same way *saccidananda*, the plenitude of consciousness and bliss, is involved in matter from the beginning, and as matter becomes more organised into ever greater complexity, it evolves into life, that is, into the living cell. As life becomes organised into increasingly complex forms in plant and animal, it evolves into consciousness in humanity. In all this it is the *Saccidananda*, the supreme consciousness, which is gradually manifesting its hidden power. In Aurobindo's view we are now in the stage of evolution from mental consciousness, that is, our present state of dualistic, rational consciousness, into "supermental" consciousness, which corresponds with what Teilhard de Chardin calls the "Omega point". The Supermind is the supreme manifestation of the ultimate Reality, which acts upon the whole creation, bringing it to fulfilment.

An important aspect of Sri Aurobindo's thought is that in the final state the differences which exist here on earth are not simply dissolved but are transcended. There is a view, which is very common in India, that when the ultimate state is reached all differences of God and man and creation disappear. But in Aurobindo's view, as in that of Teilhard de Chardin, the divine consciousness penetrates the whole creation and integrates the whole in the final state of transcendence. This is the law of evolution, that at every stage when a lower level of being is transcended, it is integrated in the higher level. As the atom develops it integrates the electrons and protons and other particles which were originally floating freely. As the molecule develops it integrates the atoms; it does not destroy them. In the same way, as the living cell develops it integrates the atoms and molecules, and as each organism develops it integrates all the different elements in itself. So also as consciousness develops the

93

whole bodily structure is integrated with the mind and forms a psycho-physical organism. As we go beyond our rational consciousness, we have to learn to integrate the rational mind and the ego consciousness into our personal being. The human person does not disintegrate as we pass into the unifying consciousness of the transcendent, but on the contrary becomes more fully personal. The human person is a centre of consciousness which is capable of infinite extension and as it grows it becomes more and more integrated with the whole complex of persons who make up humanity. We do not cease to be persons but grow into full personal being, which is always a form of relationship. The ultimate reality is the fullness of interpersonal being, which is also interpersonal consciousness.

Teilhard de Chardin always emphasised the principle that union differentiates. We become more ourselves as we enter more deeply into relationship with others. In our ordinary consciousness we are all separated in time and space, but as we go beyond the limitations of time and space we experience our oneness with others. We do not lose ourselves, but we lose our sense of separation and division and discover our integral oneness in the One Reality. This is essentially a mystery of love. When two people love one another, they do not lose their distinction of person; they become more fully personal. The whole process of evolution, as Teilhard de Chardin saw it, is a process of personalisation. The ultimate goal of humanity is a communion of persons in love. This is what was revealed in St John's Gospel, when Jesus prayed for his disciples "that they may be one, as you, Father, are, in me and I in you, that they may be one in us".[35] This is the meaning of Christian doctrine of the Trinity, that the ultimate Reality, the Godhead, or whatever name we give to the ultimate Truth, is a communion of love. In the beginning the universe was undifferentiated. The original cosmos was an undifferentiated unity; the earliest human consciousness was an undifferentiated consciousness. We emerge through all the levels of consciousness, the physical, the vital, the emotional, the imaginative, the rational and the transrational until we reach a fully differentiated unity. The ultimate reality is a differentiated unity which transcends all categories of human thought, but in which all forms of being are integrated in a transcendent unity, which as far as it can be described in human terms is a communion of love, that is, of inter-personal relationship, which recalls the description of the universe in modern physics as a "complicated web of interdependent relationships".

The New Humanity

In this chapter we will look in more detail at the biblical vision of the new humanity. Just as the Bible begins with the creation of heaven and earth and ends with the new creation, so it begins with Adam and ends with Christ. Christ is the second Adam, the new Man. The whole Bible is thus placed in the context of creation. There is the first creation and the new creation, the first Man and the new Man. The Hebrew word *adam*, which we usually take to be a personal name, in fact means "man", mankind in general. In Genesis Adam, meaning mankind, is seen as the head of creation. The whole creation was prepared and finally God created Adam, Adam here including both man and woman. The account of creation, in chapter one of Genesis, says, "in the image of God created he him, male and female created he them",[1] so the original Hebrew vision was that man and woman together are the unit of creation. Then in the second chapter, which is actually an earlier creation narrative, there is the rather crude symbolism of the woman being made from the rib taken out of man, and this is intended to show that the man and the woman are complementary to one another, that they are "one flesh". That is the basic biblical vision concerning the complementarity of man and woman.

The earliest creation account signifies that man comes out of the material creation. "The Lord God", it is said, "formed man from the dust of the earth and breathed into his nostrils the breath of life".[2] In the preceding chapters we have seen that the material creation is an evolving process, progressing from matter to life, and then to consciousness in man. The human being is the point where the dust of the earth, the matter of the universe, comes into consciousness and in the mythological language of Genesis that is described as God "breathing into his nostrils the breath of life". God created this first man out of the evolving universe and gave him the breath of the divine. The Hebrew word for breath (*ruach*) is the same as the word for spirit. From this we get the understanding of human nature, which is fundamental in the Bible and very clear in St Paul, that the human being is body, soul and spirit, *soma*, *psyche* and *pneuma*. As body (*soma*) it is part of the whole physical universe. It evolves out of the physical universe, from the matter and the life. As soul (*psyche*), humanity is the head of the universe. It is, in a sense, matter coming into consciousness and forming an individual soul but then, like matter itself, that soul is open to the *pneuma*, the Spirit, which is the point where the spirit of man opens on the Spirit of God. So the human person is, from the beginning, body and soul, while beyond body and soul it is open to, and receives its life from, the divine Spirit.

In the beginning man and woman lived in an undifferentiated unity. In the Garden of Eden humanity was in perfect unity with nature around. There was unity between the man and the woman, unity within the human person, and unity with the Spirit of God. This was the original structure of humankind and human reality. Consciousness at this point was undifferentiated. Human beings did not know themselves as different from nature or as different from God. They were still in the womb, as it were, undifferentiated unity being precisely what life in the womb is like, where there is oneness with the mother, with the earth, with creation and with the Spirit who is present in the midst of creation. So this is the original condition of humanity.

Following creation came the drama of the Fall. Ken Wilber and many others today think of the Fall as an ascent

97

rather than a descent, holding that the original undifferentiated unity had to be fragmented, man had to become
conscious, and to develop and acquire a separate individuality. This point they identify as the Fall, but that is certainly
not the biblical vision and in my view it is not the true
vision. It is rather that in that original state, body, soul and
spirit were in harmony and as human beings developed
consciousness, they learned to distinguish themselves from
other selves, from nature and from God. As consciousness
developed they became conscious of themselves as separate
from the body and separate from the mother. In that state
they could open themselves to the Spirit and allow the Spirit
to guide them, but they could equally separate themselves
from the Spirit. They could fall away from the Spirit and
centre on themselves. This falling away from the Spirit into
the ego, the soul, the separated self, and thereby separating
from God, is the essence of original sin. That is told in
Genesis in the story of the eating of the fruit of the tree of
the knowledge of good and evil. The essence of it was
disobedience. The man did not listen to the Spirit. He did
not follow the guidance of the Spirit, and so he fell away
from it into a separated self. Then the whole tragedy of
human existence takes place. Once you have fallen from the
Spirit into yourself, your separated self, you are divided.
Humanity is now divided; man and woman divided from
nature, man and woman divided from one another, and man
and woman divided from God. Total disintegration takes
place. That is the Fall of man. It is a very gradual process,
not clear at first but escalating in its implications. The
tragedy is that the more human faculties develop, the greater
the split becomes. It is a very little crack to begin with but
as human beings develop consciousness and all their powers,
this capacity to separate increases progressively. Today we
have probably reached the limit of this disintegration with
the present-day separation of persons from nature and from

God. But also, as this power to disintegrate develops and inner harmony is lost, so the same power which causes one to separate can also enable one to unite. Reason and intelligence can open one to the unity of the Spirit. Perhaps today we are witnessing a new movement of the Spirit, a reintegration of humanity, which is beginning to take place. It is significant that St Paul contrasts the *anthropos psuchikos*, the soul-man, with the *anthropos pneumatikos*, the spiritual man.[3] This is the contrast between the man who is centred on his soul, his ego, and the man who is centered on the Spirit.

The consequences of this inner fragmentation are truly apalling. Ken Wilber has put it in an extremely interesting way in his book, *The Atman Project*, (1980), where he says that the atman, the Spirit, is present to man from the beginning. Atman is Sanskrit for Spirit. If human beings respond to the Spirit they grow harmoniously; body and soul grow together in the harmony of the Spirit. But if they separate from the Spirit they still have this goal of infinite transcendence, for the spirit is infinite and eternal and beyond all. But now fallen humanity has lost the vision of the Spirit beyond and everything focusses on the self. The self becomes the centre and as such it becomes a substitute for God. That is the great tragedy. As one's consciousness and sense of a separate self develops, one loses the sense of a spiritual power beyond oneself. Everything centres on the self and one becomes God for oneself. Every human being wants to be God in this way. We all have in us the instinct for God, for the Ultimate, but we have lost the sense of the Ultimate beyond. So in each person there is repeated the fall into the separate self. The great tyrants of history, Nero or Stalin or Hitler, are examples of man making himself God. This goes all through human history. The more the powers develop, the more one's consciousness and ego develop, the stronger becomes this Atman Project. Whether it is power or wealth or pleasure or success, what is happening is that one is focussing on substitutes for God, creating a false ego substituted for the true self. That is the tragedy of the Fall of man, which we all experience, for it goes on all through human history. That is the situation of each one of us.

The effect of the Fall according to the book of Genesis was that the man and the woman were turned out of Eden and an angel with a flaming sword was placed there to bar the way to the tree of life.[4] What exactly does this loss of Paradise mean? The book of Genesis simply speaks of the sufferings which will ensue. "The earth will bring forth thorns and thistles" and the woman "shall bring forth children with pain".[5] This shows that the man and the woman would be in conflict with the world around them and with their own bodily nature. But the division goes deeper than this. It marks a fundamental split between nature and humanity and within humanity itself. The fall of humanity is the fall from the unified state of being, when humanity was in harmony with nature and with God, into the state of division and duality. It is a fall from the unified or non-dualistic mind into the dualistic mind, that is, into our present mode of consciousness. The human mind as we experience it thinks always in terms of duality, of subject and object, of mind and matter, of truth and error, and everything is perceived in terms of time and space. All our science, philosophy and theology are products of this dualistic mind, and our normal way of perceiving the universe around us is in terms of an inner and an outer world. Yet there is always something in us which yearns for unity, which is in search of the lost Paradise, and every religious system attempts to offer a way to rediscover the lost unity, to return to Paradise.

But there is no simple way of return. An angel with a flaming sword stands in the way. There are forces in the

100

unconscious which block the path. The way forward lies only through suffering and death. This is shown in the story of Noah. A flood comes to destroy the earth and everything in it and Noah and his family alone survive. This signifies that this world is destined to pass away with all humanity in its present state, but a new humanity is destined to be formed. Noah and his sons Shem, Ham and Japheth, who represent all the nations known to Israel at the time, are the representatives of this new humanity. It is important to notice that it includes symbolically all the nations of the earth. The vision of the new humanity at this stage is universal and God is represented as making a covenant with the nations, that is, with the Gentiles, as Israel came to understand them. As the biblical narrative proceeds, the new humanity is seen to centre on the people of Israel, but always the "Gentiles" are seen to be included in the promise made to Israel. Thus, as we have seen, when Abraham is chosen to be the seed of this new humanity, the promise is made that his people will be a blessing to all the earth.

From the time of Abraham the promises are seen to focus on Israel as the "people of God". The promises are renewed to Isaac and Jacob, to Moses and Joshua, to David and Solomon. But then comes the great reversal. The kingdom of Israel is divided, the people of northern Israel are taken captive by the Assyrians, and Jerusalem is captured by the Babylonians and its people transported to Babylon. But it is precisely at this point, when the fortunes of Israel are at their lowest, that the prophets come to teach them to look forward to a higher destiny. Jeremiah speaks of a "new covenant", which God will make with his people, when he will "write his law in their hearts".[6] This is the beginning of that passage to an interior religion which every religion has to undergo if it is to survive, and which is so clearly the call of religion today. From reliance on external rites and doctrines religion has to pass to the experience of God in the heart, and this movement of interiority has to be constantly renewed. This comes out above all in the figure of the "suffering servant" of Isaiah.[7] Israel had experienced the loss of everything that made up their religion, their king, their land, their temple, but it was then that they awoke to the deepest realisation of God. The concept of the suffering servant arose when they realised that God was in the midst of their suffering and their death and not in their conquests and triumph. It is through suffering and death that confidence in this world and in the triumphs of the rational mind is broken and humanity learns to surrender to God, to that transcendent Truth from which it has fallen. It was through its humiliation that Israel learned to free itself from its pride and self-sufficiency and to open itself to the other peoples of the world.

Every religion tends to centre on itself, to build up its own exclusive structures of law and authority and so to close itself to the action of God. This was the situation in Israel when Jesus came. There were many reasons for this. Perhaps the most significant was that Israel had been subject to one people after another: first the Babylonians, then the Persians, then the Greeks, and finally the Romans. The result was that Israel tended to turn in on itself, to defend its religion against the surrounding people. This gave rise to the sect of the Pharisees. The term "pharisee" means "separated", and the Pharisees were those who separated themselves as far as possible from others to be "holy" to God and to observe His law as strictly as possible. This was a worthy motive in its way, but it led to an exclusive attachment to the law. This is the danger of every religion, as we see around us today. As a religion feels itself to be threatened, it clings to its old traditions and centres on itself, so that it becomes incapable of further growth or of responding to the movement of the Spirit.

Jesus came to set Israel free from this bondage to the law

and to open it to the new life of the Spirit. He saw himself as bringing to birth a new Israel, a new people of God, which would be the nucleus of a new humanity. There is no doubt that he saw his work in continuity with the history of Israel, as God's chosen people. When he spoke of his "church" (Greek *ekklesia*), he almost certainly used the Aramaic word *qahal*, which was used of the "congregation of Israel". He could even say, "I was not sent but to the lost sheep of the house of Israel".[8] He did not reject the law of Moses or the worship in the temple or the synagogue, but he broke down the barrier of exclusiveness which had imprisoned Israel and so opened the way to a new movement of the Spirit. There was a wall in the temple of Jerusalem which separated the holy place in which the Jews could worship from the "court of the Gentiles", and no Gentile could pass beyond that wall. That wall was symbolic of the division of the world between Jews and Gentiles, the holy people of God from the sinful people outside. Jesus came to break down this wall of separation, as St Paul says: "He broke down the wall of hostility . . . that he might create in himself one new man in place of the two, thus making peace."[9] This applies not only to the wall in Jerusalem and the separation of Jews and Gentiles, but to all those barriers, particularly of religion, which divide humanity.

Every religion tends to build up a wall of separation which divides it from the rest of humanity. In some respects this is inevitable, as a religion has to preserve its own unique values. But in doing so it has to learn to respect the values of other religions. The Christian churches have built up their own walls of separation and excluded the rest of humanity from the "people of God", and even excluded one another from their own particular structure of religion. The Muslims also have their own wall of separation and even Hindus and Buddhists, though much more tolerant than the Semitic religions, yet have their own exclusive claims. Today we are seeking to find a way by which each religion can retain its own unique spiritual and moral values, while remaining open to the spiritual and moral values of other religions. This can only come about when we learn to recognise the relative value of the external forms of religion, their rites and dogmas. Each religion springs from a profound experience of the Spirit which is expressed in a sacred book or sacred teaching and develops its own distinctive rituals and doctrines, but behind all these outward forms there always remains the original inspiration of the Spirit. It is in the rediscovery of that original inspiration that we learn to find a living relationship with the other religions. It is by returning to the source of each tradition that we discover the basic unity which underlies all religion.

If we look for the basic inspiration which underlies Christianity, it is to be found in the life and teaching of Jesus of Nazareth. Jesus came to set Israel free from its bondage to the Law, that is, to its religious tradition, and to take it back to the source of all religion. It is clear that Jesus left behind no definite structure of religion. He chose twelve disciples, whom he called "apostles", and by all accounts gave Peter a position of leadership among them. He also left behind a "memorial" of his death and resurrection, the central "mystery" of his life, but beyond that it is difficult to discern with certainty any other formal structure. What he communicated to his disciples was the gift of his Spirit, which was to lead them into all truth. The essential mystery of the Gospel is this gift of the Spirit, that is, the opening of humanity to the life of the Spirit, which had been lost at the Fall, and its return to the communion with God in which the meaning and purpose of human existence is to be found. It was this which was to lead his disciples to discern the significance of his life and teaching and to enable them to become the nucleus of a new humanity.

It was St Paul who had the deepest insight into this matter

of religion and law. He himself had been brought up as a Jew "educated according to the strict manner of the Law",[10] but his conversion brought about a radical change in his understanding of the place of law in religion. He was able to discern that the whole law of Israel, though holy in itself and given by God, yet had only a relative value. All the sacred rites of Israel, circumcision, the worship of the temple, even the institution of the Sabbath were all seen as of relative importance and could be dispensed with. So he was able to say, "neither circumcision nor uncircumcision count for anything, but a new creation".[11] In this way he broke through all the restrictions of Judaism and opened the way of salvation to all humanity. As he said, "There is neither Jew nor Greek, neither slave nor free, there is neither male nor female, but you are all one in Christ Jesus".[12] Thus all the barriers, economic, social, political, even the division between the sexes, were overcome and the fundamental unity of mankind was proclaimed.

But this principle of freedom from the Law has now to be applied to all religion. Christianity in the course of time has built up its own structure of law and religion, of ritual and dogma and organisation, which have now become a barrier, separating the Christian churches from the rest of humanity. So also Islam, Hinduism and Buddhism have developed their own structures of law and ritual and are divided from one another. We have to learn to go beyond all these differences in the external forms of religion and discover the hidden mystery which lies at the heart of all religion. In Christianity it was the mystery of the resurrection which gave this insight into the ultimate meaning of religion. The resurrection of Jesus was seen as the passage beyond time and space to the eternal transcendent Reality. This was accomplished, not merely for Jesus himself, but for all humanity. The resurrection marks the beginning of a new humanity and, as St Paul says, a "new creation".[13] Just as

Israel closed in on itself and saw salvation in terms of its own limited existence, so the Christian churches have closed in on themselves and separated themselves from humanity as a whole. But in the wider perspective which we can discern today, Jesus died for all humanity and the salvation which he achieved was won for all humanity. We must never forget that in its deepest reality all humanity is one being, just as the whole creation is one being. As St Gregory of Nyssa, one of the greatest of the Greek Fathers, proclaimed, "All men from the first man to the last are one image of Him Who Is". Adam in the book of Genesis represents humanity as a whole, and when this Adam falls all humanity falls with him. So also Christ is the new Adam, the new representative of redeemed humanity, and with his resurrection humanity as a whole is redeemed from sin and death.

It is of great significance that Jesus left his disciples with the understanding that he would return again at any time and bring the world to an end. In a real sense it can be said that the resurrection itself brings the world to an end. It is the passage of human nature beyond time and space, and reveals the whole of this spatial temporal world as a passing phenomenon. We see the one Reality reflected through the changing forms of space and time, but we know that these forms are conditioned by our present mode of consciousness. When we pass beyond this limited mode of time-space consciousness, we shall see the eternal Reality as it is. As St Paul says, "now we see in a glass darkly but then face to face".[14] The whole of human history is a passage from our present mode of existence and consciousness into the eternal world where all the diversities of this world are seen in their essential unity. Our present mode of consciousness is dualistic, but as the mystics of all religions have discerned, the ultimate reality is non-dual. This new mode of being and consciousness is the *nirvana* of the Buddha, the *brahman-atman* of the Upanishads, the *al haqq* of the Muslim mystics

106

and the kingdom of heaven of the Christian Gospel. It is here and here alone that we can find the meeting place of all religion.

As we saw earlier, the sin of humanity had been their separation from the Spirit, their falling back into the separate self, and thereby coming into conflict with nature, with their fellows, and with God. Jesus comes as the man who offers himself in sacrifice in total surrender, to God, to the Supreme, and in doing this he reverses the sin of Adam. Adam, the primal Man, had fallen by disobedience, by following his own mind and will rather than surrendering to the Spirit. Jesus, the new Adam, the Son of Man, the representative Man, makes a total surrender to the Spirit, to God, to the Father, and by that he overcomes humanity's separation from the Father, from God, reuniting humanity as one body in himself. He breaks down all the barriers that have been set up and finally he reconciles creation with himself, as a new creation.

This then is the birth of a new humanity and it can be regarded as a new stage in evolution. Humanity had developed through various levels of complexity, through the hunting, the pastoral and the agricultural stages to the great civilisations. Now with Christ a new stage is taking place and a new humanity is being born. The new humanity is born "not of blood, nor of the flesh, nor of the will of man, but of God", Jesus is the new Man who is born of God, who is the Son of God.

At Pentecost the Spirit returns to man. Whereas in the Fall of man the Spirit had departed and humanity had centred on itself, now the Spirit returns. Adam, the first man, as St Paul says, was a living soul whereas Jesus, the second Adam, is a life-giving spirit.[15] Jesus has transformed the disobedience of Adam into this new man who is now the *anthropos pneumatikos*, the man of the Spirit, and he continues to communicate the Spirit to mankind. At Pentecost, it is said, there were people present from all nations on the earth. This is an exaggeration of course, but it means that people representing the entire Roman Empire, which were all the nations Israel knew, were gathered together in Jerusalem for this festival. It was symbolic of the fact that the Spirit was to be given to all nations.

Through the receiving of the Spirit this new humanity became what St Paul calls the dwelling-place of God in the Spirit.[16] In other words, we are made into the temple of God in which the Spirit can dwell. St Paul describes this in writing to the Ephesians where he speaks of the "immeasurable greatness of his power in us who believe, according to the working of his great might which he accomplished in Christ when he raised him from the dead."[17] It was God who raised Christ from the dead. Christ made that sacrifice of himself, the total sacrifice, and thereby he overcame death which was the consequence of sin. The disintegration of man was healed by this surrender on the cross which is also the reintegration of man. St Paul continues, "And made him to sit at his right hand in the heavenly places, far above all rule and authority and power and dominion, and every name that is named, not only in this world but also in that which is to come."[18] This is a reference to the cosmic powers of which we have spoken. Jesus, through the resurrection, is raised above humanity and also above the whole cosmic order, above all the cosmic powers, and, as St Paul puts it, he is made "to sit at God's right hand in the heavenly places". That refers to the transcendent order of consciousness. It is appropriate to translate these biblical images into the framework we have been using so far. We have spoken of the three worlds where the earth is the physical order, the air is the psychic or psychological order, and the sky, or heaven, the spiritual order. God dwells in heaven, in the spiritual order, whereas, significantly, the spirits are said to dwell in the air. St Paul speaks of the "prince of the power of the air".[19] The spirits of the air, along with angels and other beings, represent an intermediate state, the psychic or psychological realm. Man, of course, dwells on the earth. So Jesus goes beyond the physical and beyond the psychic world, beyond the angels and the gods, to the transcendent world, the transcendent reality itself. "He has put all things in subjection under his feet," which means, as we have seen, that the whole material creation becomes subordinate to him.

The passage continues, "and has made him the head over all things for the church, which is his body, the fullness of him who fills all in all".[20] The Church is this body of humanity which has been rescued from sin and restored to life in the Spirit and now it becomes "the fullness of him who fills all in all". The word "fullness" in Greek is *pleroma* and it corresponds to the Sanskrit *purnam*. In principle, the whole creation has been restored to that fullness. Whereas sin is disintegration and falling apart, redemption is reintegration. It is the gathering of everything into a whole, bringing it into the fullness of God. The whole of humanity is gathered into the fullness of the divine life. And further, all things, the whole creation, as well as the whole of humanity, now become the body of Christ. Christ is, as it were, the soul of that body and he reunites it in the Spirit, with God. "The fullness of him who fills all in all" means that the whole creation is now filled with this power of the Spirit, through Christ who is himself that fullness, in whom "the fullness of the godhead dwelt bodily".[21] That is the understanding of the new humanity which emerges in the New Testament.

When the Church is seen in this way it is being understood in the highest sense. We need to recover this insight and emphasise it today. The Church as it is known today may seem to bear little resemblance to it, but this is the vision of the Church in the New Testament and in the early Church

Fathers. For instance, in the Shepherd of Hermas there is a beautiful passage where the Church appears as an old woman. The Shepherd asks why she appears like an old woman and the text says it is because "she was from the beginning and for her all things were created." So the Church is the new humanity, the body of humanity, which God planned from the beginning. It falls into sin and is divided and disintegrated but now it is reunited. Its previous separations are healed, it is reintegrated and becomes the body of Christ, the body filled with the Holy Spirit. In this sense it is from the beginning and for this all things were created.[22] The whole creation and humanity is created precisely for this unity in God through Christ. That is the plan of salvation as seen in the New Testament.

All this makes it evident that this work of the Spirit has been going on in all humanity from the beginning. Certainly at Pentecost a fullness of the Spirit was revealed, but the Spirit was present from the time that man fell from Eden. The redemptive work of the Spirit was already taking place from the very beginning. In all primitive peoples and in the hunting, agricultural and pastoral peoples there was a presence of the Spirit. The Holy Spirit is present in all creation, in all humanity, drawing humanity back to God, back to Christ, back to the Truth.

Looking back at myth and ritual, which we discussed earlier, we can see that through myth God revealed Himself to the ancient world. At that point there was no *logos* since people were at the pre-rational stage. The *mythos* comes before the *logos*, for the *mythos* is the symbolic story appropriate at the imaginative level of development, whereas the *logos* requires for its understanding the reason and the intellect. Before the development of reason human beings had to learn through myth, and myth was expressed in ritual. So all ancient myth and ritual was the way in which the Spirit was made present and through which the Word was revealing

110

himself. So the Word of God "which enlightens every man coming into the world"[23] was revealing himself through the myths and rituals of the ancient peoples. When it comes to understanding this, there are two possibilities. The myth and the ritual can be accepted as a means or sacrament, through which God is revealing himself, and this is the way of true religion, or the myth and the ritual can be idolized, which means that they are made an end in themselves. We are always either open to the Spirit and take part in the work of redemption, or we close in on ourselves and settle for substitutes for the Spirit in which case we isolate ourselves from God, from the truth. So that is how the Word and the Spirit are present from the beginning, building up humanity into the new body, the new humanity.

The final point here is that this rebuilding of each person, the creation and humanity into one is conceived as coming to fulfillment in a person, the person of Christ. For many people this is a great difficulty for they cannot see the stellar universe or the universe of the atom in terms of a person. But it is in fact a very profound insight. As St Thomas Aquinas said, the person is the highest being in the universe. We understand that matter is the lowest level of organisation, it is comparatively unstructured. The atomic level, the living cell and the plant mark stages in organisation, in the development of a more complex structure. The level of animal intelligence is a further stage and finally the level of the human being is reached. Each human person has the capacity for knowledge and love, that is, a capacity to structure the universe around them and to further its organisation. A person is essentially a being capable of knowledge and love, which means being capable of receiving the universe into oneself by knowledge, that is, by symbol and language, and capable of acting on the universe by art and science. And so "person" is really the supreme reality in the universe, the point at which the universe enters into

111

consciousness. It is significant that nearly all ancient people saw the ultimate Reality in terms of a person. In Hinduism we have the *purusha*, the cosmic Person, in whom the whole universe comes together. In Buddhism we have the *tathagata*, the one who has reached Reality and who is the supreme Person. In Islam there is the "universal man", *al-insan al Kamil* and in Christianity we have Christ as the cosmic Person, the one in whom all things were created. "All things were created through him and for him . . . and in him all things hold together."[24] He is the person who personalises the universe and the universe comes to a head as it were, in him. In this way the whole of humanity is seen as growing, as St Paul put it, to mature manhood, to "the measure of the stature of the fullness of Christ."[25] The whole of humanity is growing to the full stature of the man, Jesus Christ, who is none other than the primordial Man who was there in the beginning and who has now been revealed as the Lord, uniting all humanity with God. That is the vision of St Paul and of the New Testament as a whole. In the next two chapters we will trace out this theme of the cosmic Person in Christianity, Hinduism, Buddhism and Islam, for it is one of the great themes of all the major religions.

6

The Cosmic Person in
the New Testament

In traditional Christian theology Jesus is commonly conceived as God and the central Christian doctrine is conceived
in terms of God becoming man. But this is in fact a compara-
tively late form of theology which was crystallised at the
Council of Nicaea in 325 AD. It is quite different from the
manner in which Jesus is presented in the New Testament.
I want to suggest that this theology, though perfectly correct
and legitimate in itself, is a particular kind of theological
language which was developed over many centuries in the
West and certainly corresponded with people's needs at the
time, but today presents for most people an insuperable
difficulty. Examples of this language are, "God became
man", "He came down from heaven" and "God appeared
on earth". These images, which were quite natural to people
in the past, now appear as essentially mythological and make
the Gospel message appear totally unreal and irrelevant. But
this language, as I have said, is not the language of the New
Testament itself. In this chapter it will be shown that the
New Testament has a completely different perspective. It
does not start at all from Jesus as God but from Jesus as
man. Jesus himself never speaks of himself as God. His
favourite designation of himself is as Son of man, which in
Hebrew and Aramaic is practically equivalent to Man. After ·
his resurrection his disciples came to ask themselves who
this Man was, and interpreted his life and message in the
light of the Jewish tradition as prophet, priest, king, Messiah,
Lord, Son of God, and finally right at the end of the New

Testament period began to use the word "God", but even then with great caution. In other words, to speak of Jesus as God is to use a language which was only arrived at after long reflection and has a very specific meaning. To use it as a general term without proper qualification can only be profoundly misleading.

It is particularly misleading when it is seen in the context of other religious traditions. For a Muslim to say that the man Jesus was God is the ultimate blasphemy. It is to "associate" a creature with the Creator and to deny the absolute transcendence of the one God. For a Hindu it presents an opposite difficulty. For a Hindu there is no difficulty in speaking of Jesus as God since in Hinduism every human being is potentially divine and anyone who has realised his divinity is entitled to be called God or *Bhagavan*. Jesus thus appears to him simply as an *avatara*, one of the many forms in which God has appeared on earth. For many Catholics also, it must be admitted, to speak of Jesus as God is to think that he is a divine being appearing on earth. As Karl Rahner has argued, many Catholics are monophysites without knowing it, believing only in Christ's divine nature. That is, they think of Jesus as God appearing on earth and not as he appears in the New Testament, as a man standing in a unique relation to God.

The language of later theology is a typical example of that abstract, logical, analytical thought which is characteristic of the Western mind as opposed to the concrete, symbolic, synthetic thought which is characteristic of the Bible and of all ancient thought. Thus the word "God" in the New Testament, as Karl Rahner has shown, is never used as an abstract term but normally signifies God the Father.[1] There are, in fact, only six occasions in the whole of the New Testament where the name of God appears to be given to Jesus, and all of these are qualified in some way. The only absolutely unequivocal occasion is the saying of Thomas in St John's Gospel, "My Lord and my God".[2] This is an expression of devotion rather than of theology, but it marks the exact point when the new language began to develop. A little later, at the beginning of the second century, St Ignatius of Antioch began to use it quite freely. But in the New Testament as a whole it remains abnormal and is the result of a gradual development of thought.

If we want to see how Jesus was normally conceived by his first disciples, we cannot do better than to turn to the Acts of the Apostles on the occasion of Pentecost when St Peter, addressing the people and proclaiming the message of the Gospel for the first time, declares, "Jesus of Nazareth, a man attested to you by God . . . you crucified, but God raised him up." Nothing could be further from the affirmation of Jesus as God, and Peter then goes on to say, "God has made him Lord and Christ, this Jesus whom you crucified."[3] This presents the exact terms in which the New Testament speaks of Jesus. He is a man who was crucified and whom God raised up and it was God who made him "Lord" and "Christ". "Lord" and "Christ", that is, Messiah, are the terms which are habitually applied to Jesus in the early Church. The word "Lord" or *Kyrios* can have many different meanings. It can be simply a title of respect like the English "Sir" and it can mean master or owner, but in the Old Testament, when the name *Adonai* in Hebrew was substituted for the name of Yahweh out of respect for the Holy Name, this was translated *Kyrios* in Greek and so the word "Lord" came to be used normally of God. But there are two points to be noted here. The first is that the title "Lord" normally signifies not God in himself, but God as Lord of the world. It always had the sense of power and authority. The second point is that in the mind of the early Church this Lordship, or power and authority, was given to Jesus by God. Thus Jesus says at the conclusion of St

Matthew's Gospel, "All authority has been given me in heaven and on earth".[4]

St Paul habitually uses the same language. He always distinguishes between "God and Father" and "the Lord Jesus Christ". He will speak of the "God and Father of our Lord Jesus Christ" showing how he raised Christ from the dead and "made him sit at the right hand in the heavenly places far above all rule and authority and power."[5] The metaphor of "sitting at the right hand" signifies, of course, sharing in the divine power and authority, but again this is something which is given to Jesus by God. Elsewhere St Paul is always careful to distinguish between God and Christ. Thus he can say, "God was in Christ reconciling the world to himself",[6] which would make no sense if Christ is simply identified with God. Even more clearly he writes to the Corinthians, "All things are yours and you are Christ's and Christ is" – not God but – "of God".[7] Finally there is the passage where he describes the final state of the world: "When all things are subjected to him, then the Son himself will be subjected to him who put all things under him, that God may be all in all."[8]. Clearly here the Son is the Son of Man, the heavenly man, who having accomplished his work in creation returns to the Father, the source of all.

Even in St John's Gospel, where the word "God" is actually used of Jesus, the distinction between Jesus and God is clearly affirmed. In the Prologue where it is said, "In the beginning was the Word and the Word was with God and the Word was God", a subtle distinction is made between the word "God", with the article (*ho theos*) and the word without an article (*theos*). The distinction may seem fine but it is significant. All through St John's Gospel Jesus constantly affirms his total dependence on God. Thus he can say, "I can do nothing of my own authority . . . I seek not my own will but the will of him who sent me."[9] And again he says, "The Son can do nothing of himself but only what he sees

116

the Father doing."[10] It is striking, moreover, that when the accusation is made against him that, being a man, he makes himself God, he replies not by affirming that he is God, but by saying, "Is it not written in your law, 'I said you are gods'? Do you say then of him whom the Father consecrated and sent into the world, "you are blaspheming" because I said, 'I am the Son of God?'"[11] That Jesus believed that he stood in a unique relation to God as Son to the Father there is no doubt. He can say, "I am in the Father and the Father in me"[12] and even "I and the Father are one",[13] but he could not say, "I am the Father" – that would be the equivalent of saying "I am God" and that he could never do. Finally, even at the very end of St John's Gospel after the resurrection, Jesus affirms the distinction between himself and God with the utmost clarity saying, "I ascend to my Father and your Father, to my God and your God."[14] Clearly even in St John's Gospel there is no question of a simple identification of Jesus with God.

When we turn to the earlier Gospels and ask how Jesus was first conceived to have spoken of himself, we should note that when someone addressed him as "good master", he objected saying, "Why do you call me good? There is no one good but God alone,"[15] thus clearly differentiating himself from God.

We can say with certainty that there are two figures with whom Jesus chose to identify himself. The first is that of the Son of Man. It seems absolutely clear that Jesus conceived himself primarily and essentially as the Son of Man. There has been a lot of debate among scholars about this, but that in the synoptic tradition Jesus conceived himself as the Son of Man is unquestionable. It is very revealing that he is practically never referred to as Son of Man in any other of the writings of the early Church. He himself in the Gospel always speaks of himself as Son of Man, and after that the title went out. It is almost inconceivable that the Church

117

would have invented this title and given it to him, only to drop it altogether. The term Son of Man is the most meaningful of all the titles of Jesus. The only other example in the New Testament is very soon after Pentecost, when Stephen is martyred and he says, "Behold, I see the heavens opened, and the Son of Man standing at the right hand of God."[16] That is the only time it is used apart from Jesus" use of it and after that it drops out altogether. It can be said with certainty, then, that Jesus conceived himself as the Son of Man.

What does the term Son of Man mean? First of all it means simply "man". The Psalmist, for instance, says, "What is man that thou art mindful of him and the son of man that thou dost care for him?"[17] "Son of man" there is synonomous with "man". So first of all Jesus presents himself as a man, a man along with the rest of humankind. Secondly, there is an important passage in the Book of Daniel where Daniel sees in his vision, "with the clouds of heaven there came one like a son of man."[18] This eschatological Son of Man, a Son of Man who comes at the end of time, was certainly in Jesus' mind. Before the crucifixion, at Jesus' trial before the high priest, the high priest asks him, "Tell us if you are the Christ (the Messiah), the Son of God." Jesus did not answer that directly because he did not want the title of Messiah which could so easily be misunderstood, but he says, "You have said so. But I tell you, hereafter you will see the Son of Man, seated at the right hand of power and coming on the clouds of heaven."[19] In this he is clearly identifying himself with the Son of Man in the Book of Daniel who comes at the end of time and receives a kingdom and power and glory, and everything is given to him by God.

So Jesus sees himself as man, as a man among men, and as the one who is to come at the end and fulfil all things. But he also identifies himself with the suffering servant of

Yahweh in the book of Isaiah, that marvellous figure who is the servant of Yahweh rather than Yahweh himself. It is important to be clear that Jesus does not identify himself with Yahweh but with the servant of Yahweh. And that servant of Yahweh is one who suffers on behalf of the world. He gives his life as a sacrifice for many. The fifty-third chapter of Isaiah which speaks of the servant of Yahweh is one of the greatest passages in the Old Testament. Jesus certainly saw himself as the suffering servant, and it seems clear that no one had ever before brought together this transcendent Son of Man coming in the clouds of heaven with the suffering servant who gives his life for the world. So what Jesus did here shows a tremendous insight. Jesus as a man would have been steeped in the Old Testament and would have come to see himself imaged in it. He saw himself as both the Son of Man and as the Suffering Servant of Yahweh and he went obediently to death on the cross because he knew that that was the will of his Father, for the salvation of the world. But Jesus went further. He not only saw himself as man, as Son of Man in heaven, but also he identified himself with all men. He said, "As you did it to one of the least of these my brethren, you did it to me."[20] Clearly he understood himself as representative man. Similarly, the suffering servant in Isaiah was representative of Israel. He was apparently an individual but, as we saw in chapter five, he was also representative man. So Jesus is the representative man, the brother of all, who identifies himself with all men and in a real sense represents all men. This leads us to the most interesting question of how the Son of Man is related to the original primordial Man.

It is this theme that I particularly want to develop, because this primordial man or cosmic person appears also in the Iranian, Chaldean and Egyptian traditions. In other words, these countries surrounding Israel, Persia, Babylon and Egypt all had this idea of a primordial Man, an archetypal Man, from whom creation comes. The idea of the cosmic Person is also developed in Hinduism, Buddhism and in Islam. It is very much a universal concept. It seems clear that if we see Jesus in that context we have an image which relates him much more meaningfully to the history of the world and to humanity's understanding of God. It is very doubtful whether Jesus himself had any knowledge of these traditions, but I think it is very probable that in his mind he understood himself as that primordial Man. Significant here are the passages in St John's Gospel where Jesus uses the phrase "I am". "I am" is, of course, the name by which Yahweh revealed himself to Moses and it has become customary to think that by using this phrase Jesus is identifying himself with God. The phrase "before Abraham was I am",[21] has certainly been taken to indicate that he must be God. This, I suggest, is not necessarily so. The primordial man was before Abraham and before all men, and I think it is very probable that Jesus is identifying himself there with this primordial or heavenly man, who is prior to all creation.

The evidence from Jewish tradition is very interesting. In that tradition, it is true, there is very little evidence of this primordial man until the Book of Enoch which was written a little before the time of Christ. It was certainly circulating during his time and could therefore have been known to Jesus. In the Book of Enoch the figure of the Son of Man appears and is identified with the Ancient of Days, who is the primordial ancient one who existed before creation. This supports the understanding that when Jesus said, "Before Abraham was, I am," he was identifying himself with that Son of Man, before creation. The text of Enoch also goes on to say that this Son of Man was hidden until his manifestation at the end. He was hidden from the world and would be manifested at the end, and that links him with the Son of Man in Daniel. Here then there is a Son of Man who existed from the beginning but who would come at the eschaton, the end, and is present now in the world today as the incarnate one. Another point here is that the Son of Man in the Book of Enoch is also identified with the Messiah, and that goes further in corroborating the idea that Jesus would have seen himself in those terms. Although Jesus was reluctant to accept the title of Messiah because it was open to being understood in a purely political sense, yet he could accept it in a transcendent sense.

There was a serious problem for the Jews concerning the Son of Man and Adam. Adam was a fallen man and they therefore found it very difficult to identify the original, primordial Son of Man with Adam, the first man. They did reach a stage, however, when this identification was made. Philo, the great Jewish philosopher who wrote in the first century AD , had an interesting, although quite unacceptable, theory that there were two Adams. The first chapter of Genesis speaks of the Adam who is made in the image of God and Philo says that that Adam was the heavenly, primordial man. On the other hand, the second chapter of Genesis speaks of a man, Adam, made from the dust of the earth and it was this Adam who fell and brought sin into the world. This theory of Philo's is artificial but it does show the problem presented for the Jew by this concept of the heavenly man, and it provides a clue as to why the theme of the heavenly Man was not much developed.

In contrast to the Jews the Gnostics generally took up the concept of the heavenly man and gave it their own interpretation. They held that Adam, the first man, was perfect. He was the archetypal man. The world had fallen away from him and redemption consisted in restoring everything as it had been in the beginning. The end, in other words, was the restoration of the original state. That is typically Gnostic. In the Judaeo-Christian tradition, however, there is always a movement of ascent towards an end. The world is understood as moving forward in an evolutionary ascent towards its ultimate fulfilment and there is no question of simply going back to the beginning.

The archetypal man is said to have been made in the image of God. In the New Testament Jesus is conceived as the *eikon tou theou*, the image of God. He is the one who, as primordial man, comes from heaven. Thus Jesus says in St John's Gospel, "No one has ascended into heaven but he who descended from heaven, the Son of Man."[22]

There is a very interesting passage in St Paul's letter to the Philippians where he speaks of Jesus being in the form of God, the *morphe tou theou*[23] Most exegetes take this to mean that he was God, but I prefer to follow Oscar Cullmann who, in his *Christology of the New Testament* (1967), presents most clearly and convincingly another point of view. The Greek word *morphe*, form, is the same as *murti* in Sanskrit. God has no *morphe* in Himself. Jesus being in the form or the image of God means not that he was God but that he was this primordial man who was precisely and by definition the image of God. He was the form in which God was revealing himself, the manifestation, that is, or the *morphe* of God. What happened was that he emptied himself of that *morphe*, that heavenly state, and took the form of a man. The universal man became a man and took the form of a slave and, as the suffering servant, accepted death, even death on the cross. So the heavenly man becomes a man and that man accepts suffering and death, and therefore God raised him up. God raised him up from death and gave him a name which was above every name in heaven and on earth. In other words, he was exalted to the supreme state as Lord and as Christ, but not precisely as God.

St Paul developed this further, not using the title Son of Man, but referring to Christ as the second Adam. In the first letter to the Corinthians for instance he wrote, "The first man (Adam) was from the earth, a man of dust; the second man is from heaven."[24] Here Paul is using the same image but he sees the "heavenly man" coming at the end, not at the beginning. Again, he wrote in the letter to the Romans about this first Adam "who was a type (*typos*), of the one who was to come."[25] So in Paul's view Adam is the man who fell, and he is a type of the new man in Christ who is to come and fulfill all things. Paul speaks constantly of the new man in relation to the old, a good example being his exhortation to put off the old man with his evil works and put on the new man created in the likeness of God.[26] And also in the letter to the Ephesians there is the beautiful text to which we referred above, which says that he has "broken down the dividing wall of hostility (between the Jew and the Gentile), that he might create in himself one new man in place of the two, so making peace."[27] This is the idea of Christ as the new man who re-unites broken humanity in himself, and in this sense is the new Adam.

The letter to the Colossians goes further than this when it speaks of Christ as "the image of the invisible God".[28] Christ is the image, the icon, of God who is invisible, and an image in the deepest sense is that which reflects, so the text is saying that Christ reflects, or manifests, the invisible God. It goes on in the same verse to refer to him as "the firstborn of creation", which is to say that Christ is not only the man who comes at the end, but the man who was in the beginning. This is the ancient idea that the spiritual world comes first and the heavenly man is the archetypal man, the man who was in the beginning, who is the exemplar from whom all humanity derives. The original man is precisely the archetype, or the firstborn, of creation. And "in him all things were created . . . all things were created through him and for him,"[29] but, as we saw previously, not by him. God creates all things in Christ, through Christ and for Christ, for this archetypal man. The text of Colossians goes on to say that "in him all things consist."[30] In him all things come

123

together and hold together. He becomes that centre which gathers the whole creation into unity. Finally it is said that "in him dwells the fullness of the Godhead bodily."[31] We can see now precisely how it can come to be said that Jesus is God. He receives the fullness of the Godhead "bodily", that is, in his human being. He is the Cosmic Man in whom the fullness of the Godhead is revealed.

This conception of Jesus as the Cosmic Person or Cosmic Lord, who is God's self-manifestation to the world, gives us the key to the New Testament understanding of the relation of Jesus to God. This is shown in the use of the term Son of God, as used both by Jesus himself and by his disciples after him. Whether Jesus himself actually used this language has been debated, but, as Oscar Cullman has shown, it is difficult to avoid the conclusion that it goes back to him, though he used it with great discretion. There is no doubt that Jesus experienced himself in relation to God as a son to a Father. He uses the term *Abba*, "Father", in addressing God, and it has been shown that this was a term of extreme intimacy. This "Abba experience" was fundamental in the life of Jesus. He knew himself in this relation of profound intimacy with God as his Father, and the statement in both St Matthew's and St Luke's Gospels, "No one knows the Son but the Father and no one knows the Father but the Son and he to whom the Son chooses to reveal him",[32] certainly expresses the mind of Jesus himself. He knew himself in this unique mode of consciousness, which could only be expressed by speaking of himself as the Son in a unique sense. This, of course, becomes the main theme of the Gospel of St John, who was no doubt building on the knowledge of Jesus' own intimate experience.

This is borne out in an interesting way in the letter to the Hebrews, where it is said, "God who in various ways spoke of old to our fathers by the prophets, in these last days has spoken to us by a Son, whom he appointed heir of all things

124

and through whom he made the world".[33] Here Jesus is seen, as in St Paul, as the "heir of all things", that is, as the One who "brings all things to a head" and is the end of all evolution, but also as the Cosmic Person through whom the world was made. But it is most interesting that while the writer of the Letter to the Hebrews has this exalted understanding of the nature of Jesus Christ, he at the same time has the most profound sense of his humanity.

Nowhere in the New Testament is the human frailty of Jesus brought out so profoundly as in this same letter, where it is said, "In the days of his flesh Jesus offered up prayers and supplications with loud cries and tears to him who was able to save him from death and was heard for his godly fear". Again the figure of the heavenly man and the suffering servant are brought together, and it is said, "though he was a Son he learned obedience from the things which he suffered".[34] Once again we see the rich complexity of the New Testament concept of Christ. To this we have only to add the cry of Jesus on the cross, "My God, my God, why have you forsaken me?" to realise the depth of the mystery of Christ, who though he was "in the form of God", yet emptied himself and experienced that sense of separation from God, which is the burden of fallen humanity.

In the Letter to the Hebrews Jesus is also said to be the reflection, the *apaugasma*, and the character, the stamp or impress, the expression of the Godhead.[35] The term *apaugasma* comes from the Book of Wisdom, the last book of the Old Testament, probably written in Alexandria under Platonic influence like the letter to the Hebrews itself. This again expresses the exact relation of Jesus to God as an image, a reflection, a mirror held up to the Godhead. It is this that underlies the conception of the Word, the Logos, of God in St John's Gospel. This Word is conceived primarily as the Word of God which came to the prophets in the Old Testament and has now been fully revealed in Jesus. But it also has a wider significance. The concept of the Logos was widely known in the Greek world in which the Gospel of St John was written, and there can be little doubt that the author of the Gospel was aware of it. The Logos was first conceived by Heraclitus as the Reason by which the universe is governed. In speaking of Jesus as the Logos the Gospel is clearly relating Jesus to that Primordial Word which Philo the Jew had already related to the God of the Old Testament. We come back therefore to that primordial self-manifestation of the Godhead, the Word which expresses the mind of God, which manifests his Person. But St John goes on to say that "all things were made through him and without him was not anything made that was made".[36]

This opens up a new horizon. The Word of God is the expression of the Mind of God, and in the Mind of God are contained the ideas of all created things. The Greek fathers spoke of the logoi or the "energies" (*dunameis*) in creation, which all reflect the Logos, the Primordial Word and the Primordial Energy. In that Word of God the whole creation comes forth eternally. All things come forth from God eternally in his Word and through that Word are brought forth in time and space. Again we see how this Word is none other than the Cosmic Person, the Archetypal Man, through whom everything comes into existence and in whom all things "hold together". All things come forth through the Word in time and in space and are given form by the Word which is the exemplar of all creation. And all things derive their energy from that Uncreated Energy, which is the source of all created energy. At the same time all things are being drawn back to the source of their being by the same power of the Word. As St Paul says, "It was his plan in the fullness of time to bring all things to a head in him, things in heaven and things on earth."[37]

This then is the place of Christ in the perspective of the New Testament. He is not precisely God but the Word of

God, the Image of God, the Self-revelation, the Self-manifestation of God, who is reflected in the whole creation and who brings the whole creation back to God. The nearest the New Testament can come to saying that Jesus is God is to say in the Prologue to St John's Gospel that the Word who "became flesh" in Jesus was God (*theos*) with, or in relation to, God (*pros ton theon*). This places Jesus immediately "with God", or better perhaps "in relation to" God, and it is from this that all the later theology of the Trinity derives. It is, therefore, perfectly correct to say that Jesus is God, but always with the qualification that he is "God from God", that is, he receives the Godhead from the Father, which is what characterises him as the Son; and furthermore he is not simply God, but God in man and man in God. He is the "Word made flesh". In this view the Son comes forth eternally from the Father. And this process is not merely a temporal process but an eternal reality. The Son comes forth eternally from the Father as his Self-manifestation, his Self-expression, and manifests God in the whole creation, drawing everything in time and space into the fullness of the divine being. Seen in this perspective Jesus does not appear as an isolated phenomenon, a sudden appearance of God on earth. He is the fulfilment of the whole plan of creation, drawing the manifold of creation back to unity, drawing all humanity back to God, to that fullness of being for which it was created. In this perspective also Jesus can be seen in relation to those other forms of the Primordial Person, the Universal Man, which are found in the traditions of Hinduism, Buddhism and Islam.

The Cosmic Person in
Hinduism, Buddhism and Islam

In the last chapter we traced the New Testament understanding of Jesus as the Son of Man. We saw that he is the
primordial Man, the cosmic Person of whom St Paul wrote
that "in him, through him and for him all things were
created", and "in him all things consist".[1] Through this
understanding Jesus can be seen to be related to a vast
tradition. The idea of the cosmic Son of Man is found in
Persia, Babylonia and Egypt and it has its counterpart in
Hinduism, Buddhism and Islam. This chapter will focus on
how the figure appears in Hinduism, Buddhism and Islam
and later we will follow that through to see both how Jesus
relates to these figures and what is distinctive about him.

Starting with Hinduism we begin with the famous Purusha Shukta in the *Rig Veda*. The passage speaks of the cosmic
Man or cosmic Person in whom the whole world is to be
found. It says, "This purusha is all that has been and all
that will be, the Lord of immortality." *Purusha* literally
means "man" and here it is the primeval Person, the primordial Man, in whom the whole creation exists. "So mighty is
his greatness, nay, greater than this is Purusha. All creatures
are one-fourth of him; three-fourths are eternal in heaven."[2]
The image is a little crude but its meaning is clear. He is
immanent one-fourth in this whole creation, while he is
three-fourths transcendent beyond. That is the figure of the
cosmic Man who both manifests in the creation but also
totally transcends it.

Then there is the very interesting concept that this *purusha*, this cosmic Person, was sacrificed at the beginning of the world. "The gods prepared the sacrifice with the *purusha* as their offering".[3] So the primeval man is sacrificed and the world comes into being through the sacrifice of this *purusha*. The whole creation comes forth from him and from him human beings also arise. In the Hindu tradition the four *varnas* or classes of men, come forth from the *purusha* and form the "limbs" of the primordial man. The *brahmins* come from his mouth, the *kshatrias* or ruling class, from his arms, the *vaisyas* or merchants and farmers from his thighs and the *shudras* or workers from his feet. That was the basis of the caste system in India and its being thought to have come forth from primordial man in the beginning indicates that these functions belong to the fundamental structure of human society. Further, the belief in Hinduism that the cosmic man was sacrificed at the beginning of the world links the Hindu tradition in this respect to the Christian concept in the Apocalypse of St John, of "the lamb who was slain before the foundation of the world".[4]

At the next stage the cosmic Person appears in the Upanishads. In the earliest of these, the *Brihadaranyaka Upanishad*, it is said, "In the beginning this was the Atman in the form of Purusha."[5] This means that this whole creation was originally the *atman*, the Spirit, in the form of the cosmic Person. So the whole universe, matter, life and man, all forms one original Person, the macrocosm. Within this the human person is the microcosm, the small form of the macrocosm. This concept of the Spirit in the shape and form of a person undergoes a continuous development. The text goes on to speak of this person as "the person of light, consisting of knowledge."[6] This means that this being is conscious, or rather is consciousness. There is *achit*, the unconscious universe, and *chit*, consciousness. The cosmic Person integrates *achit* and *chit*, for he is the conscious being in whom the unconscious and conscious are held together in unity. In the *Katha Upanishad*, as we have seen, the *purusha* is mentioned as the summit of all creation and there is a path of ascent to *purusha*. Beginning with the world of the senses and with outer objects you move to the *manas*, the world of the mind. This is the level of rational consciousness. Then you move to the level of the *buddhi*, or intellect, which transcends the ordinary mind and the reason. From the *buddhi* you ascend to the *mahat* which is the cosmic order, the level of the gods and the angels. Next you go to the *avyakta*, the unmanifest, the "ground" of creation; and then the text says, "Beyond the Avyakta is Purusha; beyond Purusha there is nothing."[7] So the understanding is that the cosmic Person is the Supreme Being in the universe and it is he who gathers the whole universe into unity.

In the Sankhya doctrine which emerged at this time, after the Upanishads, the universe is conceived in terms of *purusha* and *prakriti*. These are two complementary principles where *purusha* is spirit, consciousness or person, and *prakriti* is nature from which all the world emerges. In the *Svetasvatara Upanishad*, which is one of the late Upanishads dated at about 300 BC, the doctrine of the *purusha* is fully developed. Here we see the emergence of this cosmic Person as the cosmic Lord. The personal God is clearly revealed. For instance, the text says, "Those who know beyond this world the high Brahman, the vast (the *brihad*), hidden in the bodies of all creatures and alone enveloping everything, as the Lord, they become immortal."[8] The "supreme Brahman" is the name for absolute reality and this text is saying that this absolute or ultimate reality is in the midst of everything and envelops everything and that he is the Lord. He is not only the impersonal *brahman* but also the personal God. In this way the idea of the personal God emerges. The text continues, "That person, that Purusha, is the great Lord." The word "Lord" here is the same as the *Kurios* in Greek and the *Adonai* of the Old Testament, and is the one who rules the universe. He is the great Lord, "the mover of existence. He possesses the purest power of reaching everything. He is light; he is undecaying." It goes on, "He dwells in the heart of all, that Purusha not larger than the thumb, dwelling within, always dwelling in the heart of man. He is perceived by the heart, the thought, the mind."[9] So this supreme Person transcends everything, and at the same time is immanent in everything and dwells in the heart of each person. Each person is a person in that great Person. In the next chapter of the *Svetasvatara Upanishad* it says, "He is the creator and supporter of the gods, the great seer, the Lord of all." The gods are the cosmic powers and they also all derive from the supreme Person, whom they manifest. It goes on, "He transcends all understanding. No one has grasped him above, or across, or in the midst. There is no image of him, whose name is great glory."[10] Saying that there is no image of him means that he always transcends both one's thinking and any attempt one might make to imagine him. God is known as unknown because he transcends all human understanding.

Finally, in the last book of this Upanishad it says, "Let us know that highest Lord of Lords, that highest God of Gods, the ruler of rulers, the highest above, the Lord of the world, the adorable."[11] At this point Hinduism reaches a pure monotheism comparable with that of the second Isaiah in the Old Testament. This cosmic Person is clearly the object of worship, the one to be adored, and yet he dwells in the heart of all. He is both transcendent and immanent. This then is the figure of the cosmic person, the great *purusha*, which appears in the Upanishads and one can see how close it is to the figure we examined in the last chapter, the cosmic person in the New Testament.

Moving on now to the *Bhagavad Gita* we have an even more profound revelation of the cosmic Person. This comes particularly in the later books, the tenth, eleventh and twelfth, where Arjuna is given the great vision of Krishna as the cosmic Lord. Krishna says, "I am the origin of all. From me the all proceeds."[12] He then proceeds to reveal himself to Arjuna as the Lord of creation. Arjuna responds, "I see thee without beginning or middle or end, boundless in potency." "Thou art the supreme resting-place of the universe, the guardian of the ever-lasting law." The everlasting law is the *sanatana dharma*, which is at once the cosmic law and the moral law. He continues, "Thou art the immemorial person."[13] The Sanskrit for this is the *sanatana purusha*, the eternal person. So these different aspects are gathered together in the *Bhagavad Gita*. But another aspect of this eternal person is introduced when Krishna says, "I am time, devouring time." In all these traditions which we are examining the whole created universe, including time, exists within the supreme Person, within that eternal One. Time is in eternity, not outside or apart from it. Finally in the *Gita* Krishna says, "By my grace and my wondrous power I have shown to thee, Arjuna, this form supreme made of light, which is the infinite, the all, my own form from the beginning, never seen by man before."[14] This is the great cosmic vision which Arjuna is given, and he is given a divine eye, a *divyam chakshuh*, to be able to see this form of God, this manifestation. That is the supreme example in Hinduism of the revelation of the cosmic Lord.

There is a further development of this concept of the cosmic Person in the fifteenth chapter of the *Bhagavad Gita* where a distinction is made between three *purushas*. Here it must be remembered that all these words like *brahman*, *atman* and *purusha* can always be understood at three levels. The *brahman* is the supreme Reality but he, or it, manifests in the whole created universe and in the human heart. This means that sometimes the universe can be called *brahman*: "All this world is *brahman*." Or it can be said of the human being: "I am *brahman*, *aham brahmasmi*." He is thus the one Supreme manifesting at these different levels. It is the same with the *atman*. The *atman* is the Spirit, the *paramatman*, the supreme Spirit beyond all, but also the *atman* in the heart of every person, while even the body, and the physical universe, can be called the *atman* because the One is manifesting at each level. The same applies to the *purusha* where similarly there are three *purushas*. Krishna says, "There are two purushas in this universe, the perishable and the imperishable. The perishable is all things in creation, the imperishable is that which moves not." This means that the whole physical universe, which is the perishable, is a manifestation of the *purusha*, and so also is the imperishable, which is the mind, the intelligence, the intelligible order above the perishable. And he goes on to say, "But the highest Person, the *purushottaman*, is another. It is called the supreme Person (*purushottaman*). He is the God of eternity who, pervading all, sustains all."[15] So in the *Bhagavad Gita* the Purusha exists on three levels, the physical and the psychological and then beyond these that of the supreme Spirit, the *purushottaman*.

The supreme Reality can be known as the *paramatman*, the supreme *atman*, the *parambrahman*, the supreme *brahman*, or the *purushottaman*, the ultimate *purusha*, the supreme Person. In this last aspect he is the true cosmic Lord. As Krishna says, "Because I, Krishna, am beyond the perishable and even beyond the imperishable in this world, I am known as Purushottaman, the supreme Person."[16]

So that is the revelation of the *Bhagavad Gita*. Later we will go on to consider how this ultimate *purusha*, this *purushottaman*, is related to the supreme *brahman*. In the *Gita* he appears simply as a manifestation of the supreme *brahman*, the supreme Spirit, but exactly how they are related remains a problem, and the different systems of the Vedanta attempt in different ways to understand that relationship.

A figure comparable to the Hindu Purusha is the Buddhist conception of the *tathagatha*. There is a paradox, though, involved in this. Buddhism began as a very impersonal doctrine. The Buddha denied the existence of the individual human soul, teaching instead that the human being is a centre of elements, *skandas*, or "aggregates". The Buddhist view is entirely dynamic and in many ways is very close to the position of modern physics. The whole universe is understood as consisting of these elements which are dynamic, always in motion, always changing and inter-weaving with one another. The human being emerges as a coalescence or aggregate of these elements, and when the elements dissolve the human being disappears. In the Hinay-ana texts of early Buddhism the emphasis is always on the *dharma*, the law which the Buddha teaches, and compara-tively little on the Buddha himself. This is rather as in the Synoptic Gospels where the emphasis is on the Kingdom of God. Jesus preaches the Kingdom of God and himself as its Prophet. It is true that the Kingdom is present in him but his message is primarily the Kingdom rather than himself. Similarly, then, the message of the Buddha was the *dharma*. His last words were, "Take refuge in the dharma."

There is however another aspect in Buddhism. Just as St John's Gospel develops another aspect of Jesus, focussing on his person and his relation to the Father, so later Buddh-ism, the Mahayana, gradually opens up to the concept of the person of the Buddha. It is generally believed that the Mahayana doctrine emerged about a hundred years after the Buddha's death, at the Second Council. I think, however, that without doubt this aspect is implicit in the teaching of the Buddha even if it is not explicit in the early forms of it. It is equally the case that the high doctrine of St John's Gospel is implicit in the teaching of Jesus. It is therefore a mistake to think that early Buddhism had no understanding of the status of the Buddha and that this was invented later on, just as it would be a mistake to say that the Jesus of the Synoptic Gospels was the true Jesus and the Jesus of St

John's Gospel was a later invention. What happened rather in each case, was an evolution, a development, an unfolding, of what was already present. So the Mahayana, the Great Vehicle, emerged and developed through several centuries after Christ.

The great master of the principal school of Mahayana Buddhism, the Madhyamika, is Nagarjuna, generally believed to have been a southern Brahmin, who lived in the second century AD.[17] The doctrine of the Madhyamika, or middle way, developed in India during the next five centuries and eventually became the principal school of Tibetan Buddhism. The basis of this doctrine was the concept of *sunyata*, the void. The Buddha, in the early texts, speaks of *nirvana*, and *nirvana* is that which is beyond becoming, beyond the world of change. Beyond change and impermanence is that which is unchanging, permanent. *Nirvana* is understood as the "blowing out" of this mode of existence and the awakening to the transcendent reality which the Buddha did not want to name. Buddhism, in contrast to Hinduism, is a negative philosophy. Whereas the Hindu names the ultimate Reality *brahman, atman, purusha* and develops different aspects of it, the Buddha declined to give it any name at all. His reason was that once one begins to name it one then begins to talk and to argue, and one may miss the main purpose of life, which is to know the Ultimate rather than to talk about it. The Buddha therefore gave a practical way, the Noble Eightfold Path, to lead the disciple to discover *nirvana*, and he said that when one reaches *nirvana* all will be known.

The concept of *sunyata* is again a negative concept meaning emptiness, total emptiness. This doctrine which was developed in Mahayana Buddhism taught that the ultimate Reality is totally empty, and therefore all the fullness which we perceive is an appearance of that void. All phenomenal reality comes forth from the void. *Sunyata* has two aspects,

135

immanence and transcendence. *Sunyata* is understood to be immanent in the whole of the universe and along with this is the very profound idea of the interrelatedness of all phenomena. This clearly goes back to the Buddha's early teaching which stressed that all phenomena are interrelated and are dynamic rather than static forms of interrelationship. This has a strikingly contemporary ring about it and is in fact extremely close to the understanding of reality in modern physics. As Fritjof Capra points out in *The Tao of Physics*, to contemporary physicists the universe is a "complicated web of interdependent relationships." That is almost exactly how Buddhist philosophy conceived it in the second century after Christ, for that is precisely the meaning of *sunyata* as immanent in all and as the basis of this whole dynamic interdependent origination of all phenomena.

Sunyata however is not only immanent; it is also transcendent, for it is the absolute, beyond thought, beyond the senses, beyond all phenomena. Early Buddhism had maintained, in its doctrine of *anatta*, that the soul *(atman)* is unreal but that the elements *(skandas)* are real, whereas in the Mahayana teaching not only the soul but also the elements are unreal. This again comes very close to one of the main positions of modern science, which says that our senses do not give us the truth of reality; they only provide an appearance of reality. Similarly, this view holds that science does not give the final truth of reality. No scientific language is ever adequate to reality. What science provides is a certain conceptual framework within which we speak of and work with reality, but science can never lead to reality itself. Neither sense nor reason have access to reality, and the thesis of Nagarjuna was very similar in that neither sense nor reason is valid by itself. The only way we can know reality is by *prajna*, wisdom. *Prajna* is pure intuition such that, rather than knowing the reality in an external way, we become the reality. We become that which is, and realise

136

the One. This is akin to the *advaita* doctrine of Shankara where the way to know *Brahman* is by becoming *brahman*. Here in the Buddhist path we only know the one reality by becoming that reality. This means that we transcend our empirical self, our body and mind. In transcending the thinking mind and attaining total transcendence we experience the one reality, the *sunyata,* for *sunyata* is the absolute Beyond. Nagarjuna has been compared to Kant in his critique of the power of reason, but he goes beyond Kant in recognising a power of mystical intuition. It is fascinating to see how the three great thinkers, Shankara in Vedanta, Nagarjuna in Buddhism, and as we shall see, Ibn al Arabi in Islam, all arrive at basically the same theory of reality. This is why this teaching is called the perennial philosophy, for it relates to the wisdom which emerged in each of the different great traditions.

In Nagarjuna's understanding of *sunyata,* the universe viewed as a whole is the Absolute, while viewed as a process it is the phenomenal world. This means that reality is always there but that we see that reality through our senses and through our reason. When we perceive reality mediated through the senses and through reason it is only partially real. There is a sense in which what we perceive is unreal. The point is that it is the one reality which is present in all the world around us and when we come to the ultimate *prajna* we see the same reality as it really is. Neither the senses nor reason convey it, but in *prajna* we know reality and become that reality; we are one with the whole creation, the whole universe and with its source, the One beyond. This is what is meant when in the *Madhyamika* it is said that ultimately *nirvana* and *samsara* are the same. *Samsara* is the world as it is experienced, the world of change and becoming. The Buddha's teaching was concerned to show how to go beyond the world of change and becoming to that unchanging reality which is beyond. *Madhyamika* says that when we ultimately reach *sunyata*, the goal, then we discover that the whole of this universe which we perceived as changing and becoming is found in its total, timeless reality in that ultimate, in that void. The whole universe is in the void and the void is in the whole universe. In this sense it is truly said that *nirvana* and *samsara* are the same.

The identity of *nirvana* and *samsara* is sometimes illustrated by saying that when one first looks at a tree, one sees the tree as it appears to one's senses. Then one reflects on it and one realises that the tree which appears to one's senses is not the real tree, so now one no longer sees the tree. But then at a later stage one sees the tree as it really is. In other words, one first sees the appearance of reality, then one rejects appearance and finally one rediscovers the tree in its reality, not as an isolated object of sense or reason but as a part of the cosmic whole. Everything is part of this infinite transcendent wholeness which embraces the entire universe and at the same time goes beyond it.

Now we come to consider the *tathagata*. It is strange in a way that the importance of the Buddha as a person should be introduced, and yet one can see how natural it was. The basic conception is of the transcendent reality, *sunyata*, the void, and of the whole cosmos as present within that reality. The Buddha was the one who discovered this reality. Because of this he became known as the *tathagata*. *Tatha* is "that" or "thatness", and *gata* means "gone" so the *tathagata* is the one who has "gone to that", the one who has gone to the reality, who knows the reality, who has realized the truth. Because of this the Buddha is seen as a mediator between the infinite, transcendent void and the phenomenal world. He opens the phenomenal world to the void and he reveals the void in the phenomenal world. In this way he is the one who makes the world known and therefore is the Buddha, the enlightened one.

It is fascinating to see how this personal aspect of reality comes into the otherwise rather impersonal doctrine of Buddhism at this point, the *tathagata* being conceived as the Absolute manifesting as a person. A very similar process happens, as we saw, in Hinduism. There *brahman* is the Absolute and that *brahman* manifests as *purusha*, the cosmic Person. Here in Buddhism *sunyata*, the absolute void, is manifested as the *tathagata*, the person of the Buddha. In this he comes to be an object of worship and adoration. There was no real worship in Hinayana Buddhism. The Hinayana Buddhist meditates on the Buddha, imitates him and takes refuge in him but he does not worship, whereas in Mahayana Buddhism the Buddha is identified with Sunyata, the Absolute but at the same time is revealed as infinite compassion in the form of Avalokiteshvara and as wisdom in the form of Manjusri, together with the other "dhyani Buddhas", who manifest different aspects of the Buddha nature. The Buddha is in this sense conceived as omniscient. He has awakened and realised *prajna*, the supreme wisdom. He is identified with *prajna* so that he is wisdom itself. As omniscient, he knows everything in the world but he also has great concern and compassion for the world and for all humanity. Tradition has it that when the Buddha realized *nirvana* he thought first of simply passing away permanently into that state, but then he felt that what he must do was to go and preach to the world the message of the *dharma*. So out of *karuna*, compassion, he makes this knowledge known.

The Buddha then is supreme wisdom and supreme compassion, *mahakaruna*, with his concern for all humanity and for the whole world which includes all sentient beings. The Buddha came to save all sentient beings and this desire to save was born of the understanding of the essential unity of all. Behind all the diversity of this world of time and space, and behind all the diversity of human individuals and behind all suffering and death, there is ultimately a total unity.

139

Behind all difference there is always the essential unity. Our difficulty is to try to relate the two. Either we see the world in its diversity and lose ourselves in that, or we leave the world behind and we see the one unity. Wisdom is when one learns to see the whole created world, and oneself within it, in that great unity, and the unity manifesting in the whole creation. It was this that the Buddha achieved.

On the one hand, then, the Buddha is identical with the Absolute, with the *prajnaparamita*, the supreme perfect wisdom, spoken of in the great texts of the Mahayana. On the other hand he is turned towards the world in his great compassion. So he is the mediator between the absolute One and the multiple world. Again it is fascinating to see the same figure and the same pattern appearing in each tradition: the Supreme beyond, the phenomenal world and then the one who mediates between the two.

Because of this the Buddha is represented as having three bodies. The supreme body in which he is identical with Reality is his *dharmakaya*, the body of reality. *Dharma* is the absolute Reality and the Buddha has this body, or form, of absolute reality. He is the essence, the reality, of the universe. He has realised the truth; he has become the truth. In that he is freed from all duality. He has attained the unity of all things beyond all dualities. The human mind in its reasoning always works through dualities. We always make distinctions, analyse and reason, and that is how we get a dualistic view of the universe. But in *prajna*, intuitive wisdom, we go beyond all dualities and realise the absolute unity beyond all. The Buddha in his *dharmakaya* is supremely the one who has realised the unity of all, beyond all dualities.

Secondly, the Buddha manifests through *sambhogakaya*. This is his radiant or glorious body, which could be compared with the body of Christ in the resurrection. We remember that Krishna in the *Bhagavad Gita* is also said to have had a glorious body. The glorious body, the body

140

transfigured by the Spirit, is another of the many doctrines common to the great traditions. In Buddhism this radiant body, the *sambhogakaya*, is the second of the three bodies and it corresponds to the second of the three worlds. There were always the three worlds, the physical, the psychic and the spiritual. In the spiritual world the Buddha is revealed in the *dharmakaya* and in the psychic world, the world of the gods, angels and spirits, he manifests in the *sambhogakaya*. He belongs in that cosmic order, in cosmic consciousness. Thirdly, he manifests in the *nirmanakaya*, his body of this world, a human body, said to be the body of appearance. He appears in this world to benefit mankind, very like the *avatara* in Hinduism. In Krishna Vishnu takes human form to bring righteousness to the earth. The *avatara* descends from heaven, from the higher consciousness, into our level of consciousness in order to raise us to the higher level of consciousness, and the form appropriate to this level of consciousness is the *nirmanakaya*.

A further aspect of this doctrine appears in the belief that there is not only one Buddha; there are many Buddhas of whom Gautama Sakyamuni was one. He was the most revered and from him the historic movement of Buddhism started, but as Buddhism developed it was conceived that there were many Buddhas, both before and after Gautama, and also many *bodhisattvas*. The *bodhisattva* is one who has achieved enlightenment and who, instead of passing permanently into the fullness of the void, remains accessible in order to help all sentient beings to attain what he has attained. There are also other forms in which *sunyata*, the Supreme, manifests itself on earth. This point makes it very different from the Christian understanding. For Christians there is one Lord, or cosmic Person, who is revealed in Jesus and that revelation is final, but in the Buddhist conception there are many Buddhas coming into the world from age to age with an earthly body *(nirmanakaya)* manifesting the

141

dharmakaya. Similarly, in Hinduism there are many *avataras*, Krishna being only one of the many who come from age to age to reveal Vishnu, the Supreme God.

From all this we see both similarity and difference. As we compare the different traditions it is important to see the similarities. At some points it is impossible to miss how closely they resemble one another and yet there will always be differences, sometimes subtle, and sometimes profound. Among the most obvious differences are those between the many Buddhas and the one Christ, and between the many *avataras* in Hinduism with their mythical background, and the specifically historical character of the incarnation in Christ. Among the buddhas Sakyamuni was certainly historical but other buddhas and *bodhisattvas* are not necessarily historical at all. Similarly with the *avataras* many are mythological, having no basis in history at all. By contrast, in the Christian understanding, the one Supreme manifests uniquely in that one historic person and in that unique historic event of death and resurrection.

The *tathagata* in Buddhism, then, is a manifestation of the Absolute but the goal is ultimately to go beyond the *tathagata*, the person, to the ultimate transcendence. On this path one will meditate on the various forms and figures of the Buddha and on the supreme form and then go beyond and become identified with the supreme Reality beyond.

When we turn to consider the Islamic view, here again there is the same kind of paradox as in Buddhism. Just as the Buddha gives no importance to the human person and yet this full and wonderful concept of the person of the Buddha emerges, so Islam will not allow anyone to be associated with Allah. The supreme blasphemy in Islam is to associate any being with Allah. Alongside mainstream Islamic tradition, however, Sufism began to emerge a century or two after the time of Mohammed as the mystical tradition of Islam. This is very similar to the emergence of

Mahayana within the earlier Buddhism, and it seems to indicate a kind of instinct in human nature. It is of great interest that, beginning from such different points of view, Jesus in the Gospel, Krishna in Hinduism, the Buddha and then Mohammed, a strikingly similar mystical doctrine emerges in each tradition, each with its own particular character but with an obvious unity behind it. In Sufism a new vision is built up based on the Quran but developed with an extraordinary kind of mystical intuition. The supreme authority on this is Ibn al Arabi, the Islamic mystic of the twelfth century, who was also one of the great philosophers of the world.[18] Shankara in Vedanta, Nagarjuna in the Madhyamika doctrine and Ibn al Arabi in Sufism, have each a very similar doctrine. There are differences but fundamentally the same doctrine is evident. That is why this doctrine can be said to be universal and why I think it is of such importance in relation to Christianity.

In Ibn al Arabi the whole universe is conceived in terms of the oneness of being, in Arabic the *wahdat al-wujud*. That corresponds exactly to *nirguna brahman*, the non-dual being of Hinduism, and to *sunyata*, the void, the non-dual reality of Buddhism. This oneness of being is a oneness of knowledge. Just as in Buddhism *prajna* is not only knowing the Supreme but being the Supreme, so in Sufism the oneness is also perfect knowledge which entails perfect being. It is the same as the Hindu *saccidananda*. The Absolute in Sanskrit is *sat* (being), *chit* (knowledge) and *ananda* (bliss), *saccidananda*, and so to realise the Absolute is to become the Absolute. To know the Absolute is to be the Absolute. It is the total self-realisation. There is in Sufism this same basic principle of the oneness of being. Ibn al Arabi calls this absolute Reality *al haqq*, the truth, the reality, and he distinguishes that from Allah. *Al haqq* is the supreme Reality and Allah is the personal manifestation of the Supreme. Allah is the opposite pole to the creation. He is the creator and manifests

143

himself in the creation. So again there is the absolute Reality and then its polarisation into the creator God and the created world. The purpose of God in creation was a desire to be known. It is said in the tradition (*hadith*) of Islam, "I was a hidden treasure and I desired to be known". Ibn al Arabi has a beautiful phrase for this. He says, "The source of the universe is the breath of the Merciful," the *nafas al rachman*. God is the merciful and, as he manifests himself, he pours forth this "breath of the Merciful". The breath of the Merciful is the will in the divine nature to express itself, to manifest itself, to become known, that is, to realise the potentialities in its nature. The universe thus comes into being to reveal the hidden potentialities in the divine being. To Allah is attributed breath which is very like the *spiritus*, the "Spirit" of Christian doctrine, which "brooded over the waters" and brought forth the world. That is what is meant by "the breath of the Merciful".

There is, then, the supreme Reality and there is the created world, between which humankind is the link. Ibn al Arabi calls man the "isthmus", the isthmus between God and creation. The perfect man is he who unites heaven and earth. He is the one in whom the Divine sees himself and through whom the universe sees the divine. He is the eye of the universe, as the Sufis put it. God sees himself reflected in this universal Man and the universal Man enables the whole creation to reflect God. In this way he is the mediator between God and the universe. So again we have the figure of the mediator and it is particularly interesting that in a doctrine which was so far from having any link between God and the world, the mystical side of Islam introduced this concept of the perfect Man. In my view this is an extremely important point where Christianity can relate with Islam. The doctrine is not of course the same in these two great faiths but it is very similar in many ways. If we say Jesus is God the Moslem is horrified and sees this as

144

blasphemy, but if we speak of the perfect man, this mirror which reflects God and in which God reflects himself, then we are using the language of Islam, which is also the language of the Bible which sees Jesus as the "image" of God.

The perfect Man is manifested first of all in Adam. The Quran says that in creating Adam Allah gave him knowledge of all things. He gave Adam the power to name all things, which is a way of saying that he was given the knowledge of all creation. In the process of creation Adam was placed above the angels and Allah commanded the angels, which are the cosmic powers, to worship him. One of the angels refused and in so doing became the power of evil. This Adam is very like the figure we have encountered in Judaism and Christianity, the *Adam Kadmon*, who is also the original Son of Man, having knowledge of all things and to whom even the angels bow down.

Further, there is a text in the Quran which speaks of Allah bringing forth descendants from Adam. This was interpreted as taking place from the beginning, so that this Adam was seen as the primordial man in whom the whole human race is present from the beginning. Here Allah makes an eternal covenant with this Adam who is pre-existent and in whom the whole creation is to be found. So once again, in Islam this time, we discover the figure of the *purusha*, the person in whom the whole universe and the whole of humanity is to be found.

Adam, then, is seen as the archetypal Man. The whole universe exists eternally in God the transcendent, and is manifested in time and space. So God is both eternal, transcendent, and also immanent in the whole space-time universe. The eternal existence of the universe in God is existence in its archetypes. That is why we speak of the archetype of man. All the archetypes exist eternally, in the mind of God. You and I and everything in the whole creation

145

are eternally present, realized in God eternally, and then manifested in time and space.

The archetypal Man is also identified with the "idea" of Mohammed, or the spirit of Mohammed. Just as the Buddha came to be seen in his *dharmakaya*, as identified with the supreme Reality, so the prophet Mohammed was seen as the source of all prophecy and of all wisdom and came to be identified with *al haqq*, the supreme Reality. Mohammed then came to be conceived as the manifestation of the Supreme. So the same principle is at work here as elsewhere. There is the concept of God, the absolute Being, and of the universe as existing eternally in God and of the archetypal man as reflecting God in the universe and the universe in God. In all the eastern traditions this is worked out in a similar way and it is not surprising that we find almost exactly the same in the Christian tradition as represented by Meister Eckhart.

According to Ibn al Arabi this archetypal man sees beyond the "God created in belief" as the Sufis call it. Sufis have a phrase, "God who is created in belief." In fact we all create an image of God. We need some image by means of which to focus our attention on God so we form images and concepts of God. But the perfect man is the one who does not stop at the image but sees through the image to the reality beyond. In other words, he sees beyond the God created in belief to the undifferentiated truth, *al haqq*, the absolute Reality.

Every religion demands that we pass beyond all images, all forms, all concepts, to the inconceivable ineffable reality. The perfect man reflects this ineffable reality as in a mirror and embodies the spirit of Mohammed, which is the source of all prophecy. This is the point where Islam opens up to other traditions. Some Sufis hold that all religious leaders, Jesus, Moses, Krishna, Buddha and Zarathustra, were all prophets before Mohammed and they all originated from the same source of prophecy, which was embodied in Mohammed who is the seal of the prophets. The spirit of Mohammed is thus seen as the source of all prophecy because Mohammed has realized the one truth, just as Jesus, the Buddha and Krishna have.

From all this we see how there is a common tradition that the divine Reality, seeking to know itself, to reflect itself in another, created this world. For the Sufis it is important that this world is not an illusion. There is a problem here, which will be examined in the next chapter, that the created world can very easily come to be seen as an illusion, as *maya*, in which case it has to be discarded. But in the deeper tradition, this world exists in the Absolute. I think this understanding is present even in Shankara although it is not always clear in his teaching. It is very clear in Hinduism as a whole, in Mahayana Buddhism and in Islam that this world exists in the Absolute. We say that *nirvana* and *samsara* are ultimately the same. So we do not lose this world, but rather we see the total reality of this world in that absolute oneness. That is the unitive vision. Here *al haqq*, the divine reality, reflects itself and is immanent in the whole creation.

It is important to understand that the appearance of the world is not an illusion but is an aspect of the reality itself. It is part of the perfection of being that there is imperfection in it because reality embraces both the whole, the total being, and all possibilities in the whole. In God, in the Supreme, all reality is totally present but there are all sorts of particular realities contained potentially in the divine being, and the world as we see it is the manifestation of these particular realities, all of which are imperfect in themselves. A finite world is an imperfect world. All things are in God in their fullness and are perfect, but here they are manifested separately and are therefore imperfect. But that is part of the perfection of the reality, to be able to manifest all these possibilities of being, all these infinite

147

possibilities as finite beings. So reality embraces both the whole in its total unity and all the possibilities in the whole which are partial and incomplete. The perfect man is the one in whom the divine consciousness is manifest, and who embraces all these partial beings in their unity; he gathers up this whole created world, all these imperfect forms, into the perfect unity of the divine being, and is thus the mediator between the world and God.

From all of this it can be seen that there is not so much a uniform as a unitive vision of reality, common to all the great traditions. Later we will see how Christianity is related to this universal tradition of wisdom.

8

God and the World

The aim of this work is to trace the new vision of reality that
is emerging today and we are looking at Christianity in the
context of modern physics and psychology on the one hand
and of Eastern mysticism on the other. It is appropriate at
this point to recall what has been established so far. We
have seen that in modern physics the universe is conceived
as a field of energies which is structured by an organizing
power, and that this field of energies is described as a
"dynamic web of interdependent relationships." Everything
is interdependent and forms one complex network in which
the whole is present in every part. The whole cannot be
explained in terms of the parts, nor can the parts be understood apart from the whole. What we are concerned with
then is an integrated unity which includes the whole physical
universe and also the whole psychological universe, for we
know now that mind cannot be separated any longer from
matter. This is illustrated in the new understanding of the
origin of the universe in what is called the Big Bang. That
great explosion of matter/energy with which our universe
began about fifteen thousand million years ago somehow
"contained" the whole of what later ensued. The English
physicist David Bohm, as we have seen, speaks of the
implicate order.[1] He holds that what we perceive is the
explication, or unfolding, of that which was originally implicated. What has happened over thousands of millions of
years has been a gradual explication first of all of the material
universe, then of life and then of consciousness. In some way

our consciousness was already included, implicated, in that great original explosion of matter.

Contemporary psychology has taken this up and is exploring the complexity of human consciousness. It is realised that the rational consciousness by which we observe the universe and develop our physics is itself only one stage in the evolution of consciousness. We now know that we can go below our present rational consciousness to various levels of preconscious life and this can be done quite scientifically in such a way that various levels of the unconscious, or, better, the subconscious, can be accessed. It is possible, for instance, to go back in consciousness to the primordial undifferentiated state before mental consciousness as such developed. It is also possible, as we know particularly from Eastern mystical experience, to go beyond the present level of consciousness to superconsciousness. Western psychology has now taken this up. Ken Wilber speaks of the spectrum of consciousness,[2] as he calls it, from the primeval consciousness where there is simple identification with the body, to the superconscious supreme state where there is attainment of total being in total consciousness. That is the view which is emerging in the science of today.

In chapter three we looked at Eastern mysticism and saw that in the fifth and sixth centuries before Christ there was a vast expansion in human consciousness. At that point, in the Upanishads and in the Buddha, the human mind passed beyond the limits of both sense-consciousness and rational consciousness, to experience the absolute Reality. This demanded a transcending of both the mind and the senses to experience the total oneness beyond. We saw also how in the Upanishads this consciousness was explored. The name *brahman* was given to the absolute Reality which was experienced behind the phenomena of the world. Behind the phenomena of earth, plant, animal and human being, there is the universal total reality, the *brahman*. And then the

150

great discovery was made that *brahman*, the absolute Reality behind all phenomena, is identical with the *atman* which is the absolute Reality within each person's consciousness.

The next stage was that *brahman* and *atman*, came to be conceived as *purusha*, the cosmic Person. What distinguishes the person is self-consciousness. *Brahman* and *atman* are pure consciousness. Both are expressed in the term *saccidananda*, where *sat* is being, reality, *chit* is consciousness and *ananda* is bliss. *Saccidananda* is the experience of absolute Reality in pure consciousness and perfect bliss. That is what the Upanishads gradually reveal as the ultimate Reality. But in the later Upanishads, particularly in *Svetasvatara Upanishad* and then in the *Bhagavad Gita*, this *saccidananda*, absolute Reality, is conceived in terms of a Person, Vishnu and Krishna in the *Bhagavad Gita*, Shiva in the *Svetasvatara Upanishad*. A person is a self-conscious being and the understanding is that ultimate Reality is self-conscious; it is capable not only of knowledge but also of love. Krishna says, "Give yourself to me, offer yourself to me, because you are dear to me." The idea is that there is love in the ultimate Reality.

The Upanishads expressed these profound mystical experiences in marvellous language but they did not systematise the knowledge attained. A beginning of systematisation took place in the *Brahma Sutras* of Badarayana in about 100 BC. Later this was completed in the Vedanta, the various systems of philosophy developing between the eighth century and the fifteenth century AD. There were at least five different systems of Vedanta, all exploring the question of the relationship between the ultimate Reality, the personal God and the created world, each conceiving it differently.

The first system of Vedanta is that of Shankara in the eighth century and it is this that is most popular among intellectuals in India. Shankara based his philosophy on the experience of non-duality. For him that is the key to

151

everything. The ultimate Reality is experienced in consciousness as absolute non-duality. The non-dual experience of absolute Reality is, of course, the authentic mystical experience which is found in all other religious traditions. Shankara, however, found it very difficult to account for the created world, for matter and life, time and space. His tendency, in brief, is to say that all that we experience in time and space in our present mode of consciousness is ultimately illusory. We ourselves "superimpose" all the appearances we experience of this world upon the one reality. In Shankara's understanding we are constantly superimposing, for instance, the form of the building in which we are, our own bodies, trees, earth and the sky outside, upon the one absolute, infinite, eternal Reality which is always present beneath all the superimpositions. Consequently when we awaken to pure consciousness, when, that is, we get beyond our sense consciousness, all this disappears. All distinctions and differences disappear and we experience only the one Reality as pure being, pure consciousness and pure bliss. This doctrine has a certain beauty and many accept it fully, but it does mean that ultimately this world has no reality. The whole thing is only an appearance. It means also that each of us as a human individual, a *jivatnam*, has ultimately no reality. That too is an appearance of the One, valid as long as we think in these terms but losing its validity when we go beyond. Finally, in Shankara's view even *purusha* is a projection of the mind, useful and helpful in the present state but also to be transcended until we reach the absolute Reality which has no differentiation whatsoever. When speaking of Shankara, one must always remember that he was a mystic and wrote from mystical experience. He realised that to know reality the mind must transcend all images and concepts, that is, all duality, and realise the unity which underlies all multiplicity. But in affirming the transcendent unity he found no place for the multiplicity, and for this reason his doctrine was questioned by all subsequent doctors of Vedanta.

The advaitic doctrine of Shankara is held today by most Hindu professors but has never been accepted in India as a whole, and all the other systems of *advaita* oppose Shankara. This is very interesting in itself because it shows that there is something lacking in Shankara. It is not satisfactory when this world, ourselves and God are all ultimately lost in an undifferentiated Absolute. Shankara's system is opposed by all the schools of Vaishnavism which believe in a personal God. The first great School was that of Ramanuja, who lived in Tiruchirapalli in south India in the eleventh century. Over against *advaita*, the non-duality of Shankara, he proposed *vishistadvaita*, which is qualified non-duality. He held that the supreme Reality is not simply a kind of impersonal or super-personal *brahman*. It is the personal God, Vishnu, and Vishnu is the supreme Lord, the great cosmic Person. The world comes out from him and the world qualifies *brahman*, hence the term *vishishtadvaita*, qualified non-duality. *Brahman* is qualified by the world in the sense that, for instance, there can be different colours of the lotus, blue or yellow or red, but the same reality is present under all these different accidents. Similarly, the one Lord is ever the same but he appears in all the different forms of the world which qualify his being.

Another illustration Ramanuja used which is more profound is that the Lord is like the soul while the universe, including human souls, is as it were his body. He controls this whole universe from within. He is at the heart of the universe, at the heart of humanity, but they are, so to speak, part of himself. They qualify his being so that he is modified by the universe and by souls. That is not very satisfactory because it is really a kind of pantheism, though Ramanuja always strove to uphold the transcendence of the personal God. Ramanuja held also that the world goes back into

153

brahman, back to the Lord, and then it comes forth again from the tendencies, the *karmya*, forces of *karma*, in it, so that the Lord does not really create the universe. Again this doctrine of Ramanuja is beautiful in a way, with the personal God who is love and grace and who is calling mankind to union with himself, but the Lord is somehow qualified by the world and does not properly create it.

Ramanuja's teaching on this point was not considered satisfactory and in the thirteenth century, Madhva put forward the doctrine of *dvaita*, duality. In this God, the world and the soul are all different but the world and souls depend totally on God. God is *svatantra*, which means that he has his own being in himself while the universe is dependent totally on God. That is an improvement in some ways but it is too dualistic because God in this scheme is not absolutely transcendent. The world and souls exist eternally alongside God. He controls them and they depend on him but they are not exactly created by him and he is not therefore totally transcendent. So that again is not fully satisfying.

In the further schools of Nimbarka and Caitanya there arose the doctrine of *bheda-abheda*. *Bheda* means difference and *abheda* means non-difference, so this suggestion is trying to solve the problem by saying that the Lord is both different from the world and at the same time non-different. This is a paradox, which in itself is perfectly legitimate. God is one with the world and yet he is not one with the world. This difference in non-difference is said to be *acintya* – inexplicable – and that is where the matter was left in the Vedanta. None of these systems it may be said is completely satisfactory and yet each has its own unique insight.

Alongside all this, a new movement emerged in India from around the third century AD. This was Tantrism and it represents a very different approach to that of Vedanta. Whereas Vedanta came from the Vedic tradition, the Upanishads and the *Bhagavad Gita* and from the Aryan peoples who came down from the North, the Tantra came from the indigenous Dravidian people of the South. Tantrism is a religion of Shaivism and Shiva was not an Aryan god. He is always represented as dark-skinned, which means that he belonged to the dark-skinned indigenous people. He was first an outcast, living in the cemeteries and in the wilderness, and then he was gradually brought into the Vedic pantheon and came to be seen as the supreme God. At first a fierce and angry god who had to be propitiated, he later became a God of love, so that in Tamil it is said, "The ignorant think that Shiva and love are one; they do not know that Shiva is love." It is significant that, whereas the Vedic tradition was patriarchal, the ancient pre-Aryan culture from which Tantrism emerged was matriarchal and had a strong sense of the value of the body and the senses, and of sex. Tantra is both the doctrine and the practice of approaching God through matter, through the body, the senses and through sexuality. It is a corrective to the tendency of Vedanta which is to go beyond the body, beyond matter, to the pure Spirit. A great saying in Tantrism is, "That by which we fall is that by which we rise." As we fall through our bodies, our senses, our passions, and our desires, so we have to rise through them. We have to use matter and our bodies in order to attain the goal.

Many methods were developed in Tantra, some having tremendous power. There is the mantra, the sound. One approaches Reality through uttering sounds, the OM and many others, which are vibrations of energy having great power. Then there are yantras and mandalas, which are figures used as external forms through which the divine was approached visually. Above all, tantric practice involves the breath. We learn that the breath is not merely human breath but is the life force of the universe, and eventually the breath itself is the breath of God. We are then living in God, in the Supreme, through our breathing. All these methods,

155

including Hatha yoga, come from Tantra and from the concept of nature as the mother.

Prominent in Tantrism is the concept of *shakti*. *Shakti* is energy. The Vedic tradition had developed marvellously the whole idea of the mind and its transcendence but it did not understand this aspect of energy. Now Tantrism begins to get an understanding of it and is able to work with the energy from which everything comes. So it works with matter, with the body, with the breath and with sex. In the Tantra sex is seen as a means of union with God. One has to learn to control that energy. Instead of letting sexual energy dissipate in normal intercourse and in relations with others, one has to turn it back in yoga and then it becomes a creative force within. Through much practice the energy within rises up through the seven chakras and finally transforms the whole person through the transformation of sexual energy. This system has had a great revival in modern times, the late Swami Muktananda being one of the most influential contemporary exponents of it.

With Tantrism the world of the mother, the earth, and of *shakti*, the divine energy, is introduced and with this the concept of two complementary principles, Shiva and Shakti. Shiva is consciousness, pure consciousness, pure spirit, and Shakti is the principle of energy. The universe comes into being through the union of Shiva and Shakti. There are variations in teaching and practice here, the Shaktas, for instance, having formed a separate sect. For the Shaktas the mother is everything. She is both consciousness and energy, for she is the whole. The more traditional form conceives Shiva as consciousness and Shakti as energy. In Kundalini yoga the energy, the *shakti*, has to rise through all the chakras, which are centres of energy, to the *sahashrara*, the thousand-petalled lotus at the crown of the head where Shiva and Shakti are united. This symbolises the union of spirit and matter, consciousness and the unconscious, and with that union the whole person is transformed. That is all part of the new development of Tantra. It was expressed particularly in the very remarkable system of Kashmir Shaivism, a study of which has been made recently by Michael von Bruck and I owe a great deal to what he has discovered.[3]

The great authority in Kashmir Shaivism was Abhinava-gupta, who was more or less contemporary with Shankara in the eighth century AD. His system is basically *advaita*, where the ultimate Reality is pure being, consciousness and bliss, and it is experienced as total unity. But within that ultimate there are the two poles of Shiva and Shakti, consciousness and energy. What seems to be distinctive in Kashmir Shaivism is the conception of *chitshakti*, consciousness force, not simply as a power of the mind but as a power of the will. The universe comes from the *shakti*, the energy, which is organized by the mind. It is held that between Shiva and Shakti, the two poles, there is a kind of stir, a *spanda*. This stir of energy is a will, as it were. A will is, in fact, conscious energy. Energy which is unconscious in nature is not a will, but in a human being, where the energy becomes conscious, that is precisely what we call will. So there is a will in the Absolute and the universe comes forth from the will of the Absolute and expresses the Absolute in the whole universe.

Kashmir Shaivism is a very elaborate system and we will not go further into it, but the important thing is that Hinduism at this point reached beyond the Vedanta, beyond Shankara and all the others we have discussed, and discovered this power, this *shakti* within the Godhead, which gives validity to the cosmos.

The problem in Hindu philosophy is that the relation between God and the universe has never been finally resolved. In the advaitic tradition matter, life, human persons and the personal God are regarded as ultimately unreal.

157

The Absolute is *saccidananda*, being, knowledge and bliss beyond everything, and to reach the Absolute it is necessary to negate all phenomena. In other systems of Vedanta, as we have seen, the universe, the human person and the personal God are recognised as real, but the relation of the universe to God is not satisfactorily explained. Kashmir Shaivism seems on the other hand to have introduced something which gives a meaning to the whole created universe. It comes from the will of God. The Vedanta would say the universe is a *lila*, a play, but it is a play which is ultimately without purpose. In Shaivism, by contrast, it is the will which creates and which manifests God in creation. This concept of *chitshakti* seems to have been derived from tantric experience in which the energy of matter and life is united with consciousness in a profound mystical experience.

Moving on to consider Buddhism, we noted in the previous chapter that the Buddha went in the same way beyond word and beyond thought to the Ultimate, which is *nirvana*, beyond all becoming and all change. Beyond this world altogether, one experiences *nirvana*, the ultimate Reality. Later, as we saw, it was called *sunyata*, the void, total emptiness. Behind all the fullness there is, as it were, emptiness. This absolute Reality, this *sunyata*, is experienced in *prajna*, which is intuitive wisdom. Always we go beyond the senses and beyond the mind and reason, and experience Reality in pure intuition. In *prajna* we are one with reality and not separate from it. So *prajna* is that experience of the One in its utter transcendence. There is a very interesting remark on *sunyata* by D. T. Suzuki, the great authority on Zen Buddhism, quoted by Michael von Bruck: "It is not the nature of *prajna* to remain in a state of *sunyata* absolutely motionless; it demands of itself that it differentiate itself unlimitedly, and at the same time it remains in itself." Again, within the void, within the Ultimate, there is a stir, there is a principle of differentiation, and this is fundamental.

158

If there is no principle of differentiation, which is the basic point missing in Shankara, then one has absolute non-duality, pure *advaita*. In the void of Mahayana Buddhism, on the other hand, the principle of differentiation is recognised. The universe is regarded as coming out through this principle of differentiation. But, at the very moment that it comes out, in the instant that it differentiates, it returns to unity. This, of course, is not in time. It is an eternal movement outwards and an eternal movement of return, all within the Ultimate. That is why *sunyata* is said to be a reservoir of infinite possibilities and not just a state of emptiness in the sense of vacuity. "Emptiness involves form and form involves emptiness", as it is said. The Mahayana therefore does not dismiss form, matter, and the whole of life and the universe as unreal. The form is in the Ultimate, and is, as it were, the other pole of the Ultimate, so that differentiating itself it yet remains in itself undifferentiated.

Again this is paradox, like the *bheda-abheda*. When we reach this level we are inevitably involved in paradox. Paradox arises when we use language and the rational mind to express that which is beyond language and the rational mind. In this way we can get some sense of how the *sunyata* both differentiates itself in the universe and yet remains in itself undifferentiated. That is the insight. Here particularly we must not forget that this is based on experience. It is not a theory which is worked out by reason. Rather it is an experience which is interpreted in these terms. It is based on *prajna*, intuitive knowledge or active intuition.

Another way to look at it is that *sunyata* in Mahayana Buddhism is infinite interrelationship, which is indistinguishable from the Absolute. Here again we can see the connection with the understanding of modern physics that the whole universe is a "complex web of interdependent relationships". Everything that exists is interdependent and interwoven. An electron, for instance, cannot be located exactly because each electron is, in a sense, in every other electron. Everything in the universe is interrelated and interwoven which means that the idea we have of separate entities is really a product of our minds. It is said more and more, with increasing conviction, that behind all these separate entities which our minds conceive is this interrelationship where everything is interwoven in a complex web. This is precisely what the mystics experience. What the physicists had come to understand as a result of their observations, the mystics have discovered in their experience. Mystics experience the One in this interrelationship, transcending thought. Such an experience does not lead to the denial of the reality of the phenomenal world, and this is part of its great value. Ultimately all mystics affirm that fundamentally *nirvana* and *samsara* are the same. So if we see this world as it is, we will see absolute Reality. And if we know the absolute Reality then we see the whole of this world in that reality, not extended in space and time and limited as we perceive it, but in its total reality, where it is totally realised. We can realise this in our own consciousness, in *prajna*, that is to say, in intuitive insight. That is the position of Mahayana Buddhism.

Next we come to the Muslim mystics and Ibn al Arabi. We noted in the previous chapter that all distinction, difference and conflict are seen as facets of a single unique reality. This is the concept of the "oneness of being", as Ibn al Arabi calls it. It is a total *advaita*, a non-duality, yet it includes all distinctions, differences and conflicts. That is the great difference between this position and pure *advaita*. One of the sayings of Mohammed is used to explain the creation of the universe: "I was a hidden treasure and I longed to be known and so I created the world." The world is created because the Infinite had within itself possibilities and it wants to know all the possibilities of its being. The view of Ibn al Arabi here is very much like that of Kashmir

160

Shaivism. He conceives of two poles, understanding that this Infinite, this Absolute, is self-conscious. The weakness of Shankara is that to him *brahman* is not differentiated. *Brahman* is pure consciousness but it does not differentiate itself in any way. Kashmir Shaivism, on the other hand, reached the point where it saw that Shiva and Shakti have a stir within, a *spanda*, and consciousness emerges. That is a differentiated consciousness. Ibn al Arabi, then, held that there is differentiation in the Absolute, a relation of mutual conditioning. Each pole is not other than the reality itself. There is only one reality, but it expresses itself in these two poles, as it were, of self-manifestation and return to the self.

As we saw in the previous chapter, Ibn al Arabi speaks of "the breath of the Merciful" which releases all the infinite potentialities into the created world. The Lord is expressing himself, manifesting himself, knowing himself in his creation. But at the same time as he releases all his possibilities into creation and knows himself in the creation, he draws everything back to himself in a corresponding movement of unity. In Hindu doctrine this is called *pravritti* and *nivritti*. *Pravritti* is the movement outwards by which everything flows out from *brahman*, and *nivritti* is the movement of return. So the Infinite expresses itself, manifests itself, goes out of itself in the whole creation and then returns to itself. We ourselves, and the whole creation, have this dual movement of going out and returning. Each of us has come out from God and we are being drawn back at every moment. The two movements are always in operation. In the divine they are totally coincident. It is eternal, of course, rather than temporal so that the very movement of going out is also the movement of returning.

In Ibn al Arabi's view "the breath of the Merciful" releases all the potentialities, but this leads in turn to reunion so as to overcome the otherness. In releasing the possibilities the divine knows itself as other. The universe is "other" but at the same time it returns as "not other". So the Infinite manifests his otherness and at the same time realises that that otherness is himself. This is both complicated and paradoxical but it does enable one to see how this whole created universe and our personal lives are in the Godhead, and how we are personal to him, and yet how none of this divides the Godhead in any way. In the Infinite there is absolute unity. All this is in him and yet he is not divided.

The result of this movement of going out and return is that the whole universe returns to God enriched by the experience of self-consciousness. He wants to be known and he brings out this experience of consciousness in life and particularly in human beings, and again he brings us all back into his pure consciousness again. So we are created to have this experience of otherness and to return again to the One. There is always the other and the One, the two opposites, and these poles are always being reunited. The perfect man, as we saw, was conceived as the mediator between the divine subject and the object, between God and the world. Ibn al Arabi describes it as "the eye by which the divine subject sees himself", and "the perfectly polished mirror that perfectly reflects the divine light." So the perfect man is the one through whom the Lord looks out on the universe and knows himself in that perfect man, and the perfect man is the one in whom the universe comes to a head and knows itself in God. He is the mediator between the two and that is the point where we meet God and God meets us, in that perfect man. The universe is the manifestation of the one Reality in space and time and the perfect man is he who gathers the universe into unity in consciousness and reflects the divine consciousness in the world.

Now we come to Christianity. How do we situate Christianity in this context of contemporary physics and psychology and of this mystical tradition? The mystical element is a universal wisdom found in the three traditions we have examined as well as elsewhere and is, in my view, the most profound insight of humanity into ultimate Reality, into God.

Like the other great traditions Christianity also has the conception of an absolute Godhead beyond word and thought, but unfortunately we have often tended to overlook it. It is not very evident in the Bible but it is there. There is a definite mystical tradition in the Bible. Although Yahweh is a very personal God and although he is always seen in relation to the world rather than as he is in himself, yet behind that, as it were, there is always a sense of his being also the hidden God. He is hidden in clouds and darkness. This is expressed in one way in the concept of the *shekina*, the presence of God in the Temple. Within the holy of holies in the Temple there was the mercy seat and it was empty. It was a throne and there was no one seated on the throne because God cannot be figured or imaged in any way. This was the Hebrew way of conveying that God is ultimately mystery. He dwells at the centre of the temple and of the universe and is not imageable. So the whole idea that you cannot make an image of God, which is so important in Hebrew thought, was primarily a mystical intuition. God is beyond all images. Again and again, it was said that you cannot see God. No man can see God and live.[4] That again is a way of saying that he is the transcendent mystery.

In the New Testament this mystical tradition is implicit. Because in the Bible it is not very explicit, Christianity generally has a much less developed mystical tradition than Buddhism, Hinduism or Islam, but we need to be clear that the roots of it are there in the New Testament. St John declares emphatically, "No one has seen God at any time."[5] Again the letter to Timothy speaks of God "dwelling in inaccessible light."[6] This expression, which is found towards the end of the New Testament period and suggests the

163

influence of Greek thought, reveals the absolute transcendence of the Godhead. This was developed in the Greek fathers in the context of the concept of the incomprehensibility of God. There was a tendency in Arius, the author of the Arian heresy, and especially in Eunomius, who was one of the principal Arian theologians, to say that God could be described, but the orthodox Church Fathers opposed this and insisted that God is beyond all description. All the words used to speak of God merely point to that which cannot be described, that which cannot be uttered. So in the Greek Fathers, with their deep metaphysical sense, this awareness of the incomprehensibility and ineffability of God became fundamental. It is prominent in Clement of Alexandria, in Origen and especially in Gregory of Nyssa who was the greatest mystic among the Greek Fathers and who speaks of God being known in darkness. We can know him in the light through all the ways in which he reveals himself, through the Bible and the sacraments, and through Christ and the incarnation, but in himself he is beyond the light and can only be ultimately known in the darkness.

The theme of God's utter incomprehensibility was taken up by Dionysius the Areopagite, who is a key figure here. He is generally supposed to have been a Syrian monk of the sixth century who was a disciple of the Neo-platonists. He speaks of the Godhead as beyond all names, all images and all concepts, beyond being itself. Rather like the position held by Nagarjuna, this involved a systematic elimination of all names, all images and all concepts. The only way to know God is by unknowing, by going beyond concepts, beyond the rational mind and receiving a ray of the "divine darkness". This is mystical language. One has gone beyond and has experienced God in the darkness, as the light beyond the darkness, and as the light in the darkness, as it were. So that is the essential Christian mystical experience.

Dionysius the Areopagite was for a long time accepted as having been a disciple of St Paul. This was a fortunate mistake because it led to his being taken into the whole Catholic tradition, where he became one of the authorities for St Thomas Aquinas and the medieval doctors of the Church generally. In fact his teaching became fundamental Catholic doctrine. It was largely lost at the Reformation because the reformers went back to the Bible alone and in the Bible the mystical tradition, although present as we have seen, is not so strong. In the Catholic tradition it has always been there, although to some extent it has been underemphasised, especially in recent times, but it is in fact at the centre of the tradition.

In the Bible itself this incomprehensible Godhead, which is one with the mystical vision of India and of Islam, is revealed in Jesus of Nazareth. That is the essential Christian faith. The ineffable Godhead, the one absolute reality, was revealed in the historic person of Jesus of Nazareth at a particular time and at a particular place. It has to be emphasised that, in the biblical faith, it is a matter of the infinite being manifest in the finite, the eternal in the temporal, in a specific historical time and place. This is a key point by which the Christian revelation is distinguished from the Hindu and the Buddhist view. For the Hindu the *avatara* is first of all not historical. Many *avataras* are purely mythological, the tortoise, the fish, the boar and the lion, for instance. Even Krishna and Rama, the supreme *avataras*, are not fully historical. They are legendary figures, probably with some historical background, but in their case the historicity is not important. Any Hindu will say that whether Krishna lived or not he is a symbol of the divine, a symbol of the Godhead. As such he is of infinite value, whereas his historicity, or otherwise, is not significant.

It is the same with the Buddha. Buddha was a historical person, no doubt, but for the Buddhist this is not important.

There were hundreds of buddhas and *bodhisatvas*, all symbols of the great *sunyata*. But in the Christian tradition the infinite reveals itself in a historic time and place and this gives value to history and time. In the Eastern traditions time is cyclic. In Hinduism everything comes out from the *brahman*, as the *Bhagavad Gita* says, and it returns and comes forth again in endless cycles. But in the Judaeo-Christian tradition all time is moving towards an end, the *eschaton*, which is the final fulfilment of all things. This is why Jesus is said to be not an *avatara* who can come again and again, nor a buddha who has many other buddhas before and after him, but rather the one who brings the whole purpose and meaning of the entire universe to a head. It was the divine plan, "in the fullness of time, to bring all things to a head in him, things in heaven and things on earth."[7] That is one of the central affirmations of the gospel.

The infinite, then, is manifest in Jesus, in this historic person coming within the historic context of Israel. He was the prophet who was expected to initiate the Kingdom of God, the priest who was to reconcile man with God, and also the king, the ruler, the messiah, who was to rule as God, in the place of God. Jesus was born in that historic context and was recognised to be the fulfilment of all these roles as God's revelation on earth. That is the understanding of Jesus within the Hebrew context. Further, Jesus' earthly life ended at the crucifixion and the crucifixion is an historic event. "He was crucified under Pontius Pilate," as the Creed says. It is really an extraordinary thing that it should be of the essence of Christian faith that Jesus was crucified under Pontius Pilate at a particular time in history and under a particular Roman governor. This kind of thing is absolutely alien to Hinduism or Buddhism. When Krishna or Rama, or Buddha in the Mahayana, lived is of no account whatsoever; they are manifestations of the eternal, not confined to any time or place.

166

Jesus, on the other hand, manifests the infinite God in historic time and place and in his historic death, dying on the cross. There are many ancient myths of the god who dies and rises again but these are symbolic figures and their meaning is deep but different. Jesus' death, on the other hand, is not simply symbolic. He was an historic person, and the descriptions we have of his suffering and death, in the four different accounts in the Gospels, are given in minute detail. On that historic death and on the resurrection the whole Christian faith centres. The experience of the disciples after the death of Jesus, that the body was not to be found in the tomb and Jesus' appearances to them, convinced them that he was risen from the dead. They understood that, unlike Lazarus who was raised from the dead but simply carried on with his limited life in this world, Jesus was alive for evermore, transcending this world. What this means is that in the death and resurrection of Jesus the matter of this world was transformed. In other doctrines, in other great faiths, matter is often conceived simply as an appearance and the appearance disappears when we have reached the one reality. But in the Christian understanding the matter of the universe is transformed. The atoms, the molecules, the cells of Jesus' body, which are part of this cosmic energy, were changed. Matter is a temporary condensation of energy and that structure of energy which made up the body of Jesus on the cross was transformed into a new structure. It maybe suggested that in the resurrection that structure of energy became a psychic body, which is a more subtle body. His body was first of all what is called a gross body which anyone could recognise, and then it became a subtle body, which could not always be recognised. This subtle body could appear and disappear, as we know from the Gospel narratives. Finally he becomes a spiritual body at the Ascension. He transcends matter at both the gross and the subtle levels and enters the spiritual level and, with that transformation, the matter of this universe is taken up into the Godhead. That is the Christian mystery. It is amazing when we begin to grasp it, that the matter which exploded in the so-called Big Bang fifteen or even twenty billion years ago at that point was finally transfigured. In fact the transfiguration has been going on all through history and we ourselves are involved in this transformation of matter, as consciousness is working on matter. The Christian understanding is that in Jesus consciousness finally took possession of matter, and this means that matter was spiritualized. In him the matter of the universe was, in other words, made totally conscious and became one with God, in the Godhead.

It is also important to emphasise that the soul of Jesus did not disappear. In the view of Shankara and so many others the *jivatman* disappears at death. You simply realise yourself in the total reality and there is no *jiva*, no individual, any more. But the soul of Jesus, that unique Jew of the first century with all his personal characteristics, is eternal in the Godhead. It is not that he disappears into the Godhead. Rather, both the body (*soma*) and the soul (*psyche*) are taken up into the spirit (*pneuma*) in the transcendent one and are totally transfigured in the One. This is beyond our comprehension but we can perhaps try to conceive how it takes place.

We see that in Christ the world of space and time is not annihilated; it does not disappear but it is transfigured, and that is precisely what St Paul means by the New Creation. The New Creation is this present creation transformed into the spiritual creation, matter no longer obeying the present laws which, as we know, are related only to this particular stage in evolution. All material laws are simply stages in evolution. At the inorganic level there are certain laws operating, and then new laws come into being as the earliest living creatures emerge. Later, new laws develop pertaining to the animal level and, later still, other new laws develop pertaining to human persons. The next stage is the transcendence of finite being, as we enter into the divine consciousness and into the divine mode of being. That is the New Man of St Paul, which is also the heavenly Man and can be related, as we saw, to the perfect Man of the Muslim tradition and the *purusha* of the Hindu. But there is this great difference here in Christianity, that the individual human being of Jesus does not disappear in the Ultimate but rather is fully realised. As with Kashmir Shaivism and Mahayana Buddhism, the Christian tradition recognises interrelationship in the Absolute. Shankara denied any relationship or differentiation in the Absolute. For him the Absolute is *saccidananda*, pure being, pure consciousness and pure bliss, with no differentiation whatever. Kashmir Shaivism, on the other hand, maintains the differentiation into Shiva and Shakti which we have discussed, and the *spanda*, the pulse or stirring of will between them which is self-conscious within the One. The One is totally one without duality, yet there is also differentiation. This is expressed in the gospel when Jesus says, "I am in the Father and the Father is in me."[8] If Jesus had been an *advaitin* he would have said, "I am the Father" or "I am God." Jesus never says that. In saying, "I am in the Father and the Father in me", "I know the Father and the Father knows me," "I love the Father, the Father loves me," Jesus is affirming total interpersonal relationship.

It is very significant indeed that physics now sees the whole universe as a web of dynamic interrelationships. When we come to the human person, our lives are also a network of interrelationships. At the human level the child is related to the mother and then to father, brothers and sisters, friends and so on, in a web of relationships. The question is, do these relationships disappear in the ultimate? In this Christian understanding there are relationships in

169

the ultimate and Jesus himself expresses this by saying, "I am in the Father and the Father in me", and also when he prays "that they may be one as thou in me and I in thee, that they may be one in us."[9] Jesus' prayer is that as he is in the Father in his personal relationship, so we also may be in him and he in us, which means that we also enter into that interpersonal relationship within the Godhead.

There is a very important concept here. As in Kashmir Shaivism and in Buddhism there is the principle of differentiation in the Ultimate, so in the Christian view the *logos*, the Word of God, is the principle of differentiation in the Godhead. The Father is the source, the one, the origin, from which everything comes, and the Father knows himself in the Son. He expresses himself and differentiates himself in the Son. So there is interpersonal relationship there in the ultimate, in eternity. But also, at the very moment that he differentiates himself in the Son he unites himself with the Son in the Spirit, just as in the other doctrines there are the two movements, the going out and coming in, which are identical in the Godhead. We speak of this as being in time, of course, but time is a category of the created universe, not of God. So in the Trinity the Father eternally knows himself, differentiates himself, in the Son, and is eternally united with himself, in the Holy Spirit. So here is the same principle of differentiation in unity that we saw in the other spiritual traditions.

Putting this in another way may perhaps make it more intelligible. The Father expresses himself in the Son, totally and perfectly, but in the Son and in the Word all the potentialities of creation are present and therefore in expressing himself in the Son, the Father expresses the possibilities latent in himself in his Word. St Thomas Aquinas, and the Christian tradition generally, calls these possibilities "ideas" in God. This is based on Plato, where the notion of ideas meant that everything in this world exists first as an eternal idea. Every plant and tree and animal and person has its eternal idea, its archetype, in God. These ideas in God are identical with God. There is no differentiation at that stage. God knows himself in all these. He knows himself in you and in me, eternally. Eckhart says, "God only spoke one word, and in that word the whole creation came into being." Then by an act of the creative will, like the will that stirs between Shiva and Shakti in Kashmir Shaivism, these possibilities of being, these finite possibilities, appear in space and time in the universe as we know it and reflect their archetypes in the One. And as they emerge from the eternal into time they are being drawn back from time and space into the eternal. We are all in that movement of *pravritti* and *nivritti*. So everything comes forth from the Father in the Word and everything is being drawn back to the Father in the Spirit.

The difference in the Christian position here is that everything that returns to the Father returns through the Son and the Spirit and so comes back transformed. That is the whole rhythm of the universe. It comes out through the Word into time and space. The Word is the intelligence, the mind, which organizes the universe, and the Spirit is the energy which develops the universe. The Spirit is drawing everything back to its origin, bringing atoms, molecules, cells, plants, animals and human beings, back to their source in God. We ourselves are precisely at that point where we have come forth through the Word and are experiencing ourselves in this world of differentiation, and we are being drawn back by this movement of the Spirit towards our source. That movement of the Spirit takes place in every person. Each person emerges into creation in time and space but there is within each the *pneuma*, the point of the spirit, which enables one to know oneself and to experience oneself as open to the divine mystery and as being drawn towards something beyond the self. As Karl Rahner says, the sense of self-

171

transcendence is fundamental to human beings. We all have an urge to transcend ourselves. That is why people want to do things like climbing mountains and going to the moon. It is a need to transcend, to get beyond the self. That is also why we fall in love. We want to get out of our self into another. Clearly we are drawn out of ourselves all the time, but this impulse towards self-transcendence is only fulfilled when we are drawn back to our source, when we give ourselves back totally to the origin from which we come. That is the ultimate meaning of the impulse of love.

In this process of being drawn back in that way to the source, sin is the refusal to respond. Sin is the refusal to love. Love is drawing us back to itself. It has given us our being, put us in this world with all its problems, but it is always drawing us back. This instinct of self-transcendence is the movement of love. Also each person's creation is a movement of love. The Father wills us, loves us into exist-ence. He conceives us in the Word and wills us in the Spirit, and he expresses his love in bringing us forth. We are an effect of that divine love, and the very love which sends us forth from him draws us back to him all the time. If we respond, then we grow in this world and gradually we are transformed, as Jesus was in the resurrection, and we return to the Father. Sin, on the other hand, is the refusal to go back to the source. We want to stay where we are and we cling to ourselves, or we cling to our mother or the earth or to money. Clinging to anything stops our return. Grace is when we open ourselves and allow ourselves to be drawn out of ourselves, to return to God in this movement of love. Sin is always a refusal of love and grace is always a response to love. Love moves the universe as Dante put it, "The love which moves the sun and other stars." The universe comes into being through that motion of love in the Godhead, that *spanda* or pulse of will, which wishes to express itself in love and in the desire to be loved. God wants to make himself

172

known and he wants us to know him, to return to him in knowledge and love.

In the final state creation and humanity return to God. That movement is taking place and, while sin obstructs it to some extent, redemption overcomes it. Redemption in Christ has overcome the disintegrating forces of sin and has restored mankind to unity. In him we are able to return to the source. We are able to return to God and to exist eternally in God, each participating in the one divine reality, yet remaining distinct. This is the Christian vision. We do not merge in the Godhead like a drop of water into the ocean as is sometimes said, but we enter the Godhead. We are transfigured by God, as Jesus was in the resurrection, and we become one with God, but we do not lose our distinction.

There is a very interesting illustration of what this means in the work of Beatrice Bruteau,[10] where she emphasises that love is the instinct by which we go out of ourselves to another, and identify ourselves by our participation in another. In doing this we develop and grow. A person is a dynamism of love and we become a person as we give ourselves to others. In other words, we grow by relationship with others. The world is in fact a web of relationships, and each one of us is a centre of relationship. If we isolate ourselves we die; we are breaking the rhythm of the universe and that is sin. On the other hand, if we open ourselves in love we go out to the other. As we relate to another person, when we first encounter them they are an object, but as we begin to know them we begin to share their thoughts, feelings, desires, fears and hopes. We begin to share with one another. Bruteau says that our ultimate desire is to be totally one with that other, so that we share and participate in unity. But this certainly does not mean that we dissolve into the other. Here, as Pierre Teilhard de Chardin emphasises, "union differentiates." This means that the more we are united with others, the more we become ourselves. So each is in the other and in the One who unites all the others together. The basis of this is the Christian understanding of the Trinity. The Father is in the Son in a total self-giving to the Son, and the "I" of the Son is one with the Father. Similarly, in the Holy Spirit the "I" of the Father and the "I" of the Son are united in the "I" of the Spirit. It is a total interrelationship of unity; in other words, total non-duality and yet with this profound differentiation. That is also what we experience in our lives in the experience of love, when we can share and participate in the identity of the other. The ultimate state is when we all reach that state of pure identity in difference.

A good illustration of this in the Hindu tradition is the "net of Indra", which is a network of pearls so arranged that every pearl reflects every other pearl and the whole of which they are parts. So in the ultimate state each person reflects the One who is present in every person and in everything. This is a total interrelationship of interpenetration and of transparency. These are only words that we use to try to present this mystery to ourselves but they are important because all the time, particularly in India, one is faced with the opposite tendency, which is to think that when one reaches that ultimate state all differences disappear. It is thought that there are no more individuals and no longer a personal God, but only *saccidananda*, being, knowledge and bliss. That is a profound mystical intuition and Shankara, certainly, realised the unity of all things, but he was not able to reconcile it with differentiation. On the other hand, as we have seen, Kashmir Shaivism, Buddhism and Sufism have all been able to discern how the differentiation is part of the unity. All hold in different ways that the One differentiates himself and yet remains undifferentiated. That is the mystery.

All this has a very practical meaning, which is that our life in this world has eternal value. Each one of us as a person is a unique manifestation of the One, and each has

174

a unique destiny to experience the divine and to experience unity with all the others. It means also that our life in this world day by day, and hour by hour, has eternal value. And it means that history itself, the evolution of humanity and of the world, is all part of this divine drama. The whole universe is to be taken up into the divine along with the whole of humanity in all the stages of its history. All is part of this movement of the divine in matter, in life, in humanity, and we are all being drawn into that, such that our ultimate state is a total fullness of being as we experience the whole.

Again, modern physics affirms that the whole is present in every part. When we begin consciously to enter that state we become aware of ourselves as parts, as it were, of that whole, but also the whole is present in each one of us. Each one is a microcosm, and the macrocosm is present in each one. We are all within that total unity which is ultimately non-dual. This is an absolute unity and yet it embraces all the diversity and all the multiplicity of the universe. It must always be remembered that these are only words which we use to describe a reality infinitely beyond our conception, but they are useful in so far as they point us towards that reality, both theoretically and practically. It is important not least because this affects our practical lives. If we think that the universe is ultimately unreal and that our own lives are unreal we will live accordingly. But it will make all the difference to how we live when we realise that this universe is created by God, that it has infinite eternal value, that each one of us has an infinite eternal value in the sight of God and that we all form a unity which yet embraces all diversity. So we are fulfilled in that Absolute in our own individual being, and in the whole cosmic order and the fullness of Reality.

9

The Ascent to the Godhead

In this chapter we are going to explore the ascent to the Godhead. We have seen in chapter three how a breakthrough in consciousness took place in the sixth century before Christ with the Upanishads and the Buddha. This was a breakthrough beyond the senses, beyond the imagination and beyond the mind, to the experience of the absolute, transcendent Reality. From that time there has been in India an exploration of these higher levels of consciousness which has gone further than anywhere else in the world. It is an exploration of inner space which is much more significant than the exploration of outer space. It is the discovery of the levels of consciousness in human existence, leading to the ultimate reality. This is something which has profound meaning for the whole world, and today many people are discovering it in the West as well as in the East. In the West particularly there has recently been the great discovery that there is this inner world to be explored, although knowledge and experience of it was by no means absent before, as we shall see here and particularly in chapter eleven.

We will trace this breakthrough to the transcendent reality in the Hindu tradition. The Buddhist tradition is no less rich, particularly in the Mahayana and in the Vajrayana of Tibet, but to explore that would take us too far afield. So we will concentrate on the Hindu development and see how that tradition has come to explore this reality. It begins with the discovery of *brahman*, the one Reality behind all phenomena. Then comes the realisation that this one reality behind all phenomena is one with the Reality behind human consciousness. Whether we move from the outer world to discover the Reality behind it, or from the inner world to discover the reality within, we encounter this one Reality, the *brahman*, or the *atman*, the Self, as it is called.

What is involved then is the search for the Self, the inner Reality of the human being. This is expressed very well in the *Isa Upanishad*, which, as it were, summarises the doctrine, "He who sees all beings in his self, (*atman*) and his self in all beings, he loses all fear."[1] This is to discover one's self and the whole creation within and this is the goal of this yoga, as it came to be called. So we see at this stage the beginnings of the path of yoga. Here it should be noted that Vedanta is the doctrine and yoga is the practical method of how to explore, how to discover ultimate Reality. We have seen in the previous chapter and elsewhere some aspects of the Vedantic doctrine of the knowledge of that Reality.

The first indication is in the *Katha Upanishad*, one of the earlier Upanishads dated at about 500 BC, where we see, first of all, the structure of the universe and of human consciousness, as it had come to be understood at this period. There it says, "Beyond the senses (*indriyas*) is the mind, the *manas*. Beyond the mind is the intellect, the *buddhi*. Beyond the intellect is the *mahat*, the great self. Beyond the *mahat* is the *avyakta*, the unmanifest, and beyond the unmanifest there is *purusha*."[2] This is what Ken Wilber calls the "spectrum of consciousness", the degrees of knowledge, which starts from the senses, the *indriyas*, through which immediate experience comes. The mind then works on the senses and the aspect of mind working on the senses is the *manas*, this term being derived from the root *ma*, to measure, so the *manas* is "the measuring mind". This is the lowest level of mind. Beyond this is the *buddhi*, the intellect or higher intelligence. This is the mind which knows transcendent reality and the first principles of being and of truth. Aristotle called this the *nous* and St Thomas Aquinas called it the *intellectus*. Whereas the *manas* is equivalent, in St Thomas's understanding, to the *ratio*, the logical, analytical, discursive aspect of the mind which goes from one thing to another, the *intellectus* is the pure intelligence.

So far we have gone beyond the senses and the mind to the intellect, but the next stage opens new ground for most in the West. This next stage is that of the *mahat* which is the great Self, the cosmic Self, or cosmic consciousness. Cosmic consciousness arises from the understanding that the world of the senses, the physical world, is a unity in which everything is interconnected. As the science of today says, the whole physical world is a web of interrelated being, and we are part of that web of interrelationships. So also our individual consciousness is part of a larger consciousness in which we all participate. That is the cosmic order, the cosmic consciousness. In that, as we shall see later, are included all the higher realms of being, the angels, the gods and the cosmic powers.

Beyond that world of the *mahat* is the *avyakta*, the unmanifest. Before anything comes into manifestation, to be known by the mind, it is first unmanifest. It is in the seed. That is what is called *mula prakriti*, the root nature or the cosmic nature, in which all is gathered up. Using the language of David Bohm we could say that this is the implicate order. The *mula prakriti* is where all things are implicated in one, like a seed from which the whole creation comes. From the *mula prakriti* the whole creation comes into manifestation in the world that we see. Then beyond the *avyakta* is *purusha*, that great cosmic Person whom we have been considering, and he is the end. Beyond *purusha* there is nothing. He is the goal. So we move from the senses and the mind to the intellect, to the cosmic consciousness, to the unmanifest and finally to the supreme person. Later, as we shall see, further distinctions are made within that ultimate, that person. But at present the *purusha* is the end.

The *Katha Upanishad* then shows the path to this supreme goal. The text says, "A wise man should keep down speech in mind". Speech is that by which we go out of ourselves, communicate to others, and when we begin to meditate we have to withdraw from speech into the mind, into the *manas*. Then "he should keep the mind within the self which is knowledge."[3] That is, we should bring the *manas* into the *buddhi*. The *manas* is discursive, it goes from one thing to another, whereas the *buddhi* is single-pointed, *ekagraha*, one-pointed. It is "the still-point". It is the key point where we open on the transcendent. It must be realised that not only does modern Western philosophy not go beyond that but, in fact, it has hardly reached that point. In the West the mind simply stops at the *manas*. But in the Hindu tradition, beyond the *buddhi* is the *mahat*, the great Self, so we open up on the transcendent, cosmic order. It was common knowledge to all ancient people that beyond the human is this cosmic order. The angels in the medieval Christian tradition were part of this, and there were nine orders of angels, nine orders of consciousness, beyond the human. The human is the lowest level of consciousness and beyond are all the other orders. In the Hindu tradition there is this vast cosmic order beyond. It corresponds to a large extent with the world of ideas of Plato, while in Plotinus it is the *nous* which includes all the ideas from which the whole creation comes forth. It is here in Plato and Plotinus that Western philosophy comes nearest to the eastern tradition, although these developments tended to be lost later on in the West.

So one goes beyond the *buddhi* to the *mahat*, which is cosmic consciousness. Then the *Katha Upanishad* says he should keep that "in the self which is peace",[4] the *shanta atman*. One goes beyond the world of the gods and of the angels which are at the limit of creation to the uncreated, to the source, which is *shanta*, peace, the peace which passes understanding. One goes beyond understanding, beyond

179

the mind. So that is the path of yoga. One of the first uses of the term yoga itself is found a little later on where the text says, "When the five instruments of knowledge, (that is the five senses) stand still, together with the mind, the *manas*, (when one's senses are still and the mind is still) "and then the intellect, the *buddhi*, does not move." When, in other words, one has brought one's whole being to the still point, then "that is called the highest state."[5] When all the external activity ceases, then the interior reality begins to unfold.

We need to notice how this is completely contrary to the Western tradition which imagines that when one gets to the intellect one has come to the end. In the Eastern tradition the intellect is really only the beginning, when one has gone beyond the gross world and is entering into the subtle world and into the transcendent. The *buddhi* is the path to that, but the highest state is beyond both the mind and the intellect; it is the transcendent state. Then the *Katha Upanishad* goes on to say, "This firm holding back of the senses is what is called yoga." So yoga was first the holding back of the senses. Later, in the yoga of Patanjali, yoga is defined as *chitta vritti nirodha*, the cessation of the movements of the mind. When the mind stops moving and centres in itself, then yoga begins. And yoga means union, uniting. "Yoking" is the same word in English. It is the integration of the whole person. All the elements in our nature have to be brought into that unity. At that stage one experiences oneself, one's *atman*. So that is the path which is mapped out at this stage in the *Katha Upanishad*.

This development may be traced next in the *Mandukya Upanishad*, which explains this higher state of consciousness in a remarkable way. The text speaks of four levels of consciousness, the waking state, the dream state, the state of deep sleep and the fourth is *turiya*, the transcendent state. In our waking state, which we imagine to be real, we are in the world of the senses and of the mind, and that is the lowest level of consciousness. In the dream state we go beyond the outer world and begin to experience the inner world. This does not mean ordinary dreaming but the deeper, inner experience of our inner world, the subtle elements. Beyond that is *sushupti*, the state of deep sleep, when one goes beyond one's bodily senses and beyond one's mind, into a deeper centre, but of course one is not ordinarily conscious of it. The fourth state, *turiya*, is when one enters into that deep centre in full consciousness. That is the aim of meditation, to go beyond the waking, the dreaming and the deep sleep state into this transcendent consciousness.

The text then has a remarkable description of the fourth state, which is considered the most significant in all the *Upanishads* and in all Hindu tradition. It says the fourth condition is *atman*, the Self in its own pure state, the awakened life of supreme consciousness. It is neither outer nor inner consciousness, or semi-consciousness (that is, not the ordinary outer waking consciousness nor the inner consciousness nor something in between the two), nor is it the consciousness of deep sleep. It is neither consciousness nor unconsciousness, for at this stage one has gone beyond the opposites, the dualities, altogether. "It is *atman*, the Spirit, that cannot be seen or touched, that is above all distinction, beyond thought, and is ineffable."[6] In other words, one goes beyond one's senses, one's imagination, one's mind, and beyond word, until one comes to the Absolute beyond. And union with him is the supreme proof of his reality. This appears totally unreal to the ordinary mind, but when one experiences it one knows the supreme Reality. One knows it by itself. One cannot know it by one's reason or by one's intellect, but only when one enters into it does one know it. The great seers, Ramana Maharshi, for instance, in modern times, are those who experience the inner reality and know the self (*atmavidya*). He, this inner reality, is "the goal of evolution", the end of the whole evolution of consciousness, and "he is non-duality, *advaita*". Dualities are made by reason, and at this stage one has gone beyond one's reason so that there are no more dualities. He is peace and love, *shanta* and *shiva*. *Shanta* is the ordinary word for peace, while *Shiva* means "the blessed one", "the kindly one". *Shiva*, which is here used as an adjective, means "benign" or "kindly". It can be translated "love", although that may be a little strong. So that is the Ultimate as described in the *Mandukya Upanishad*.

In the *Svetasvatara Upanishad* there is a description of yoga which is one of the earliest we have. The *Svetasvatara Upanishad* is one of the later *Upanishads*, contemporaneous with the *Bhagavad Gita*, in other words about 300 BC. Here there is again a description of yoga. The *Yoga Sutras* of Patanjali were put together about 400 AD but based on a tradition going back to at least 400 BC. In the *Svetasvatara Upanishad* it says, "If a wise man holds his body with its three parts erect (i.e. the chest, neck and head) and turns his senses with the mind towards the heart . . . "[7] This is the art of yoga. One sits if possible in *padmasana*, the lotus posture, with the head, neck and spine erect so that one forms a column or pillar corresponding to the pillar of the universe, and one relates oneself to the whole cosmos at that centre. Then one turns the senses, with the mind, towards the heart. This is bringing the senses and the *manas* towards the heart, "the heart" being the term used for this inner centre both here in the Hindu and in the Hebrew tradition. "He will then in the boat of Brahman cross all the torrents which cause fear."[8] One goes beyond all this world of conflict and violence into the inner peace, the *shanta atman*.

The text goes on to describe how one controls one's breathing and restrains one's mind, which is like a chariot drawn by vicious horses. This is a common description of the human being; the body is the chariot, the horses are the senses, and the mind is the reins. One has to control the horses, the senses, through the mind. "Let the wise man without fail restrain his mind, that chariot yoked with vicious horses."[9]

The conclusion of this in the *Svetasvatara Upanishad* is, "When by means of the real nature of his self he sees as by a lamp the real nature of Brahman, then, having known the unborn, eternal God who is beyond all natures, he is freed from all fetters."[10] Here we have another description of this final state. In that state first of all one realises oneself, *atmavidya*, one has knowledge of the self. By means of the real nature of this self one enters into one's true being, beyond mind, beyond intellect, into the inner self. Then, as by a lamp, one sees the real nature of *brahman*. Instead of seeing a mere appearance of sense objects around one, or of mental objects, one sees the Reality. And the Reality within and the Reality without are the same. One realises the non-dual Reality.

There is a further stage here. "Having known the unborn, eternal God (*deva*)." This brings us to the third aspect, that this Reality is not only *brahman* behind the universe, and not only *atman* the self within, but is also recognised as God, as personal being. This is a new stage, that the one Reality is the transcendent mystery of being and the transcendent consciousness, but also, and for that very reason, a person, because a person is a conscious being. Ultimately person is fully conscious being. So here this third element is introduced into the experience of the one reality. The text says a little later, "That person is *purusha*, not larger than a thumb, dwelling within, always dwelling in the heart of man."[11] This is another way of expressing it. Beyond the outer senses, beyond the mind, beyond the intellect, in that inner centre, the heart, is this *purusha*. When he is said to be the size of a thumb it means he has no dimensions, he does not belong to this world of space and time. "He is perceived by the

heart, the thought and the mind."[12] The terms in Sanskrit
are *hrdaya*, the heart, *manisha*, the thought, and *manasa*,
the mind. These terms become more precise later on, and
although here they are used in a general sense there is the
recognition of this faculty by which we can know the self
within, the true person, the God within.

Finally at the end of the *Svetasvatara Upanishad* it says,
"through the power of his *tapas* and through the grace of
God, the wise Svetasvatara truly proclaimed Brahman."[13]
One of the means by which *brahman* is attained is by *tapas*,
which originally meant "heat". It is the inner heat which is
generated in yoga and meditation, and so it comes to mean
all disciplined yogic activity. It is through one's own effort,
tapas, and through the grace of God, that one comes to know
Brahman. This conception of grace occurs also in the *Katha
Upanishad* where it says, "Not by much learning, not by the
Vedas, not by understanding, is this Atman known. He
whom the Atman chooses, he knows the Atman."[14] So it is
not only through the power of one's own *tapas* and *sadhana*,
efforts and discipline, that the *atman* is attained, but one
encounters the grace of the *atman* coming from above, which
draws us to itself. So that is the witness of the *Svetasvatara
Upanishad*.

Now we come to the *Bhagavad Gita*, and here a further
great advance is made. The *Bhagavad Gita* recognises a
three-fold yoga, *karma, bhakti* and *jnana*. In the earlier tradition, which we have looked at so far, the yoga was *jnana*
yoga, where knowledge and consciousness were being
sought. The discipline was concerned with how to awaken
the higher levels of consciousness and come to the Supreme.
But the *Bhagavad Gita* recognises that there are other ways
to the one Reality, and the first is *karma*. *Karma* is basically
"work", and in the earlier traditions it was said that work
cannot enable one to reach the Supreme. But *karma* has
several different meanings and the first one is ritual action.

That was the original meaning of *karma* in the *Vedas*. The point that the seers of the *Upanishads* made was that one cannot reach this level of consciousness by ritual action. This was the basis of the teaching of Shankaracharya when he said that it is not by ritual (*karma*) but by knowledge (*jnana*) that one knows the One. So it is necessary to go beyond ritual. But the *Bhagavad Gita* gives a wider sense to *karma*; it is not only ritual action but also social action and moral action.

The situation in the *Bhagavad Gita* is that Arjuna, who represents the human self, is seated in a chariot facing the battle and Krishna, the Lord, comes to counsel him. Here the chariot represents the body, Arjuna is the mind and Krishna is the spirit within, the Lord who has come to counsel him. What Krishna says to Arjuna is that he must fight the battle. He must face life and do his work in the world. This was a very important development because at an earlier stage it had been said that one should separate from the world, separate from all activity and meditate in silence and solitude, and then one attains the Supreme. That is one path, the way of the ascetic, the *sannyasi*, and that path is also recognised by the *Gita*, but it now opens another path which is a way for the householder, the ordinary person living his ordinary daily life, if the work is done in the spirit of yoga. There are several conditions for doing one's work in the spirit of yoga. Attachment is what the Buddha called *tanha* or *trishna*, clinging to people, clinging to things. This attachment is really the attachment of the ego in the self-centred person. There is a true self which is open to God and to others, and there is a false self which clings to itself and, centring on itself, sees everything in the context of itself. That is the great obstacle to all meditation and to all transcendent experience.

It is very important that, while the *Gita* teaches detachment, it does not say that one has to suppress one's senses.

In later traditions it often seems to be that one has to try to suppress the senses, but the *Gita* teaches being detached, enjoying the senses but not being attached to them in the least. It is possible to be totally free in this enjoyment. At the same time one is not to indulge the senses, for then one is carried away by them. This is the middle path of detachment from the senses and it is attained by sacrifice. *Sacrum facere* is to make a thing sacred. The thing sacrificed is made over to God. What the *Gita* now introduces, following what the *Svetasvatara Upanishad* had begun, is the concept of the personal God who is going to be the guide to the higher stages of contemplation and of inner experience.

In this case the personal God takes the form of Krishna and the whole of one's work in life must be dedicated to him in sacrifice. One offers everything one has and everything one does to the supreme Lord. Above all one offers oneself, one's ego. Detaching oneself from people and things, one sacrifices everything one does and thinks and is to the Lord within. It is done out of *bhakti*, devotion. It is done out of love. This is very important, that at this stage the path of meditation is not only a path of knowledge, *jnana*, consciousness; it is also a path of love, and while love is primarily for the Lord it also does include others, the "welfare of the world".

The final stage of *karma* yoga is when one has surrendered everything and oneself to the Lord in total devotion and love and one is able to say, "I am not the doer." One realises that it is not oneself who is acting but the Spirit, the Lord, who is acting in one. Then one is free from the ego; that is liberation. So that is the path of *karma* yoga in the *Bhagavad Gita* and the first six books of the text are primarily concerned with this.

The next six books are concerned principally with *bhakti* yoga, which is devotion to the personal God. Krishna is the form of the cosmic person, the Lord of the universe, and he is also the personal Lord, the one who is not only knowledge but also love. And so he says, "Offer to me all thy works. Rest thy mind on the Supreme. Be free from vain hopes and selfish thoughts and with inner peace fight thou thy fight."[15]

A little later the text describes the process of yoga. "Day after day let the yogi practice harmony of soul (which is yoga) in a secret place, in deep solitude, master of his mind, hoping for nothing, desiring nothing."[16] In other words, at that stage one is free from desire and is simply open to the transcendent. The text goes on, "Let him find a place that is pure and seat that is restful, neither too high nor too low, and let him practise yoga for the purification of the soul, with the life of his body and mind in peace, his soul in silence before the one."[17] This is the process of yoga; the *prana*, the life energy, and the mind have to be in peace, and then the *buddhi*, the intellect, is silent before the one Reality, the one Self. The text continues "with upright body, head and neck which rest still and move not, with inner gaze which is not restless but rests between the eyebrows".[18] That is a common technique. One tries to focus the mind between the eyebrows, one of the *chakras*, which we will come to later.

The text continues, "Then with soul in peace and all fear gone, and strong in the vow of holiness (*brahmacharya*), let him rest with mind in harmony, his soul on me, his God supreme."[19] *Brahmacharya* is basically chastity but it is much more than that; it is purity of heart. So this is not simply pure consciousness but consciousness focussed on the personal God, the Lord, the Creator. "And that yogi who, lord of his mind, ever prays in this harmony of soul, attains the peace of *nirvana*, the peace of supreme that is in me." *Nirvana* is a Buddhist term for the transcendent reality and the *Gita* speaks of "the *nirvana* which is in me."[20] In other words one finds one's inner peace, inner tranquillity, in the Lord himself. This culminates in the saying, "Give me thy mind, give me thy heart, give me thy offering and thy adoration and then, with thy soul in harmony, and making me thy goal supreme, thou shalt in truth come to me."[21] In the *Katha Upanishad* the goal was *purusha*, but *purusha* had not been clearly defined. There *purusha* was hardly different from *brahman* and *atman*. But here in the *Gita* the *brahman-atman* is seen as the personal God, the Lord. "He is your goal supreme."

Finally, at the end of the *Bhagavad Gita*, Krishna sums it all up by saying, "This is my word of promise, thou shalt in truth come to me for thou art dear to me."[22] This is very important. At this stage in the process one is going beyond oneself, beyond the created world, and then one encounters the personal God. One encounters love. "You are dear to me." That is a further stage in revelation, when one discovers the reality of the person within. The text says, "Leave all things behind", which is literally all *dharmas*, "and come to me for thy salvation. I will make thee free from the bondage of sin. Fear no more."[23] This is the path of *bhakti*, of devotion to a personal God, which is of course, very close to the Christian path which we will be considering in the next chapter. It has to be seen in the context of both *karma* yoga, the yoga of work and service, and *jnana* yoga, the realisation of the absolute Reality. That is the path of the yoga of the *Bhagavad Gita*.

The next thing to consider is the yoga of Patanjali and the earlier yoga system which goes back to at least 400 BC. The earlier yoga *darshana*, or system, is based on the Sankhya philosophy, which again is one of the earlier philosophies of about the same period, 500-400 BC. The two basic principles of the Sankhya are *purusha* and *prakriti*. *Purusha* is spirit, consciousness, hardly person, at this stage. *Prakriti* is nature or matter. *Purusha* is masculine and *prakriti* is feminine. The aim of the earlier yoga was to separate *purusha* from *prakriti*. The understanding was that *purusha*, the mind or consciousness, has descended into involvement in matter, in nature, in the senses, and the goal of this yoga is to separate the mind from the senses, from the body, from the material world, until one reaches *kaivalya*, isolation, separation. The idea was to separate from the world and to realise the *purusha*, the person within. This is a very limited way and later profound changes were made in it. But that was the earlier stage when one was simply trying to get out of this world, out of the body and into the Self within. At this stage there was not only one *purusha*; there were many and one was trying to discover one's own *purusha*, person, which would be one among the many.

This method went on developing for hundreds of years until we have the yoga of Patanjali, which is the system of yoga that is normally followed. In this system there are eight stages. The first two stages are *yama* and *niyama*, which basically are the moral law that must be practised in everyday life. Under *yama* are five abstentions: *ahimsa*, not to do violence; *satya*, to be truthful in word and deed, i.e. not to lie; *asteya*, not to steal; *brahmacharya*, which is both chastity and purity of heart; and *aparigraha*, not to covet. It is important that in this approach to the Godhead one has to base oneself on the moral order. The Ten Commandments in the Judaeo-Christian understanding have the same function. This moral aspect may be left behind when one goes further, but as the basis it cannot be neglected.

The *niyama* are like the counsels of perfection: *saucha*, cleanliness, purity; *santosha*, contentment with pleasure and pain, good and evil, in other words, inner equanimity; and *tapas*, which here is discipline, effort, practice. Then there is *svadhyaya*, literally self-study, which is taken to mean the study of the scriptures. This is important at this stage, for one of the means by which one opens oneself to a higher level of consciousness is by meditating on the scriptures because they come from the higher level. All sacred scriptures come from a higher level of consciousness. They are expressed in the language of the senses and the mind, but one has to look through that language to the mystery that is being revealed, whether it is in the Vedas or the Bible or the Quran. In immersing oneself in any of the scriptures one is always encountering a higher level of consciousness and this tends to raise one to that level. The final *niyama* is *ishvarapranidhana*, devotion to *ishvara*, the cosmic Lord. In the yoga of Patanjali, however, *ishvara* is only a perfected being; he has not assumed the fullness that is found in Krishna. He is only one who gives assistance. He helps one to meditate and to have some figure of a personal God. This yoga has gone through many stages and some people just have a particular deity which they use as a method of transcendence. This is very different from the *Bhagavad Gita*.

The next two stages are basic in the yoga of Patanjali: *asana* and *pranayama*, control of the body and the breath. This is *hatha* yoga and it was worked out to a fine art. Through control of the body and the breath one also controls the mind. The mind has to be concentrated on what one is doing. In all yoga the mind must be attentive to every movement of the body, so it is constantly integrating the body and the mind. B. K. S. Iyengar, the great master of *hatha* yoga today, in his *Light on Yoga* brings that out very clearly. For him it is a discipline of the body through which we reach the discipline of the mind and eventually attain to full experience of Reality. We begin with the body which is in contrast to the earlier tradition where very little attention was paid to the body. In that tradition *purusha* separates himself from *prakriti* and she finally disappears. In other words, this world and the body finally disappear in pure spirit. So the earlier tradition was very one-sided, but now with Patanjali there is the beginning of seeking a balance. One recognises that the body and nature have their place in one's yoga. There is control but one never suppresses or forces the body. In yoga it is always a matter of balance

190

and harmony, harmonising all the senses, harmonising the muscles and the whole physical organism. This reaches perfection in certain yogis where there is almost perfect control of the body.

Pranayama is control of the breath or life-energy and this is extremely important. Through the breathing the mind is controlled also, creating harmony between body and mind. Again, *pranayama* has vast possibilities and extraordinary powers may be developed. The breathing controls the senses and the inner powers. One of the features of *hatha* yoga is the *siddhis*, the powers, which begin to develop. As the body and the breathing is controlled, the senses, instead of going out in the ordinary way, begin to be concentrated within and then one can have very deep experiences, similar to sense experiences, but taking place within. One begins to receive visions and locutions and revelations of different sorts, and then one begins to develop the *siddhis*. Being able to control the senses, one can control matter through the senses. The yogic powers of controlling matter through the senses are well established. Satya Sai Baba is a good example today and there are many others who, through yoga, have attained the power of controlling matter. What one is doing is drawing the powers of one's being away from the outer world into the inner world, to the source where matter is controlled. Ultimately all matter is controlled from within and one reaches that point where one can consciously control matter. There is danger in this state, of course, because controlling the body and matter is not an end in itself and it can be used as a form of magic to do harm to others as well as to assist them. The stage at which the *siddhis* develop represents an intermediate stage. All this so far is the bringing of the body and the senses under control in *hatha* yoga, through *asana*, the seat or posture, and through *pranayama*, the control of the breathing.

Next there is what is often called *raja* yoga, the discipline

191

of the mind. Having controlled the body and the breathing, one has to control the mind. The four stages are *pratyahara, dharana, dhyana*, and *samadhi. Pratyahara* is withdrawal from the objects of the senses. The senses are drawing us out all the time; most people live through their senses, which draw us to the outer world. So in meditation one first recollects oneself, withdrawing the senses from their objects, and one begins to concentrate the senses. The next stage, *dharana*, is concentration and is central to the whole process. Having gathered the senses within, one now has to concentrate the mind. The mind, the *manas*, is always moving from one thing to another and the art of yoga is to fix the mind, either on an outer object or on an inner image, or even on a thought. One can use different methods but one has to find a way to concentrate the mind and achieve *dharana*. This is a fundamental mental discipline.

The next stage is *dhyana*, meditation proper, and this is when the mind is so concentrated that it continues in that state of inner concentration. It is said to be like a flow of oil. The mind flows steadily in that unity of concentration. The word *dhyana* became *chan* in Chinese and *zen* in Japanese as the art of meditation was taken from India to China and eventually to Japan.

The final state is *samadhi*, when one goes beyond. At this stage one becomes what one contemplates. First of all one concentrates on an object and the mind fixes on that. The object may be external, it may be interior, it may be God, and finally the mind is united with that object. In *samadhi* there is no longer a separation between the mind and what it contemplates. One emerges in the object of meditation. In the final stage the knower, the knowing and the thing known become one. It is a state of non-duality where one discovers the ultimate oneness. But all this is technique, a method of reaching that oneness. The danger of it is that it may be thought to be an end in itself. What can be done by mental concentration is limited. One may get the *siddhis*, one may have remarkable powers, but these are not ultimate. It is only when one goes beyond oneself altogether that one discovers the Ultimate. It could be that through *samadhi* one opens oneself to the transcendent and receives grace, but there is always an element of danger here. A great yogi can be a great egoist in that he has really not gone beyond himself; he has only found his self and concentrated at that point. So this can be a dangerous path and certainly it is not the end. Patanjali also calls that final stage *kaivalya*, isolation. One has separated oneself from everything and is centred now on that deep centre, that deep point. It is a marvellous state but also a dangerous one, because it is incomplete. So that is Patanjali's method of yoga.

We come next to the very interesting development which took place in the fifth and sixth centuries after Christ, that of the Tantra. The basic principle of Tantra is that instead of going beyond your body, senses and mind, and going to the One beyond in isolation (*kaivalya*), one works through the senses, through the body and through the material world. This is an opposite method and a complementary one. Today what is represented by Tantra is of extreme importance because the danger in Hinduism has been this separating away from the material world, from the human world, to concentrate on the Supreme beyond, and that leads to a rejection of the material world. The material world becomes known as *maya*, which is often translated as illusion. The word *maya* is from the root *ma*, to measure, from which the words "matter" and "mother" (*mater* in Latin) are also derived. So the earlier system was fundamentally a separation from matter, from the mother, from the feminine in the attempt to go beyond. It is a marvellous path in its way but it is one-sided. But now with Tantra the balance is restored as matter, the mother and the feminine are restored to their proper place.

In Tantra the aim is to reach the Supreme through all the levels of one's being. A start is made with the basic level, which is the energy, *shakti*. In the earlier tradition there is no mention of *shakti*. *Prakriti* is equivalent to *shakti* in that she is both nature and the feminine principle, but in the earlier tradition the aim was always to go beyond *prakriti*. The result of that was the devaluation of matter, of the body and the feminine. Now with Tantra the balance is restored; the mother and the feminine, matter and the body, come back. *Prakriti* is now seen as the energy behind the whole universe and behind one's own personal being. *Shakti*, energy, is what sustains the universe and she is the mother. The method is now to bring consciousness into every level of one's being, from the most basic level to the highest. This is a totally different practice and today it is becoming more and more attractive because we now realise the dangers of separating from nature, from matter, from the body, the senses and the feminine. If one concentrates too much in the mind this can result in what is basically a kind of schizophrenia, and that is precisely what has happened in the West; we have over-developed our minds and have underdeveloped the other complementary parts of our being. Tantra is seen today as being of particular importance in that it is a practice in which the balance and complementarity of the opposites is restored.

Tantra consists in bringing the consciousness into all the levels of being. The understanding is that *shakti*, the divine energy which is in all nature, in all matter and in one's own body, is rooted at the base of the spine like a coiled serpent. In this form it is called *kundalini* or serpent power. That *kundalini* has to rise through the seven *chakras*, the seven levels of consciousness, until it reaches the supreme consciousness beyond. *Shiva* is pure consciousness and *shakti* is the energy. As this process takes place *Shiva* and *Shakti*, the male and the female, are married, united, and the whole person is transformed. That is the path of Tantra.

There are seven *chakras*. The first is the *muladhara*, the root *chakra*, which is the link in each person with *mula prakriti*, with mother nature. This *chakra* is located at the base of the spine, and so it is understood that at the base of the spine we are all related to the physical web of the universe. The whole universe as we know it, from the atom to the star, is a web of interdependent energies, and our physical bodies are part of that web of energies. At the *muladhara* we are linked with all the energies of the universe. As that *chakra* opens we become aware of this energy. Ancient people lived much more from the *muladhara*. They were immersed in the physical universe. This was a limitation to some extent and they had to grow out of it, but we have grown so far out of it that we have lost consciousness of it. We now have to recover that deep physical consciousness, consciousness of matter and of our integration in the material world. So we have to allow the *muladhara* to open and become activated.

The next *chakra* is the *svadhisthana*. This is the life consciousness, or sex consciousness, and this was a very important element in the Tantra which eventually led to its falling into disrepute and being rejected. In Tantra part of the practice was to develop sexual energy as one means of uniting with the Godhead. There is both physical energy and life energy, which is the energy which is in all the plants and animals and in all the life of nature. We also share in that energy and through this *chakra* we are related to, and united with, this whole life energy of the universe. The aim is to convert this energy. We do not simply let it out in its normal channel, and neither do we suppress it (which would be disastrous); rather we try to draw it within. The energy has to rise through all the *chakras* and in this rising it becomes an inner force, *ojas*, as it is called. This is a very practical discipline. People today are trying to find a way between suppressing sex and indulging it. The third way is to have

195

a disciplined method for transforming the energy. This is done largely through control of the breathing but also through the mantra, the breath and the word.

Access to the third sphere of psychic energy is through the opening up of the *manipura chakra*. This is the level of emotional energy. Here again we are all linked emotionally, first with our mother and father, family, blood relations and so on. These are very close emotional ties, and we know now how a person's life may be conditioned by these emotional experiences which begin in the womb and develop during the first two or three years. As this *chakra* opens up the emotional energy has to be controlled. Normally when the *chakras* open the energy is not controlled; tantric yoga is precisely the control of the energy in the *chakras*, not letting the energies dissipate themselves but learning to bring them within. In this way the emotions are brought within this current, this force, and allowed to rise up to the deeper centre. It needs to be emphasised that to do this is to control the emotions. It is not a matter of suppressing the emotions or of indulging them, but rather of learning the middle way of control. Again the method is the same. It is done by sitting, by breathing and by concentration of the mind. To concentrate the mind, those who are religious concentrate on God, on Jesus if one is a Christian, on Shiva or Vishnu if one is a Hindu. One concentrates the mind at that point and then the energy is allowed to rise to that point. It is given a direction. It is not safe to awaken the *chakras* if one is not directing the energies which are released. It is dangerous because one may awaken powers which cannot be controlled. But, by focussing on the Supreme in one way or another, one guides the energy towards the still point.

The fourth *chakra* is the *anahata*, the heart *chakra*. This is the *chakra* of affection. The emotions are unstable, affection is stable. It is the centre of the will and of the reason, the *manas* or lower mind. Most people live from the heart *chakra*; feelings, affection and practical discipline come from the heart. It is a deep centre and to focus on it is a very valid way, but it does not take one very far. This is the middle level of consciousness, the mental consciousness in its rather limited aspect and that is where many people remain.

Next comes the *visuddha*, the throat *chakra*, which includes the verbal and sound-based consciousness: words, language, poetry, music and so on. All this opens up in the throat. So there is a progression as one emerges from the deep consciousness, through emotional ties with one's mother and family, through the heart where one is opening up to a wider sphere of knowledge and of practical reason and will, and now one is opening up through one's feelings, and imagination, and through music and poetry, to a wider sphere altogether.

Then one comes to the *ajna chakra* and this corresponds to the *buddhi*, the intelligence. That is where one focusses the mind, so one is drawing all the energy up through this point. The *buddhi* is where one opens on the transcendent and that is why in meditation one tends to concentrate on the *ajna chakra*. There can be concentration on the heart and this is good, but there needs also to be concentrationon the mind, the intellect, the *nous*. At that point one comes to the *buddhi*, the point of awakening and of enlightenment. The Buddha is the enlightened one. This is the point of the so-called third eye, where one is beginning to open to the transcendent. Until that eye opens one is still living in the created world, the world of the senses and the mind; one has not yet gone beyond. The *ajna chakra* is the passage to the transcendent.

The seventh and final stage is the *sahasrara*, the thousand-petalled lotus at the crown of the head. The *chakras* are pictured in different ways. One way is to see them as lotuses having different numbers of petals at each level. At first the petals are turned down. Then, as the energy rises, the petals are pictured as turned up symbolising the opening of the lotus, the opening of the chakra, at that particular level until one's whole being is transformed as the energy flows through it. The *chakras* are also associated with colours and with sounds. There is a whole science of colour and sound and energy, and the interrelationships between them have been very profoundly studied.

At this point, then, the energy rises to the supreme *chakra*, the *sahasrara*, and there one opens on the transcendent. This is the realm of what is called transpersonal psychology, which relates to the consciousness beyond the ego. Beyond the gross world, the world of the senses, is the subtle world. We in the West have very little understanding of this subtle world. It has become clear that practically all Western psychology is simply concerned with the lower levels of consciousness and Western psychologists are for the most part unaware of the higher stages. There are several stages beyond. The first is the lower subtle world where the mode of experience is through the subtle senses. Instead of only relating to the outer world through the gross senses one begins to develop subtle senses. One perceives the psychic world, which is a different level of reality enfolded in the physical world. The physical world is the outer shell and beyond that is the subtle psychic world.

In the Hindu tradition there is a way of talking about this transformation which is in terms of bodily sheaths, or *koshas*, in which the human consciousness is involved, of which only the first is physical and the rest are subtle. The first sphere is the *annamayakosha*, the food *kosha*, which is the material body. Then there is the *pranamayakosha*, the level of the breath or life energy. Inside this is the *manomayakosha*, the mental body, or mind energy. In the West this is generally thought to be the final stage of development, whereas in reality it is only an intermediate level. Beyond the *manomayakosha* is the

198

vijnanamayakosha, and that is where one comes to the *buddhi* or intellect. Finally there is the *anandamayakosha*, the supreme bliss consciousness. As one passes beyond all the limitations of the lower levels of consciousness, one experiences the bliss of the *sahasrara*, the highest level of consciousness, the *anandamayakosha*. At that stage one is open to the cosmic consciousness, the cosmic order, and that is where one becomes aware of the gods and the angels.

Very few people in the West have any experience of gods and angels, or any other presences. They tend to think that talk of such entities is all a matter of fairy stories; in fact they think that fairies are only stories. But in fact all these entities correspond to experiences in the subtle or psychic sphere. Beyond the physical there is a subtle psychic world and the subtle senses perceive the psychic world within the physical. That is why there are anecdotes of fairies, elves, spirits and elementals, of which people in the past were aware. Then there are the higher levels of various spheres of spirits, until one comes to a higher level still where there are the gods, the *devas*. This is the cosmic order, the level of cosmic consciousness, and it is what St Paul refers to as the cosmic powers. The writers of the New Testament were just as aware as any other ancient people of this whole world of angels and demons. It must be remembered that, as in the gross physical world, so here in this more subtle world, the entities encountered are both positive and negative. One may encounter not only the gods and angels, but also the *asuras*, the daemonic powers and negative forces. So the subtle, psychic world is a dangerous world, to be entered only with the guidance of one who has experience in it, a guru or experienced spiritual director.

The subtle world can be divided into lower and higher levels. The lower level is the psychic world in general. Many people today are discovering latent psychic powers and are experiencing, for instance, extra-sensory perception of various sorts. These things are interesting in their way but they are always a little ambiguous. Then there is a higher, or deeper, level of the subtle or psychic where we come to the gods and the angels. Here one is encountering the greater powers. We must remember that all the time we tend to think of this as vague and unreal, presuming that the real world is the world we see around us, when in fact the physical world is but the outer fringe of reality. It is real, it has a reality, but it is a limited reality. The whole scientific world, the world of stars and galaxies and electrons and protons and so on, all that is the outer fringe of reality. When one comes into the psychic world one enters a deeper level of reality. This is a matter not of speculation but of experience. Just as the outer world, can be experienced, so one can experience the inner world. One becomes aware of the world of the saints and the angels and the gods as one enters into this deeper realm of reality.

As the exploration proceeds the whole of that psychic sphere is transcended as one enters into the causal. The causal level of reality is where all the psychic powers and entities find their centre in the One, the cosmic Person, the cosmic Lord. Reality is not a chaos but an order and it centres in the One, and that is why in meditation one focusses on the One who gathers all the sense world, all the mental world and all the psychic world into unity. In meditation one is trying to enter into that supreme unity. That Supreme is the cosmic Person, the Krishna of the *Bhagavad Gita*, the cosmic Lord of creation. It is also the *Tathagata* of the Buddhist tradition and the *dharmakaya* of the Buddha. This would correspond with the *nous* of Plotinus, as that in which the whole cosmos is unified and in which the gods are present, while the previous level would correspond to Plato's world of ideas. So this structure is found in all the different traditions.

Finally it is necessary to go beyond the cosmic Person to

the absolute transcendence, the One beyond all. That, in the Hindu tradition, is *nirguna brahman*, *brahman* without attributes. As long as one conceives the absolute in relation to this world then it is *saguna brahman*, the Lord, the Creator, the Saviour, the good, the true, the beautiful and so on. But now one has to go beyond that to the Ultimate from which everything comes. One goes beyond thought altogether, beyond concepts, and that is what the Buddhists call *sunyata*, the total emptiness beyond. So one has always to go to that beyond, which is *nirguna brahman*. That, in the Christian tradition, is what we call the Godhead, the Godhead which is beyond all, the divine darkness beyond all light. And so finally one reaches the Supreme.

There is a very important point here and that is that as one makes this ascent through all the levels of consciousness one always has to integrate each level as it is transcended. The danger of the other view is that as one goes beyond the senses, the mind, the intellect and the cosmos to the Supreme, one has the impression that all these lower levels are left behind. But in the deeper tradition, both Hindu and Buddhist as well as Christian, one assumes, or gathers up, all these levels of consciousness. The real art of Tantra is the raising of all these levels of consciousness, from the base level through the life level, the emotional and imaginative, the intelligent, the psychic and the causal, the whole is gathered into unity in the Supreme. The Supreme cannot be spoken of, for it is the utter transcendence. The difficulty is that there are no words for it at all; we can only use words to point to the Beyond.

The final stage of the ascent to the Godhead can be summed up in a quotation from Ken Wilber, who has worked deeply in this area. In a very impressive passage he writes of this ultimate transcendence. Wilber is one of the few who have really grasped what is involved here. So many stop at an emptiness, at a void, and leave out the world.

201

Wilber uses the Buddhist term *svabhavikakaya* for this ultimate state of consciousness, while in the Hindu tradition it
is called *sahaja samadhi*. It is the state in which we have
returned to our own nature. Having found the Ultimate the
person is totally at one with the whole world. One gets the
impression that one is going out of this world to the Supreme
but now comes the discovery that when one reaches the
Supreme, it embraces every level of reality. Every level of
reality is included in it. This is how Wilber speaks of it: "As
unknowable, unobstructed, unqualified consciousness, it
shines forth in completion from moment to moment, like an
infinite series of ever newly perfected states, forever changing
in its play, forever the same in its fullness." In other words
this is perfect rest and perfect activity, the two poles united
in one. "It appears to be the end limit of evolution but is
actually the prior reality of every stage of evolution from
first to last. This was present from the beginning." In other
words, whereas one thought one was rising from one level
to another, on coming to the end one realises that one has
come back to the beginning. "In just this way it is always
and perfectly unattainable, simply because it is always
already the case, timeless and eternal. It is just that and all
attempts to attain it, even in the causal realm, are finally
undone. It is understood to have been fully present from the
start." Again and again it is said that one cannot reach
liberation; one is free and through all the stages one is trying
to get to a state where one already is. It is a matter of
discovering who we are and what the universe is. "It is
understood to have been fully present from the start, never
lost and never regained, never forgotten and never remembered, always already the case prior to any of that. As
infinite, all-pervading, all-embracing consciousness, it is
both one and many, only and all, source and suchness, cause
and condition, such that all things are only a gesture of this
one, and all forms a play upon it." Wilber goes on to say

that it demands wonder. Wonder is one of the signs of the awakening to *brahman*. The *Kena Upanishad* says, "He is seen in nature in the wonder of the flash of lightning; he is seen in the soul in the wonder of the flash of vision."[24] This is that wonder which goes beyond everything, the sudden awakening. So, "As infinity it demands wonder, as God it demands worship, as truth it demands wisdom (*jnana*), as one's true self it calls for identity." In other words, one finds one's self. "In its being it has not instructions and this no-trace continues for ever. Bliss beyond bliss beyond bliss, it cannot be felt. Light beyond light beyond light, it cannot be detected. Only obvious, it is not even suspected. Only present, it shines even now." That is the Ultimate. One has returned to where one was at the beginning, but now in total consciousness. So that is the evolution of consciousness leading to the ultimate state, or ascent to the Godhead, as it has come down to us through the Hindu and the oriental traditions.

10

The Experience of God in the Old and New Testaments

In chapter nine we were concerned with the Hindu experience of God, seen as the ascent to the Godhead, as it is expressed in the Vedas, the Upanishads, the *Bhagavad Gita* and the Tantra. We need now to compare with that the Judaeo-Christian experience of God. It is important to be clear that when we speak of experience of God, what is meant is the subjective aspect of that which objectively we call revelation. Revelation and experience are always interdependent. As the human soul opens to the divine mystery, so the divine mystery reveals itself to the soul. Humanity has always been faced with the divine mystery. From the very beginning human beings have been in the presence of that mystery which is, in fact, nothing but the mystery of existence and they have been exploring this mystery. All ancient religion, wherever it has arisen, from the earliest times onwards, is an exploration of this mystery. The process is that on the one hand the mystery is revealing itself as the human soul opens to it and on the other hand the human person is striving to apprehend the mystery.

When we come to the Hebrew experience, it is clear that the Hebrew religion also springs from the encounter with the sacred mystery. The word in Hebrew for the sacred mystery was *elohim* which, as we saw in chapter four, is a plural form which must originally have meant "the gods". For the early Hebrew the word *elohim* must have signified the whole world of the gods, that is the sacred mystery itself. The sacred mystery was apprehended first of all as a god, an *el*, and there were many *els* at one time, many gods. But a decisive moment came, presumably with Abraham, the founder of the people of Israel, when they broke through to the experience of a transcendent God, not at first as a strict monotheism but as a kind of henotheism, where, *mutatis mutandis* as in Hinduism, a form of God was conceived as unique to Abraham and his descendants. This experience of God as the transcendent One continues to develop from the time of Abraham through Moses and the early prophets, until finally it attains to a strict monotheism in the later prophets. What is characteristic of this revelation is that, whereas in Hinduism this supreme Reality was always seen as manifesting in the cosmos and in the human soul, in Israel the same supreme Reality is experienced primarily as manifesting in history, in the history of a particular people. That is the unique character of the revelation to Israel. As we will see, whenever God the Supreme reveals himself in Israel it is always in relation to the history of the people.

God reveals himself initially to Abraham, saying, "Go from your country and your kindred and your father's house to the land that I will show you. And I will make of you a great nation, and I will bless you . . . "[1] The revelation is based on the promise of a people, and it is associated with an historic event leading to the emergence of an historic nation. That context of the initial revelation to Israel continues right through to the end. But on the other hand, while the revelation is concerned with history, with the growth of a people who are to bring a blessing to humanity, it comes in the form of a personal experience. A later revelation to Abraham is very striking in this respect. The text says, "As the sun was going down a deep sleep fell on Abram (as he was called then); and lo a dread and great darkness fell upon him."[2] That was clearly a deep mystical experience. Darkness is one of the aspects of mystical experience as one goes beyond the created world and encounters the divine

Reality. Here Abraham is given an insight into the future of his people, but at the same time he experiences the presence of God in a flame of fire, one of the typical symbols of the sacred mystery. "When the sun had gone down and it was dark, behold a smoking fire and a flaming torch passed between these pieces."[3] The story of the three angels who come to Abraham at Mamre is another example of a mystical experience. Abraham entertains the three strangers and then realises, as in so many ancient traditions, that in entertaining strangers he has entertained the Lord.[4] These "strangers" are symbolic, of course. In fact a great deal of the Hebrew revelation belongs to what the Buddhist calls the *sambhogakaya*, which is the middle region of consciousness. The *nirmanakaya* is the manifestation in this world, the *dharmakaya* is the Absolute and the *sambhogakaya* is the realm of spiritual manifestation, that is, the sacred, or as the Hindu calls it, the *mahat*. This latter is the cosmic order, the level of cosmic consciousness, and it is in this level that the angelic beings are encountered. So these men who appeared to Abraham in that way were "angels", or manifestations of the world of the sacred. Abraham's sacrifice of Isaac, or rather non-sacrifice, was again a profound experience. He felt the call to sacrifice his son, the urge to human sacrifice being a typical archetypal symbol of the unconscious, but it was felt to be a call from God which he obeyed and thus the meaning of the symbol was transformed and human sacrifice was abolished. It is not the human body which has to be sacrificed, but the human will. As a result of his faith and self-surrender he was justified and the child was saved.

When we come to Jacob we find again a similar very profound experience of the sacred. For instance, in one passage it says, "Jacob went on his way and the angels of God met him; and when Jacob saw them he said, 'This is God's army.' So he called the name of that place Mahanaim."[5] People at this stage were generally living in that world of the sacred where one encounters the angels, the gods or the demons, which is the realm of psychic manifestation. In this Israel was no different from other contemporary people. A similar experience is recorded in the story of Jacob's ladder, taking place in this instance in a dream.[6]

A little later on there is the extremely significant passage which reads, "Jacob was left alone; and a man wrestled with him until the breaking of the day. When the man saw that he did not prevail against Jacob, he touched the hollow of his thigh ... Then he said, 'Let me go, for the day is breaking.' But Jacob said, 'I will not let you go, unless you bless me.'" This wrestling with an angel was clearly a mystical experience, an encounter with a spiritual power in the darkness. Jacob encounters this conflict within himself, which is the meaning of the wrestling, and he overcomes. Because of this his name is changed. "He (the angelic being) said, 'Your name shall no more be called Jacob, but Israel, for you have striven with God and with men, and have prevailed.'"[7] This was a genuine mystical experience, since Jacob declares, "I have seen God face to face." At the same time it marks him out as a father of the people of Israel, which is given his name.

At this early stage the God of Israel is known as *el Shaddai*, which is commonly translated as "God almighty" but it may mean "the God of the Mountain". In any case, there was not a clear monotheism at this point. In other words Jacob encountered the Absolute in that *el* but its relation to other gods had not yet been clarified. It is when we come to the Exodus that we get the breakthrough to a more explicit monotheism. Moses' encounter with God at the burning bush is an excellent example of God's self-revelation, of which the human counterpart is mystical experience in the psychic level of consciousness. "He (Moses) led his flock to the west side of the wilderness ... And the angel of the Lord appeared to him in a flame of fire out of the midst of the bush; and he looked, and lo the bush was burning, yet it was not consumed . . . When the Lord saw that he had turned aside to see, God called to him out of the bush, 'Moses, Moses!' And he said, 'Here am I!' Then he said 'Do not come near; put off your shoes from your feet, for the place on which you are standing is holy ground.'"[8] This is a profound experience of the sacred mystery. The sacred is experienced normally through phenomena such as these, which are basically at the subtle, psychic level. All through the Exodus story such psychic phenomena occur, the burning bush and the fire and the cloud on the tabernacle, the manna and the water from the rock, not to mention the so-called plagues of Egypt. The people at that time were living in the world of the sacred, in this psychic realm which is between the spiritual and the physical, of which Western people today have very little experience. And so the Lord reveals himself to Moses in that way at the burning bush and immediately commissions Moses to deliver his people. This is again a mystical experience but related to a historic situation. The Lord had revealed himself to Abraham, calling him to the new land, and now he says, "I have seen the affliction of my people . . . and have heard their cry . . . " and he tells Moses that he is to take them out of Egypt into the land of the promise. The revelation is directed towards history: it is an historic event. But again it is also a genuine and very deep encounter with the sacred mystery.

Moses and the people of Israel continue through the desert and come to Mount Sinai, and there he has another profound mystical experience. "On the morning of the third day there were thunders and lightnings, and a thick cloud upon the mountain, and a very loud trumpet blast, so that all the peoples who were in the camp trembled. And Mount Sinai was wrapped in smoke, because the Lord descended upon it in fire . . . and the whole mountain quaked greatly . . . And the Lord called Moses to the top of the mountain, and Moses went up.'"[9] So again there was a mystical experience related to cloud, darkness and smoke, subtle phenomena but signifying, as St Gregory of Nyssa shows in his life of Moses, an encounter with God in the darkness beyond phenomena.

The cloud mentioned in this narrative is one of the great symbols of the Biblical revelation. It goes before the Israelites through the desert and comes to rest on the tabernacle, a pillar of fire by night and a pillar of cloud by day. That again is a phenomenon which belonged to the level of the *sambhogakaya*, the symbolic, psychic order, but in it the presence of the person of Yahweh, the personal God, was recognised. The Lord Yahweh was present in the cloud. This comes to a climax when he appears to Moses in the tabernacle or "tent of meeting". The "cloud of glory" (*shekinah*) would descend on the tabernacle and Moses would go to meet God in the tabernacle. The text says, "When Moses entered the tent the pillar of cloud would descend and stand at the door of the tent, and the Lord would speak with Moses. And when all the people saw the pillar of cloud standing at the door of the tent, all the people would rise up and worship . . . Thus the Lord used to speak to Moses face to face, as a man speaks to his friend."[10] The phrase "face to face" is the Biblical way of speaking of the most intimate experience of God, so much so that the Church Fathers, St Augustine and St Thomas Aquinas, for instance, questioned whether Moses had the beatific vision, that he actually saw God. We would certainly say that he did not, that at that stage God's self-revelation was still under a veil. But it clearly signifies a profound intimacy with God, which was a genuine mystical experience.

Moses' experience of encounter with God deepens as he says to the Lord, "Show me now thy ways, that I may know thee". He wants to know God. The Lord answers, "My presence shall go with you, and I will give you rest." To live in the presence of God was to know him, and at this time "the angel of the presence" symbolised the presence of God. But Moses is still not satisfied and he says, "I pray thee, show me thy glory." The glory, the *qabod*, is really the essence of God, or perhaps one should say, the manifestation of the essence of God. The glory is like the radiance from the sun, the radiance of light. The Lord says to Moses, "You cannot see my face." The text has just used the expression "face to face" but here this expression is qualified by saying, "man shall not see me and live." For the Hebrew it is a matter of the utter transcendence of God. Whereas the Hindu is always concerned with the immanent presence and with a growing awareness of it and experience of it, the Hebrew, by contrast, is always aware of God's utter transcendence, totally beyond the self, and, of course, it remains true that one cannot see God until one has died to oneself. The text continues, "The Lord said, 'Behold, there is a place by me where you shall stand upon the rock, and while my glory passes by I will put you in a cleft of the rock, and I will cover you with my hand until I have passed by; then I will take away my hand and you shall see my back; but my face shall not be seen.'"[11] These are anthropomorphic images, of course, but they can be seen to symbolise a most profound experience. It is, in fact, very close to what we normally hold, that in this life one never sees the face of God. One never sees the divine being itself but rather one always sees it "under a cloud", glimpsing only, as it were, the back or the shadow of it. One does not see the reality in its fullness.

Coming to the book of Deuteronomy we enter a further stage of revelation, influenced by the later prophets, and we can see how the image of God emerges as the supreme Creator. So far it has been a matter of God revealing himself in the history of a people and in the kind of personal experience we have discussed, which was always related to the history of Israel. But now it goes further. "Behold, to the Lord your God belong the heaven and the heaven of heavens, the earth with all that is in it . . . The Lord your God is God of Gods and Lord of Lords, the great, the mighty, the terrible God . . . "[12] Here we have the supreme personal God manifesting himself as Creator and as Lord of Lords. It may be recalled that in the *Svetasvatara Upanishad* we saw the same development. *Purusha*, the supreme Person, revealed himself as the Lord of Lords, the God of Gods, the Ruler of Rulers.[13] Here Israel comes to the same understanding, that the Supreme Reality is this personal God, the supreme Lord. That is the great theme of Deuteronomy. We must worship that One alone. That is the difference between the Hindu and the Hebrew, that the Hindu discovered the personal God, the *purushottaman*, but for the Hindu the personal God could have many forms. Shiva or Vishnu or Krishna or Rama were all forms of the personal God, and they remain so today. The Hindu has his *ishtadevata*, the form of God through which he chooses to worship the Supreme. It was altogether different in Israel, and this remains true also for Christians and Muslims: God has only one form. Yahweh (or Christ or Allah) is his form and one must worship God under that form only. A large part of the battle of the prophets of Israel was to prevent the worship of God in any other form. The danger of worshipping God, that is, the sacred mystery, under different forms is that you can lose the sense of the transcendence of God. Once one considers God as manifesting in animals or in imperfect human beings one can very easily form a false image of God, and so the prophets wanted to preserve the purity of their experience of God and proclaimed Yahweh alone as the form of the divine mystery.

We come now to consider the experience of the prophets. The prophet (*nabi*), was originally like the shaman, one who has an experience of God. The revelation to Samuel is an

211

example of this. Samuel is a boy born out of a vow to God and he is consecrated to God in the tabernacle at Shiloh. One night he hears a voice calling him and, not yet having awakened to the presence of the divine mystery, he goes to Eli, the priest, and says, "Here I am." Eli says, "I did not call; lie down again." The Lord calls him twice more and each time he goes to Eli until Eli understands and says, "Go, lie down; and if he calls you, you shall say, "Speak, Lord, for thy servant hears.' "[14] This is an example of an awakening to the divine mystery. The boy in the tabernacle had the experience of the divine presence revealing itself to him. It is sad that what comes out of this experience is that Eli and his sons are going to be killed and tragedy is to strike the people of Israel. But again the relation of mystical experience to an historic event is clearly shown.

When we come to David we enter into the sphere not only of history but also of politics. David is called to be king over the people, and it is revealed to him that God will give him a son who shall sit upon his throne and his kingdom shall last for ever. Again the promise is in the context of Israel's history as a nation, but at the same time it transcends history. The kingdom is to last "for ever". Solomon, his son, builds the Temple and again there is a mystical experience. When Solomon builds the Temple and consecrates it, the cloud of glory, which had rested on the tabernacle and had followed Israel through the desert, descends upon the Temple. The whole Temple is filled with the cloud of glory and nobody dares to enter it.[15] Again this is a psychic phenomenon which symbolises the presence of the God of Israel and is a sign that he is dwelling now in that Temple in Jerusalem at the very centre of their political life.

Elijah and Elisha are both involved in the political affairs of their time, and yet at the same time they are open to extraordinary mystical experiences, particularly when Elijah is taken up to heaven. Elisha, his disciple, wants to be with

212

him when he departs and Elijah says he may accompany him. So they walked together and "as they still went on and talked, behold a chariot of fire and horses of fire separated the two of them. And Elijah went up by a whirlwind into heaven."[16] Again this is a subtle, psychic experience. In the experience of Elijah it was not of course a physical chariot or a physical fire, but rather a psychic chariot and a psychic fire. In Hindu tradition psychic phenomena of this kind are generally accepted and in Yogananda's *The Autobiography of a Yogi*, for instance, there are many examples of a similar nature which are reported as having happened recently. So these experiences are simply part of the universe in which we live, though people today have generally lost contact with them.

When we come to the later prophets whose revelations were recorded we can consider the experience of Amos and Hosea, two prophets of the eighth century BC, through whom the supreme transcendence of the God of Israel is revealed. Through Amos came the great revelation of God's creative power. So Amos says, "For lo, he who forms the mountains and creates the wind, and declares to man his thought – the Lord, the God of hosts, is his name."[17] This is the creator God, utterly transcendent, who creates the world and at the same time knows the thoughts of men, that is to say, who is Lord both of the physical world and the world of men. At the same time this God of creation is the God of righteousness. "Seek good, and not evil, that you may live;" and, "Let justice roll down like waters, and righteousness as an over-flowing stream."[18] This is a demand for judgement, justice and righteousness. So the link between human conduct, moral behaviour, and God is clearly established.

God is the God of justice and he demands justice, but he is also the God of mercy. This comes out beautifully in Hosea. Through Hosea there is a profound and sensitive revelation of the *hesed* of God. There is no exact equivalent of

213

hesed in English, but it is often translated as loving-kindness. Hosea experiences God in a love relationship, in a bridal relationship. The Lord says, "I will betroth you to me for ever; I will betroth you to me in righteousness and in justice and in steadfast love and in mercy." Linked with this bond of love is knowledge. He goes on, "I will betroth you to me in faithfulness; and you shall know the Lord"[19] That is the *gnosis* which is knowledge of the Lord through love. This is the theme of all mystical experience. Interestingly this passage goes on to say, "I will answer the heavens and they shall answer the earth and the earth shall answer the corn and the wine and the oil and they shall answer Jezreel." That means that this God of heaven above is also the God of the earth and when this relationship of love and righteousness is established with him, then the earth also prospers and bears fruit. This is an expression of the cosmic dimension in Israel's experience of God. Whereas in Hinduism it is the dominant theme, in Israel it is secondary but it is always present. The God of Israel is also the Creator of the world and he controls the world from above. He is never immanent in the same way as the Hindu God is, but he has this power over the whole creation and the creation responds to his will. The other significant passage in Hosea is where he says, "When Israel was a child, I loved him, and out of Egypt I called my son."[20] This brings out again how the God who reveals himself as love is also the God who acts in history.

When we come to the great prophets of Israel, Isaiah, Jeremiah and Ezekiel, we are here very clearly in the world of historic reality. The prophet is one who knows God and who knows also God's will for humanity. Revelation here is always concerned with the will of God for the world and for humanity, but nevertheless the prophets themselves have the most profound experiences. Isaiah, for instance, has this experience in the Temple. "In the year that King Uzziah died I saw the Lord sitting upon a throne, high and lifted up; and his train filled the temple. Above him stood the seraphim; each had six wings: with two he covered his face, and with two he covered his feet, and with two he flew. And one called to another and said, 'Holy, holy, holy is the Lord of Hosts; the whole earth is full of his glory.'" This again is a deep mystical experience under the symbolic forms of the Temple, the throne and the angels crying, "Holy, holy, holy". Through this is brought out an aspect of God's self-revelation which emerges particularly in Isaiah, namely, the holiness of God. To be holy means to be separate. When you take anything and offer it to God, what you are doing is separating it from common use and it then becomes a holy thing. If a person is consecrated to God, separated from the world, he is regarded as a holy person. God himself, in Israel's understanding, is the supremely separated one, the one who is beyond everything in utter transcendence. So holiness is the essential attribute of God. Isaiah responds to the manifestation of the Lord on the throne by saying, ". . . I am a man of unclean lips, and I dwell in the midst of a people of unclean lips; for my eyes have seen the King, the Lord of hosts."[21] The holiness of God reveals one's own sin, one's own unworthiness. The holiness of God is realised as a moral transcendence.

The two moral attributes of God which come out clearly in Isaiah and in the other great prophets are justice or righteousness (*zedek*) and mercy or loving-kindness (*hesed*). The God of Israel is primarily revealed in the moral order, whereas the Hindu revelation is primarily in the cosmic order. In Hinduism God is the cosmic Lord, the Lord of creation, although *dharma* the moral law, is also recognised as deriving from him. Krishna in the *Bhagavad Gita* is said to be the Lord of *dharma*, righteousness. In Hinduism, however, this aspect is subordinate whereas in Israel the primary character of God is his righteousness, which means his justice, his concern for justice in this world. He is righteous in himself and demands righteousness of those who serve him. This demand for justice as an essential condition for true religion is one of the basic principles of the prophetic revelation.

In the later chapters of Isaiah Yahweh, Israel's God, is revealed as the only God. It is in these chapters, which belong to a later period after the exile, that the strongest expressions of monotheism occur, as, for instance, "I am the Lord, there is no other. Beside me there is no God."[22] It is quite definite that in Israel the Lord Yahweh was the one Lord alone to be worshipped, the God of Gods, Lord of Lords. No God other than Yahweh was to be worshipped. This principle came down to the Christians also and to the Muslims. We need to be aware that such strongly emphasised monotheism created a problem later, because when only one form of God is recognised all other forms are denied. Hostility develops towards all other forms of God, and then inevitably great conflict arises with other religions of the world where God is worshipped under other forms.

Whereas in Isaiah God is the God of holiness and of righteousness, in Jeremiah God is again like the God of Hosea, the God of love. Jeremiah has a wonderful experience right at the beginning when the Lord appears to him and says, "Before I formed you in the womb I knew you, and before you were born I consecrated you." Somewhat like Isaiah responding to the vision of the holiness of God by feeling unclean and sinful, Jeremiah here responds by feeling like a child before God. He responds to the call to be a prophet by saying, "Ah, Lord God, I do not know how to speak for I am only a child." But the Lord says, "Do not say "I am only a child" for to all to whom I shall send you you shall go, and whatever I command you you shall speak."[23] Again this mystical experience, as always is directed towards the people, to action and service, but it is essentially an experience of divine love. "I have loved you with an everlasting love; therefore I have continued my faithfulness to you."[24]

Coming to Ezekiel we find many examples of visions and other subtle experiences, of which his great vision of the chariot is the best known. Ezekiel is very much a visionary, so again we need to remember that all these visions belong to the psychic world. He has a vision of a strange chariot that later developed into the mystical tradition of the *merkabah*, the chariot in which God reveals himself.[25] Although fully mystical doctrine did not develop in the Bible, it developed later in Judaism with the Qabala, which has a complete mystical theology. It is latent in the Old Testament, particularly in the figure of the *merkabah* and also in the *shekina*. The *shekina*, or "cloud of glory", was the sign of the presence of God. In the inner sanctuary of the Temple, which is seen symbolically as the inner place where God dwells, there is the mercy-seat and the seat is empty. What is conveyed by this is that God has no form. His presence is hidden in the inner sanctuary, associated with the mercy-seat but without any form at all. That is why Israel was never allowed to form an image of God but had to relate instead to the formless God. In India, of course, God is worshipped under every kind of form, but he is regarded ultimately as formless. In a Shiva temple, in the sanctuary, there is always the *lingam*, which is a stone very roughly carved without form. The other gods may have their hands and feet and fully human appearances, but in Shiva, rep resented by the *lingam*, there is the image of the formless Godhead.

After Ezekiel Jewish mysticism became increasingly apocalyptic. The prophets were seeking God's intervention in the history of Israel to bring all things to fulfilment. That is the revelation to Israel, that God has chosen this people

217

and is working with them, that he has brought them out of Egypt and led them into the Promised Land, and he has now promised them the Messiah who is to come to be their king. God was going to fulfil all things in them and they, his people, eagerly looked forward to that final fulfilment. But then, as their own fortunes declined and nothing seemed to happen and as their king was taken captive and the Temple destroyed, the goal of fulfilment was projected more and more into the future. It came to be believed then that the Lord would intervene from above and manifest himself and wonderful visions were recorded, as in the book of Daniel, in the form of an "apocalypse", a revelation of a new age in which everything would be fulfilled. That was the stage at which Jesus actually came into the world, as Israel looked for the coming of God from above, and for the final fulfilment.

It is into this tradition, then, with all its expectations, that Jesus comes. It must always be remembered that the God of Jesus is Yahweh, the God of the Old Testament. But of course Jesus brings a new understanding of the nature of God and his relation to humanity. In the later stages of the Old Testament the utter holiness of God was seen as making him utterly separate, totally transcendent. The danger of an utterly transcendent God is that he becomes too remote. He is so much above you that the only way in which you can properly relate to him is in awe and worship and in humble obedience. Jesus brought God down to earth, as it were, in his experience of God as Father. It is generally agreed that his Abba experience was unique. Jesus experienced God in utter closeness to himself and addressed him as "Abba", which is a term of great intimacy. So what happens with Jesus is that this transcendent God of infinite holiness and infinite righteousness, but also of infinite mercy, becomes present to man. He was present in some way in the Temple no doubt and in the king, and had been experienced in his closeness to the people of Israel. But now in the New Testament there is this bringing God down to earth, and making him present in a human being.

Jesus comes to reveal God's presence in himself. He reveals this first of all in terms of the Kingdom or rule of God which he declares is present in himself, but he also reveals God's presence in terms of sonship. He expresses his relationship to God in this way, "No one knows the Son except the Father, and no one knows the Father except the Son . . . " This is a unique *gnosis*, a unique knowledge. Only the Son knows the Father and only the Father knows the Son. So it is quite clear that he experienced God in a unique way. It is important that we put Jesus into the context of history. Just as we tried to see the Hindu revelation in the context of its history, so we try to see Jesus in the context of his history, and he comes as a man who experiences God as his Father in this absolutely unique way, and sees himself as the Son. But it must not be forgotten that, as we saw before, in the Son he also includes his brethren, all humankind, so that in him and through him this new relationship to God is opened up to all. So he says, "No one knows the Son except the Father, and no one knows the Father except the Son and anyone to whom the Son chooses to reveal him."[26] Jesus makes known this relationship of intimacy, of relationship to God, so that we also can share in that relationship and can know ourselves as children of God.

In St John's Gospel this relationship of the Father and the Son is expressed in the terms, "I am in the Father and the Father in me." That is a relationship of total interiority. But Jesus goes on to pray for his disciples, "that they all may be one; even as thou, Father, art in me, and I in thee, that they also may be in us . . . "[27] So here we have this revelation of total intimacy such that he is *in* the Father and the Father *in* him, and that he wants to share that relationship with his disciples so that they also are in the Father as

219

he is. This is the centre of the Christian revelation. The God of Israel, the transcendent holy One manifesting himself in Jesus, reveals this relationship of Father to Son, of Son to Father, and communicates that relationship to his disciples in the Spirit. That is the central Christian revelation and the central Christian experience. It must always be remembered that what is revelation from one point of view is experience from the other. There is no revelation coming down from above without any relation to human experience. It always has to be experienced in order to be revealed. It is only through our experience that we know God.

Jesus can say then, "I and the Father are one."[28] He knows himself as one with the Father, and yet, as we saw, in distinction from the Father. He does not say, "I am the Father" but "I and the Father are one". This is unity in distinction. This mutual interpenetration combining unity and distinction developed, as we shall see in the next chapter, in the whole course of Christian mysticism, as one of its fundamental elements. This is what distinguishes the Christian experience of God from that of the Hindu. The Hindu in his deepest experience of *advaita* knows God in an identity of being. "I am Brahman," "Thou art that." The Christian experiences God in a communion of being, a relationship of love, in which there is none the less perfect unity of being.

When Jesus reveals himself as one with his disciples he uses the striking image of the vine. "I am the vine. You are the branches. Abide in me, and I in you."[29] We cannot hope for a more intimate relation than this, the vine and the branches. He is the vine and we are the branches of the vine. We share in his life, not separate from him but as truly part of him as branches of the vine. So Jesus comes to reveal that life in God and to communicate that life to us so that we also, in and through him, become sons of God and experience the Spirit as he does. And so later on St John in his letter can say, "Our *koinonia*, our common life, is with

220

the Father and with his Son Jesus Christ".[30] We as a community share in the knowledge and love of the Father and the Son. We share in their life.

Jesus communicates to his disciples the mystical experience he has of his relation to the Father and they form a community, a *koinonia*, with him. *Koinos* means "common" and *koinonia* is "common life", "community". The Christian mystical experience is always in terms of community. The Hindu experience is essentially individual and has no positive relationship to the community whereas the Christian experience, although certainly personal and individual, is always also implicitly or explicitly a community experience. This is very important. It comes out clearly in the Acts of the Apostles when, after Pentecost, the Spirit descends on the disciples. Jesus had promised them that when he departed he would send the Spirit and that the Spirit would abide with them. So the Spirit descends and then it is said that the disciples were all "of one heart and soul". The experience unites the people together in one. Then another dimension of the experience is revealed. "They sold their possessions and goods and distributed them to all, as any had need."[31] So the descent of the Spirit forms the community and the community is such that in it everything is shared, even at the economic level. This is a particularly Christian understanding. It is the descent of God into the whole context of human life. That is the primary importance of the historic dimension, that God is always seen in relation to the human world, to human history and to human relationships. As St John brings out very strongly in his letter, anyone who does not love his brother whom he has seen, cannot love God whom he has not seen.[32] So this love of God is totally expressed in the love of our neighbour. Love of God and love of neighbour can never be separated. Comparing this with *bhakti* in Hinduism, *bhakti* is always a personal relationship to God, a self-transcendence, going beyond and being one with God, but, although the relation to the neighbour is certainly there, it is not normally expressed. It is an experience of identity, not of relationship. The relationship to the neighbour is implicit but not explicit, whereas in the Christian context the relation to the neighbour is always explicit and fundamental. And so it is an experience of God in the Spirit which brings this experience of being of one heart and one soul with others, and this then spreads out into daily life in the sharing of the goods of the world. These three aspects characterise the Christian mystical experience in the New Testament.

In St Paul we find these three aspects very clearly brought out. First of all St Paul develops the doctrine of the Spirit. In the Synoptics and even in the Fourth Gospel it is very little developed, whereas in St Paul it is basic. In the first letter to the Corinthians he makes very clear the relationship between the human spirit and the divine Spirit. He says that God is "revealed to us through the Spirit. For the Spirit searches everything, even the depths of God." Through Jesus, particularly through his death and resurrection, the Spirit has been communicated and now this Spirit encounters our spirit. The text continues, "For what person knows a man's thoughts except the spirit of the man which is in him? So also no one comprehends the thoughts of God except the Spirit of God".[33] So in us there is a spirit by which we know ourselves and by which also we can know God. At that point of the spirit we are open to the Spirit of God. There is a very important distinction between the Hindu and the Christian understanding here. In the Hindu tradition there is *jivatman*, the individual self, and there is *paramatman*, the supreme Self. But in the normal understanding, as seen in the advaitic school, the individual self is identified with the supreme Self. "I am Brahman." "Thou art that." It is an identity with the Absolute. That is a genuine and profound mystical experience without a doubt.

222

By contrast, in the Christian understanding the human spirit is never identified with the Spirit of God. The spirit in man is rather the capacity for God, the capacity to receive, and always the experience of God comes as a gift, as a grace from above. So the spirit of man receives the Spirit of God. This St Paul brings out in the letter to the Galatians where he says, "God had sent the Spirit of his Son into our hearts crying Abba! Father!".[34] That is an exact description of the Christian mystical experience. God had sent the Spirit of his Son into our heart or into our spirit. In the Spirit we are united with Christ the Son. We become sons in the Son and we are able to say, "Abba, Father". We share in Jesus' experience of the Father. We enter into the dynamic of the trinitarian experience. In the Spirit we become one with the Son and in the Son we are able to know the Father. The whole Christian tradition is based on the experience of the Trinity. The Trinity is not a dogma revealed from on high but an experience, an experience first of all of Jesus in his relation to the Father, and then of the disciples of Jesus who share his experience in the Spirit.

In the letter to the Romans Paul clarifies this by saying, "When we cry Abba, Father, it is the Spirit himself bearing witness with our spirit that we are children of God."[35] The Spirit of God enters into our spirit and actually transforms it, and our spirit is revealed as a capacity for the Spirit of God. Through that we realise ourselves as children of God. This is very close to the Hindu experience of the *atman*, but in the Christian understanding the spirit in man is a capacity, a receptive power; it is not identical with the Spirit of God. We receive the Spirit and in that Spirit we know ourselves as sons. Experiencing this sonship, in relation to the Father, we return to the source in the Father. But this experience of God in the Spirit can only take place when we have died to ourselves. "You have died and your life is hidden with Christ in God," says St Paul.[36] We are dead. We died to

223

ourselves in baptism and this dying goes on in the whole Christian life which is a continual process of dying to ourselves, to the ego, and identifying with our real Self which is hidden with Christ in God. In other words, it is a continual going beyond creaturely existence to experience the true Self in Christ in its ultimate transcendence, hidden in God. It is a going beyond, into the Ultimate. The way St Paul expresses this is authentic mystical doctrine.

If we now finally compare the Hindu and the Christian mystical experience we see in the Hindu the profound exploration of the Spirit, the *atman*, the Spirit within, and we see how this implies the transcendence of the lower self, the ego, and the experience of the ultimate Self. Furthermore, that ultimate Self is conceived in the form of a person, *purusha*, to whom we give our love, our *bhakti*, and we realise that that person loves us. As Krishna says in the *Bhagavad Gita*, "You are dear to me."[37] God loves us. So there is in Hinduism a profound experience of self-transcendence, opening to the divine, experiencing the divine as the very inner Self but at the same time as one who is the object of love and who gives love. Then there is the stage of going beyond that, as we saw, to the ultimate oneness, to ultimate unity. The Christian experience is distinctive in that identity with God is not claimed. In the Hindu experience the immanence of God is dominant and there is more concern with realising God as within one and oneself as within God, whereas for the Christian, coming out of the Hebrew background, God is always transcendent and one never identifies oneself with God. There is always a distinction between God and the human person. The point is, however, that in Jesus, although that distinction is always present, total unity in distinction takes place. Jesus as man is one with God, with the Father. He knows himself as the Son in a unique way and calls us also through the Spirit to become sons, to experience the ultimate oneness with the Father. However all this is a

224

gift of God, a grace, transforming us. It is essentially a communion of love. It is a communion so profound that we know ourselves as one with God as Jesus is one with the Father, but at the same time it is a communion of love, of personal relationship, of being "all in each and each in all".

Thus we experience God in unity and distinction in the mystery of the trinity, but we also experience ourselves as living in one another as members of the body of Christ. St Paul particularly develops the striking image that we are members of the body of which Christ is the head. Just as Jesus spoke of the vine and its branches, St Paul speaks of the head and its members. Each of us experiences through the Holy Spirit, through the power of love, this unity in the body where we are distinct members of the one body. We share the one life, members of the one Person, but each distinct in his or her place. We are, as St Augustine put it, persons within the Person, a communion of persons in love.

This mystical community experience also penetrates into the physical world. It is the whole creation that, as we saw, has been restored to unity with God through Christ, and our whole person, including the physical body, is not discarded but is rather transfigured. That the body itself is' holy is a fundamental aspect of Christian experience. St Paul speaks of the body as the "temple of the Holy Spirit" and declares that "the body was not made for immorality but for the Lord."[38] This is deeply significant. It means that sexuality is itself holy. It is a divine energy within us. It can be used for immorality but it can also be consecrated to God, whether in marriage or in virginity. In both cases it is the same energy which is being used, either externally in a physical relationship or internally in a spiritual relationship. The ultimate aim of life is, in fact, to convert this physical energy into a spiritual energy, so that the body itself becomes what St Paul calls a "spiritual body", that is, a body which has been wholly penetrated by the divine Spirit. This is the

225

meaning of resurrection. Every human body is created for
the resurrection, which means for the gradual transformation of the physical energy of the body into a spiritual
energy which is no longer subject to the ordinary laws of
matter. Matter, as we know it, is conditioned by space and
time, but the body in the resurrection is beyond space
and time. This was revealed in the body of Christ at the
resurrection. He appeared to his disciples in a "subtle"
body, a body which is already not determined by ordinary
space and time, but could appear and disappear at will.
Then at the ascension he passed beyond space and time
altogether and entered into the eternal order of being, transcending this world.

We have to keep constantly before our minds that this is
the ultimate goal of humanity. This is the "new heaven"
and the "new earth", prophesied in the Old Testament and
revealed in the Apocalypse of St John.[39] This world of space
and time and the human mode of consciousness which goes
with it is destined to pass away. In fact, as the Buddha saw
so clearly and as modern physics recognises, it is always
passing away at every moment. The time-space world is an
appearance, determined by a particular mode of consciousness, of the one infinite and eternal reality, which manifests
itself under these conditions. We have constantly to learn to
see beyond the passing forms of this world to the eternal
reality which is always there. It means passing from our
present mode of consciousness, which is conditioned by time
and space, into the deeper level of consciousness which
transcends the dualities external and internal, subject and
object, conscious and unconscious, and becomes one with
the non-dual Reality, the Brahman, the Atman, the Tao,
the Void, the Word, the Truth, whatever name we give to
that which cannot be named. It is this alone that gives
reality to our lives and a meaning to human existence.

Christian Mysticism
in Relation to Eastern Mysticism

In this work we are exploring the divine mystery which is behind human life. The thesis is that corresponding to the sacred mystery there is a universal wisdom which comes down from ancient times and which was formulated in India, China, the Arab world, and in Christianity. At the Renaissance, and particularly with the rise of modern science and philosophy, it was largely lost in the West. Only very recently have we in the West come to realise the existence of this universal wisdom and only now are we beginning to recover some of it. In the previous chapter we looked at the experience of God in the Old and New Testaments and this chapter will trace the development of this experience in later Christian mysticism, looking particularly at the similarities and dissimilarities between this and the mysticism of the East. A few key points set out the basis of this development.

In the Hebrew tradition there is a profound sense of dualism. God is understood as totally separate from creation and from humanity. While there is a tendency in Hinduism towards pantheism where God is identified with nature, the tendency in the Hebrew tradition is precisely the opposite and it is the utter transcendence of God that is emphasised. Further, this dualism is emphasised by the conception of sin. Humanity is separated from God not only by being part of creation but also by sin. Within this scheme the relation of the human person to God is seen in terms of obedience and disobedience, law and righteousness. This brings out the moral character of the Hebrew revelation. In exploring the divine mystery behind human life it becomes clear that each tradition has its own insight into the mystery. The Hebrew insight is particularly a moral insight and therefore God is seen as essentially holy, that is, separated from sinners but at the same time just and merciful. On the human side the demand is for faith, justice and humility. There is a beautiful passage in the prophet Micah which reads, "He has showed you, O man, what is good; and what does the Lord require of you but to do justice, to love kindness, and to walk humbly with your God?"[1] That is the Hebrew way to God. It is essentially a moral approach.

Another characteristic of the Hebrew tradition is that God is always conceived in personal terms. He is angry and repents. He is jealous and vengeful. He is full of hatred but also loves and forgives. And yet, as we saw, behind that there is a mystical tradition, an experience of God beyond all human limitations, eternal and unchanging, beyond human comprehension. Always, in all the traditions, we are in the presence of a mystery, and it is recognised that all human language is inadequate to express it. Even so, it is the language of God as person that in the Hebrew tradition is used to convey something of this mystery.

The New Testament is built upon the tradition of the Old. The emphasis is on the moral character of God, and personal language is used to speak of the divine mystery. Jesus himself thinks and speaks in the context of this tradition. On the other hand, whereas in the Old Testament God is totally above creation, in the heaven of heavens above, and is, as it were, looking down upon humanity on earth, Jesus in his person bridges that gulf. In him God becomes man, so that he becomes the mediator between God and humanity. As we saw in the last chapter, Jesus has a unique experience of God as Abba, Father, which he expressed in saying, "No one knows the Son except the Father, and no one knows the Father except the Son and

228

anyone to whom the Son chooses to reveal him."[2] This experience of God, which is unique to Jesus, he now communicates to his disciples by the gift of the Spirit. Christian mysticism is that experience of God in the Spirit coming through Christ from the Father. This makes us members, as we saw, of the mystical body of Christ. The whole of humanity is brought together in principle in this unity of the Spirit, recovering the unity which was lost through sin. This being brought back to unity extends to the body itself. Not only the soul but also the body is recreated and renewed as a spiritual body (*soma pneumatikon*), in the mystical body of Christ. The whole person, and eventually the whole creation, is restored to unity with the Father, in the Spirit, through the Son. That is the basic pattern of the Christian revelation and of the Christian experience of God.

To trace the development of Christian mysticism we move out from the Hebrew, Semitic tradition into the Graeco-Roman world. In the Hebrew tradition, as we saw, there was profound mystical experience but there was little reflection on it. It was experienced and then expressed in symbolic language. Here we must make a clear distinction between symbolic language and abstract language. All ancient revelations, the Vedas, the Quran and the Bible, for instance, are expressed primarily in symbolic language. This is because God cannot be properly expressed: we can only speak of him in terms of analogy. Symbols are concrete images. Jesus is constantly referred to in the Scriptures in symbolic terms, for instance as Son of God, Son of Man and Messiah. When he proclaims the Kingdom of God this is a profoundly symbolic image. People normally approach God through symbols, through the external symbols of rites and ceremonies and then through mental, imaginative symbols. In this way, through the symbol or sign, they approach the transcendent beyond. But now, as capacity for abstract, logical thought develops, rational, abstract language can be used

229

to examine the symbols. This is a very important stage in all religious traditions. Working on the symbols and images of experience, the rational mind comes into play and begins to analyse and discern the exact meaning of the symbols and images. That process began to take place at a very early stage in India, as we saw with the Upanishads and the *Bhagavad Gita*, although symbolic language was still used to a large extent. It was thoroughly developed in Sankara and the later doctors of Vedanta who elaborated a fully philosophical mystical doctrine. Nagarjuna and the Buddhist philosophers and Ibn al Arabi and the Muslim philosophers, did the same for Buddhism and Islam respectively.

In Christianity the same process took place as the gospel moved out into the Graeco-Roman world. In contrast to the mind of the Hebrew, the Greek mind is essentially rational and analytical. It was the Greeks who introduced rational, analytical thought to the West. Consequently, when the Church spread out into the Roman Empire, the Greek mind began to work on the original Hebrew revelation and to express its experience in categories derived largely from Greek philosophy.

There are indications that the Greeks were influenced by Indian thought. Pythagoras lived in the fifth or sixth century before Christ, around the time of the Upanishads and the Buddha. It is said that he had been to India and there is little doubt that he shows Indian influence. He believed for instance in reincarnation, a doctrine which was rare in Greece at that time, and he practised vegetarianism and taught the practice of silence in an organised community, elements which seem to derive from the Hindu and Buddhist traditions. If so, and this cannot be proved, there was a positive influence on the West from Indian mystical experience at that time.

Plato himself was profoundly influenced by Pythagoras and inherited this mystical tradition. But again Plato, in his written works, always used the language of rational, analytical thought, though there is obviously behind it a mystical vision which comes out especially in some of his letters. There is certainly a tradition of some hidden mystical wisdom in Plato, but what stands out in his writings is their highly rational, intellectual character.

The other great influence on Christianity was Stoicism. Heraclitus had developed the notion of the *logos*, the reason which orders the universe and in which human reason participates, and this became the central doctrine of the Stoics. Human reason in this view enables us to know the reason, the *logos*, of the universe. The Christian writers in the second and third centuries inherited this tradition and began to express their Christian faith in these terms. Justin Martyr, for instance, in the second century speaks of the Word or Logos having been known to Heraclitus and Socrates before it was revealed in Christ. But the first person of importance to our purpose is Clement of Alexandria. Alexandria was a centre where there were many influences from the East. It is almost certain that there were Hindu and Buddhist monks in Alexandria in the first and second centuries AD. So there was an influence from India already there. There was also Gnosticism. The Greek word *gnosis* is the same as the Sanskrit *jnana*, and it means knowledge in the sense of divine wisdom. There were gnostics, both Jewish and Christian, who believed in an elaborate, secret knowledge outside orthodox Judaism and Christianity but Clement, and Origen following him, maintained that the true knowledge of God, true *gnosis*, was to be found in the Church. Clement used the language of Stoicism and Platonism, including, of course, the language of the *logos*. In the Fourth Gospel St John writes, "In the beginning was the Word (*logos*) and the *logos* was with God and the *logos* was God." In using the term *logos* he was certainly referring back to Hebrew *dabhar*, the Word of God which came to the

231

prophets. But *logos* was at this stage a very common term in Greek philosophy. So this was the point where the Christian writers opened themselves to the Greek philosophical tradition. They said that the same *logos* which had been revealed in Israel had also been present in the great Greek philosophers, in Heraclitus and Socrates and the Stoics, and that that *logos*, that wisdom which orders the world, had been manifested fully in Jesus Christ. So that was the point of insertion where the Christian wisdom encountered the Greek wisdom.

Clement of Alexandria also made much of a characteristically Stoic term, *apatheia*. *Apatheia* does not mean our modern apathy or indifference. It means rather a state beyond the passions. Here we touch again the typical Indian experience that if one wants to reach the knowledge of God, the transcendent, one has to be free from one's passions. So *apatheia* was a freedom from passion which created purity of heart and opened one up to the transcendent. The link with the "purity of heart" of the Gospel is clear. In Clement for the first time we have the understanding that this could lead to divinisation or deification (*theopoiesis*) which means to be made God or rather to be made one with God. This understanding of deification becomes a major trend in Christian mysticism and is of great importance, for it links it immediately with the Indian tradition.

Another aspect in Clement is his understanding that behind the physical world is the world of the angels. This as well, as we shall see, develops further in Christian mysticism and exactly parallels the idea in Hinduism of the *mahat*, the cosmic order. Beyond the physical world is the cosmic order, the psychic world, the world of the gods, and in Christian tradition that is encountered as the world of the angels.

Clement was followed as leader of the great school of Alexandria by Origen, who was the major Christian philos-

opher of the early centuries.[3] He is said to have been a
disciple of Ammonius Saccas, of whom very little is known
except that he was a teacher in the school of Alexandria and
was the master of Plotinus, the founder of Neo-Platonism.
Origen himself was a thinker of immense originality and
was a great exegete of the Bible. He developed a profound
Christian theology, interpreting the Scriptures in the light
of Middle Platonism, the predominant philosophy of his
time.

Origen conceived of God as absolute unity and simplicity
above thought and essence. This was a typical Greek view,
and it links up again of course with the Eastern view of God.
In the East God is known to be above and beyond the
rational mind and therefore not accessible by thought. Corresponding to the distinction made above between symbolic
and rational language, there is the distinction made now-
adays between the functioning of the right and left hemispheres of the brain. Symbolic language is the language of
the intuitive mind and is associated with the right hemisphere, while the analytical, rational mind is associated with
the left. For true understanding and spiritual growth what
is important is the bringing together of these two modes of
knowing. The point is sometimes made that in the Hebrew
right-brain activity was dominant while the Greeks developed predominantly left-brain thinking, but now they
come together in the Christian mystical tradition.

Starting from his understanding of the transcendent Godhead above thought and essence, Origen develops an interesting concept of the Trinity. For him God the Father is
God in his own right. He is *ho theos*. In Greek *theos* is God
and normally it has an article with it, so *ho theos* is the usual
way of referring to God. In the New Testament God the
Father is always known as *ho theos*, God, but in the Prologue
to the Fourth Gospel the Son, the Word or *logos*, is called
theos, without the article and this makes a subtle distinction.

233

Origen makes much of that distinction, since for him the Father is God in his own right, the absolute Godhead, whereas the Son is an emanation from the Godhead, and he speaks of the Son as the first-born of all creation, using the language of St Paul.[4] The Son, as we saw in the previous chapter, is the mediator between God and man, and the first-born of creation. But Origen also says that he dwelt with God and is God, *theos*, and is the archetype of all mankind and of the whole creation. This is very profound. The *logos* is with God and is God in a real sense but is not *the* God, the source, the origin. Rather he comes forth from the Godhead as God and is the archetype of all creation, the mediator between God and man and the first-born of creation. This subordinationist trend in Origen gives the impression that the Son is lower than the Father and subordinate to the Father, a view rejected by later theology. Although an element of subordinationism is certainly there in Origen, it is only a tendency rather than his full doctrine.

For Origen, beneath the Godhead, the Father, and beneath the *logos* there is the world of spirits, and in his thinking there was an earlier creation which was a spiritual creation. He believed that there was in the beginning a spiritual creation of angels and of human beings in an original unity, and this for Origen and his followers was the origin of the universe. Then by a rather curious view, which we would not accept today, Origen held that human beings received their bodies on account of a fall. Having fallen from their spiritual nature they were given physical bodies and from then on they had to work out their destiny through the body. This was another of Origen's teachings that was not accepted in later Christian tradition, but for him the human person falls, as it were, into matter and then has to work out his or her salvation through this material world, gradually rising above it and returning to the source, to the Father.

Origen has also a profound conception of the world as a

234

spiritual being. He speaks of this world as an "immense, gigantic world which should be regarded as one being, kept alive by God's power and the *logos,* as a single soul." This is particularly remarkable today because increasingly we are coming to understand that the entire universe is an integrated whole. It is one being where everything is inter-related, from the electrons to the furthest stars in the galaxies, and where intelligence or consciousness is present in some way from the beginning. There is a total integration, a total unity. As David Bohm expresses it, all things were originally implicated or enfolded in one and they become explicated or unfolded in the universe as we know it. So Origen, and the ancient world generally, had this vision of a world which is one being, kept alive by the power of God and the *logos* or wisdom of God, as a single soul, a single living entity. Teilhard de Chardin in our day has done much to recover this vision of the universe.

Origen goes on to say that "the sun and moon and other heavenly bodies are living beings." Perception of this truth is beginning to be recovered today. We no longer see the material world as separated from the spiritual, but rather we are coming to grasp that the whole material world is pervaded by consciousness. David Bohm, for instance, also says that ultimately you come to a field of energies pervaded by consciousness and having the nature of compassion or love. So that is Origen's vision that the sun, the moon and the stars are living beings, not just dead matter. There is no such thing as non-living matter; all matter is alive in some sense. As has been repeated so often, everything has a three-fold character. Everything has a physical character where it obeys mechanical laws and can be studied by the physical sciences. Then every material thing has a psycho-logical or psychic character, a relationship to the human psyche and a kind of latent consciousness in it. Examples of this are sensitivity in plants and the kind of relative intelligence of animals. This is leading more and more people today to recognise that the planet is a living being, now called Gaia, and that we are all members of this living whole.

Returning to Origen, beyond the physical order of living beings is the order of the angels and this, as has been made clear above, corresponds to the world of the gods, which is the cosmic order in Hinduism and in all ancient tradition. In Origen's understanding angels watch over the elements, the world and everything in it. So the whole universe is ordered by the angels. This became traditional doctrine and it was only lost at the Renaissance. We must always remember that until the Renaissance it was generally understood that this physical world is pervaded by consciousness, by what Aristotle and the Arabian philosophers following him called "intelligences", and which in the Christian tradition were referred to as angels. In this way angels were seen as ministers of God which order the cosmos. Origen goes on to spell this out, saying that the growth of plants and trees, springs and rivers, animals and land and sea are all under the direction of the angels. It is interesting that there is a community at Findhorn in Scotland where events certainly appear to substantiate something like this. The leader of this community was highly sensitive and she learnt to grow all kinds of plants by communicating with the spirits or devas, as she called them, of those plants and of the trees and of the earth. As a result of this the community had the most remarkable results in that magnificent vegetables, flowers and fruits were produced from the otherwise infertile, sandy soil. So there is a growing realisation today of this psychic world as people are rediscovering facts which had been lost.

For Origen and his generation, then, it was quite clear that the angels were present in all the cosmos, ordering its course. Angels, of course were regarded as both good and evil and this was held to explain the evil and the violence

236

which are so evident in the cosmos. There are thus two contrary forces at work in the cosmos, angelic and demonic. In Origen's view angels are set over people and over nations. Every person has his angel, and Origen believed further that we each have both a good and an evil angel. There are good angels which are motivating us to good and evil angels which are tempting us. These angels belong to the psychic world and we can speak of them in, for instance, Jungian terminology, as forces in the unconscious. Seers, like Sri Aurobindo of Pondicherry, have explored and studied the psychic world, and Sri Aurobindo's conclusion was that the psychic level has a system of laws as coherent as those operating in the physical world. This then was the world of thought to which Origen belonged, and to understand him we must remember that the whole ancient world generally accepted this vision of the physical world pervaded by the psychic world and that beyond all these is the supreme Reality which embraces both the physical and the psychic, creating the unity of the whole.

In his understanding of the spiritual life Origen based himself on three fundamental principles which are basic in Christian mysticism. The first was creation. Whereas in gnostic systems creation is often seen as a fall of the spirit into matter, in the Christian view matter is created by God and is good. There are evil forces, certainly, as a result of sin but essentially the creation as created by God is good. Secondly, providence was important for Origen, and by this he understood that the creation is guided by divine providence and not by fate, as the Greek philosophical schools generally taught. His third principle was that of free will, and his doctrine of the spiritual life centres on the free will of human persons and on their openness to the will of God. Origen then sees that the whole creation and matter is good as given by God, but everything is affected by the fall of human beings from the spiritual into the material

237

state. Now the plan of redemption is to restore humans to their original spiritual state and to restore the whole creation to its unity in God.

Within this understanding human beings are seen to be created in the image of God. This is a biblical concept and it becomes one of the main themes of Christian mysticism. Origen identifies the image of God with the spirit in man and speaks of it as being incorporeal, incorruptible and immortal. When we sin we fall away from the image of God and we are restored to it by grace. The spiritual life begins when a person recognises their dignity as the image of God. At that point one awakens to the spirit within, realising that one is created in the image of God and that God is present to you in that image. In a beautiful phrase, Origen says that such a person "understands that the real world is within." That is exactly the doctrine of the Upanishads and of Buddhism, that the real world is the world within. We project a world outside ourselves which has an appearance of reality, but the real world is always within. Through grace one discovers that in one's own self as the image of God the whole creation is contained.

It seems then that Origen holds that the soul is naturally divine and partakes of the *logos*. This was a typically gnostic view which is found also in Hinduism, that the soul is essentially divine, that it has fallen away from its divine state and it is being restored to that divine state by grace. One can never be quite sure, but it seems as if Origen was exploring what for him were new ideas. If that were so he could put forward a view like that, but it need not necessarily have been his final position. The orthodox tradition has always denied that view, holding instead that the soul is not divine but that it has a capacity to be made divine by grace. We are made in the image of God to be restored to his likeness.

In Origen's teaching there are the so-called "three ways"

238

of the spiritual life which were derived from the Greek philosophical tradition: ethics, physics and *theoria*. Ethics or moral philosophy is the way of moral life, which is always basic in all the great religious traditions. Physics or natural philosophy is the knowledge of the creation, the material world and the angelic worlds. *Theoria* or contemplation is the vision of God. The process is that we prepare ourselves first by the moral life. We then open ourselves to wisdom, to *gnosis*, and come eventually to the contemplation of God.

The first stage Origen describes, using biblical imagery, as the passage through the desert. The children of Israel leave Egypt, which symbolises the world of the senses and the passions, and they go out through the desert freed from the passions and from sin. The first stage of the spiritual life is to attain freedom from sin, from the passions and from attachment to the world, and that is known as the purgative way. The next stage is when one ascends above phenomena, beyond the external world and one discerns the divine Reality. Origen speaks of "knowledge of divine things and the causes of human things." One goes behind the phenomena of the world and awakens to Reality and to the world of the angels. That second stage, then, is the awakening of the mind and the discernment of the Reality beyond. Finally, the third way of which he speaks is ecstasy. For Origen this may have been only a sense of wonder, of awe. Ecstasy in the full sense as it is spoken of later, for instance, in Gregory of Nyssa is going beyond oneself and finding oneself in God. Origen, however, does not seem to have been a mystic in the full sense. He certainly worked all this out very carefully, but particularly when referring to the last stage it does seem to be more an intellectual knowledge and, as it were, an intellectual love.

We move on to St Gregory of Nyssa who was the great master of the spiritual life and who laid the foundations of all Christian mysticism.[5] His teaching was based largely on

239

that of Origen, of whom he was a disciple, but he took Origen's doctrine much further. He represents the whole Christian life in terms of the paschal mystery, that is to say, in terms of death and resurrection. The process begins in baptism when we die to sin and are illuminated by grace. It is confirmed in the rite of confirmation, which signifies the return of the soul to itself and the awakening to the divine image within, and it is consummated in the Eucharist when we are fulfilled by communion with God in love. The pattern of death and resurrection, repeatedly enacted in the believer, emphasises that this mystical path, this experience of God, is always connected with Christ and the church. It becomes a total Christian mysticism in that sense.

Again, for Gregory of Nyssa the main theme is the restoration of the image of God, the *ikon*. The human person is made in the image of God and recovers that image when it returns to itself. Here again there is a strong similarity with the Hindu tradition. The Greek goal, as proclaimed by the Delphic oracle, was "know thyself" while the basic movement of the Indian tradition was to discover the *atman*, the inner Self. For Gregory the first step in this movement is when we return to ourself and become *monoeides*, which means uniform or, one might say, single-minded. In India we speak of *ekagraha*, of being one-pointed, where we go beyond all diversity and discover the inner centre where we are one. So that, for Gregory, was the first stage. The aim was to return to yourself and to recover this oneness within.

Then in Gregory of Nyssa there is the theme that knowledge of self brings knowledge of God. This again is a basic principle in Hinduism. It was taught also by Plotinus but there is an important distinction here. For St Gregory and the whole Christian tradition after him, the knowledge of God in the self is knowledge by grace. It is not that simply by finding oneself one finds God. Rather, by finding oneself one opens oneself to God and the divine light penetrates the

soul. It is always a gift of God, a grace. That is why it is
held that we have a capacity for God. We are not God but
we have a capacity for God and can receive the life of God
into ourselves. That is Gregory of Nyssa's understanding.
He also uses the concept of *apatheia*, passionlessness,
which he relates to purity of heart but which also is conceived as the effect of divine grace. One does not first become
passionless and then find God, but God himself enables
one to free oneself from passion and attain to this purity
of heart.

Like Origen Gregory teaches that there are three stages
involved in this process. The first stage he relates to Moses'
experience when he goes out and encounters God in the
burning bush. This stage Gregory calls *photismos*, illumination. It is the illumination which occurs at the beginning
of the journey and it is really the awakening of faith. In the
experience of faith one is led to leave Egypt, which stands
for the passions and the world, and to go forth into the
desert. The second stage here is very interesting. In Origen
the passage through the desert was a matter of going through
many temptations until one eventually came to the Promised
land, whereas in Gregory of Nyssa it is quite different. For
Gregory one goes through the desert under the cloud which
is the sign of the presence of God and one comes to Mount
Sinai. With Moses one ascends Mount Sinai, and enters into
the darkness of the mountain. Here a new theme in Christian
mysticism emerges, that of knowing God in the darkness.
Knowing God in the darkness is death to the senses and
reason. Origen was still living very much in the context
where reason was highly valued and he never gets fully
beyond it. Gregory of Nyssa, on the other hand, passes, like
all mystics, beyond the level of reason. Mystics consistently
emphasise that we have to die to our senses and to our
reason and, having passed beyond both, we awake to the
contemplation of reality, *ta onta*, the real things or the reality

beyond the phenomena. In other words, we go beyond phenomena and come to know the realities beyond the phenomenal world. This is a knowledge of God through nature. By contemplating the world of nature, we discover the hidden presence of God. This ascent also involves experience of the angelic realm. For Gregory of Nyssa this leads to the knowledge of *logos*, the Word of God, who is manifesting himself in nature and in the world of the angels.

Another important point here is that the original unity of man is rediscovered. Humankind was originally one but was divided by sin. Now when we recover our own unity we rediscover the unity of the whole of humanity. This is awakening to the inner unity of man, not only the individual but the universal man. The archetypal man is rediscovered in oneself.

The third stage of the journey comes with the realisation of God, experienced in the darkness as a presence. Whereas in the illuminative way we see the world with intellectual sight, here we go beyond our intellect. It is the experience which is really an experience of love, love beyond knowledge, experienced in the darkness. A very important concept emerges here which is that as one grows in the knowledge of God within, one becomes increasingly aware of the God beyond. This does not normally appear in the Eastern tradition. In the East one turns within and discovers one's true self and that Self is seen as one with God. But in the Christian mystical tradition, as one increasingly experiences God within, one becomes more and more aware that he is infinitely beyond. So there are two movements, discovering God within, and then going beyond oneself in love. That is real ecstasy, *ekstasis*. Gregory distinguishes between *enstasis* and *ekstasis*. *Enstasis* is where one finds God within, whereas in *ekstasis* one goes beyond oneself and experiences the Reality of God beyond oneself.

In all this God is represented as inaccessible, dwelling in

the darkness, in that inner sanctuary where the divine presence reveals itself. The equivalent in Hinduism is the lotus within the heart where the Infinite dwells. So this is the inner sanctuary and Gregory speaks of it as the *ousia*, the essence or ultimate substance and ground of everything. The process is to pass beyond all diversities into the darkness, into the inner sanctuary and there discover the very being of God. There are two movements here, *eros* and *agape*. *Eros* is the urge towards God, which is rather like *bhakti* in Hinduism. This is love drawing one out towards God. The other movement is *agape*, which is God's love pouring into one. And the two meet. As one goes out to God, so God comes into one, and vice versa. And this, in Gregory's view, is a constant movement. The more one loves, the more one knows God, the more there is to know. So one is constantly going out to God and returning to oneself and then having to go out again because there is infinite growth taking place. This constant going beyond is what Gregory means by *epekstatis* and it is a very original conception. Finally we should say that this awareness of the presence of God in the darkness, is always related both to Christ, the *logos*, who reveals God, bringing him to light, as it were, and to the sacraments of the Church by which we open ourselves to the presence of Christ and through him to the Father. So Gregory always works with this total vision of the Father as God beyond creation, and the *logos* and the Holy Spirit penetrating the whole creation and humanity, and then leading human persons back through the Church and the sacraments to the divine.

We come now to Dionysius the Areopagite who is generally supposed to have been a Syrian monk of the sixth century.[6] He wrote under the name of Dionysius, the disciple of St Paul, and as a result came to be accepted as of supreme authority in the Church. In him we find for the first time a radical criticism of language. In this respect he is very close

to Shankara and to Nagarjuna. Nagarjuna was the great
Buddhist philosopher of the second century who made the
most thorough analysis of language concerning the Absolute
and came to the conclusion that no language was even
remotely adequate. All language defeats itself and one has
to go beyond words and experience God beyond thought.
Dionysius' radical criticism here is a good example of the
rational Greek mind being exercised on mystical experience
and rejecting every term that might be used as a definition
of the Godhead. He says that "the Godhead surpasses all
condition, movement, life, imagination, conjecture, name,
discourse, thought, conception, being, rest, dwelling, limit,
infinity, everything that exists ... " Consequently all
language used about God is defective. Dionysius says that
one has to "go beyond all these, beyond name and form,
beyond being and concept, into the divine darkness" and
he speaks here of "knowing by unknowing". This became a
traditional phrase, *The Cloud of Unknowing* being the title of
a great work on mysticism produced in the Middle Ages,
and this doctrine passed into the tradition of the Church.
So in Dionysius we find this process of going beyond being
and beyond all concepts into the darkness and there knowing
by unknowing, by transcendent knowledge.

On the other hand, this infinite Beyond is manifesting in
the whole creation and particularly, for Dionysius, it is
manifested in the celestial hierarchies, the hierarchies of the
angels. So again we have this understanding that from the
absolute, infinite One there comes forth, through the Word,
this spiritual creation, the world of the angels. Dionysius
speaks of nine orders of angels. This concept of the angelic
hierarchy is based on the biblical tradition but it indicates
an awareness of a cosmic order representing different levels
of consciousness above the human. For him this whole
celestial hierarchy comprises angels ranging from the lower
level of the angels related to man and the universe, to the

highest angels totally absorbed in God, the cherubim and seraphim, the angels of knowledge and of love. Then there is the ecclesiastical hierarchy. This hierarchy of the angels descending from the Trinity is reflected in the church and forms the ecclesiastical hierarchy. In the Greek Orthodox Church this understanding still remains, and it comes out in the liturgy with its magnificent rituals and the profound symbolism reflected in the paintings and mosaics and in the whole structure of the church. So there is a total mystical reality of the Church as a reflection of the divine mystery on earth. There is a famous story worth recalling of how, in the eighth century, some people came from Russia to learn about Christ. They went to Rome and were taught there about the doctrine of the Church, and then they went to Constantinople and there saw the liturgy. They returned to Russia saying, "We have seen heaven on earth." And so Russia joined the Orthodox Church. For Dionysius it is fundamental that the one infinite reality is manifesting at all the different levels of creation, of humanity, of the angels and finally in the Trinity.

Dionysius says about the languge we use to speak of God, that all words like Father, Son, being, light, Word, Spirit, are communications or revelations, but "their ultimate nature which they possess in their own original being is beyond mind and beyond all being and knowledge." So all words we use about God are symbols in which divine reality is present but is beyond the grasp of the mind. This is an extremely important point. Here we are at the heart of mystical theology. God cannot be known directly. He is only known through signs and symbols by which the divine mystery makes itself known. All the terms of the biblical revelation are symbolic of that which utterly transcends them. This links with the Buddhist and the Muslim view, no less than with that of Hinduism, that in the Ultimate Reality, in *sunyata* (the void) of Buddhism and in the *al haqq*

245

(the truth) of Ibn al Arabi as in the *brahman* of Hinduism, both unity and difference are recognised. It is not a matter of simple unity because all the differences of the universe are somehow present in that Ultimate Reality. So Dionysius says that all this creation with all its differences comes forth from the divine being and in this way "it is differentiated without loss of difference and multiplied without loss of unity, and from its oneness it becomes manifold while remaining in itself." That was exactly what Suzuki said of *sunyata*, the void, as was said of *brahman* in Hinduism and the *al haqq* in Sufi doctrine. It is one total unity and yet all the differences of the universe come out from it while it remains the same. This is a paradox which cannot be properly expressed. The reason it is insisted upon is that if it is not held – and in each tradition there is a continuous movement of thought seeking to express the paradox, to balance the opposites – the implication is that ultimately the whole material universe and the whole human universe are unreal. *Brahman* or *nirvana* alone is real, all else is unreal. But in this more profound view all the multiplicity of creatures and of humanity, with all their differences and distinctions, have reality in the Absolute. They are present not in the way they appear here to our limited human time-space consciousness, but in their eternal, absolute Ground of being and consciousness, and therefore all human and created realities have real being in the Absolute.

Dionysius applied the same critique of language to the doctrine of the Trinity. He says, "It is not a unity in Trinity which can be known by us or any other creature, and we apply the names of unity and Trinity to that which is beyond all being." In other words, we simply use these names to point to a reality which is beyond everything we can describe. This understanding is still very prominent in the Eastern Orthodoxy and it is fundamental. The Trinity is the Absolute, the Godhead, the Supreme Beyond, the unap-

246

proachable light, which cannot be named. It is unity in Trinity beyond all human comprehension. Behind all this is that view which maintains that when we speak of God we first use positive terms such as God, Father, Creator, Lord, Saviour, Spirit, grace, love, beauty, truth. Speaking of God in positive terms such as these is known as affirmative theology or the *via affirmativa*. Next, however, we deny or negate all those terms. We go on to say God is not God in any sense that we can understand, nor is he truth in any sense we can understand, nor Father, nor Son, nor Spirit, nor anything. God is utterly beyond. This stage where we deny all that was previously affirmed is known as the *via negativa*, the negative or apophatic way. But we then go beyond both the positive and the negative way to the way of transcendence. Here God is God, Father, Son, Word, truth and love but in a totally transcendent sense, beyond human comprehension. We can only point to that Reality but we cannot express it. That is essential Christian mystical doctrine. With these basic teachings Dionysius laid the foundations of mystical doctrine in the Church. His views were taken up by the great scholastic theologians, St Thomas Aquinas and Bonaventure, and are still fundamental today. So here in Dionysius there is a fully-developed mystical theology, comparable to that of the Hindu, Buddhist or Muslim understanding.

In India Eckhart is very popular among Hindus because he comes nearer to Vedanta than any other Christian, but unfortunately Eckhart expressed himself very freely, especially in his German sermons. There is also the further complication that he did not write them himself. They were taken down by others and so the texts we have now may not express his position accurately. His language is often deliberately paradoxical and can easily be misunderstood. Ruysbroeck, the Flemish mystic, however, has practically the same doctrine as Eckhart but he writes more from experience and his teaching is correspondingly profound. Eckhart was more of a philosopher and gives the impression sometimes of playing with words. Ruysbroeck, on the other hand, is obviously writing from a deep experience of reality and his doctrine is all the more impressive.[7]

In Ruysbroeck there are some very original ideas. The basic Christian understanding is that man is the *ikon*, the image of God. We have seen this to be fundamental in Origen and in Gregory of Nyssa, and it comes also in Dionysius. But now in Ruysbroeck there is the further understanding that this image of God in man has its archetype in God. Each of us has an eternal archetype in God where we are one with God in our eternal archetype.

This comes very near to the doctrine of Ibn al Arabi. He expresses almost the same view in his teaching that everything in creation and everything in man exists eternally in God. Creation comes forth eternally in God as God, without any difference, and then it comes forth differentiated in time and space. Originally it is God in God. So the image of God exists eternally in God, in its archetype. Ruysbroeck says, "God utters himself in the Spirit eternally without intermediary and in this Word he utters himself and all things." In the utterance of the Word which comes forth from the Father eternally the whole creation, the whole of humanity, you and I and all created things, are present. Everything and all beings are present in that eternal Word, eternally present with God, in God and as God. We are all participating in the Infinite at that stage, beyond creation. This is what is meant by our uncreated being in the Godhead. Eckhart had the same idea but he expressed it less carefully while Ruysbroeck puts it extremely well. He speaks of "a waylessness and darkness in which we never find ourselves again in a creaturely way." We lose ourselves in that divine darkness. And he goes on to speak of God, this "God beyond", as it were, as "a simple nudity, an incomprehensible light". The one who has reached this point "finds himself and feels himself to be that light, gazing at that light, by that light, in that light. Here one has entered totally into the Godhead and one knows in the light and by the light. This is exactly how it is put in the Upanishads and in the *Bhagavad Gita,* where it is said that one knows the *atman,* through the *atman.* The *atman* cannot be known by any other means. God is grasped and held through God.

Ruysbroeck then asserts that we have our eternal archetype in God which comes forth forever from the Father in the Son and returns in the Spirit. But then we have a created existence as we come forth from God in creation, in time, and in our created existence we reflect an eternal archetype. In the depth of our being that eternal archetype is always being reflected. So each of us has that reflection of God in the depth of our being, and that is the true image of God in us. So he says, "All creatures come forth from the Son eternally and they are known as other, yet not other in all ways because all in God is God." So all creation comes forth in God and is other than God in one sense, but yet is not other for it is still God in God. There is no created difference at this point. "Our created being abides in the eternal essence and is one with it in its essential existence." Our created being has its eternal being in God, which is exactly the doctrine of the most profound thinkers in Hinduism, Buddhism and Islam. It is important to realise that this is not simply the teaching of a particular person but of a universal tradition. When the human mind reaches a certain point of experience it comes to this same understanding and this is what constitutes the perennial philosophy, the universal wisdom. "It has an eternal immanence in the divine essence without distinction and an eternal outflowing in the Son in distinction." It exists without distinction eternally in the essence and then it comes forth eternally in the Son from the Father in distinction. So Ruysbroeck can

say, "The image of God is that in which God reflects himself
and all things, and in this image all creatures have an eternal
life outside themselves, in their eternal archetypes." All
creatures have this eternal archetype in God, beyond themselves, and we come forth from the eternal ground of the
Father in an unmanifest state into manifestation in the Son.
In the eternal ground of the Father we are unmanifest and
in the Son we come forth into manifestation. "And in the
divine light they see that as regards their essential essence
they are that Ground from which the brightness shines forth
and they go forth from themselves above reason in an
intuitive gazing, and are transfigured into the light which
they see and which they are, and they behold God in all
things without distinction in a simple seeing, in the divine
brightness." This is a coming back to the original unity.
Everything comes forth from that original unity, from the
Father, in the Son and the Spirit. We come forth in time
and space with all our differences, all our conflicts, with all
the sin and the evil of the world, and then we are drawn
back by the love of God. Love is drawing us out of our sin
and out of the limitations of this world to the inner image,
to the archetype within, and then in that image, in Spirit,
we return through the Son to the Father and we reach unity
again. We know ourselves in God, as God.

Ruysbroeck goes on to say that "the wisdom with all that
is in it turns towards the Father, the ground, and then there
comes forth the Holy Spirit and this mutual love enfolds
and drenches both in action and fruition, the Father and
Son and all which lives in both." The Son comes forth from
the Father as his eternal wisdom and then there is this return
in the Spirit in the mutual love which enfolds them in one.
So within the Godhead there is the distinction, the coming
forth, and there is the return. That is eternal, not, as it were,
spread out in time but it is one act, both coming forth and
returning. "In this return in love in the divine ground every

divine way and activity and all the attributes of the persons are swallowed up in the rich compass of the essential unity. All the divine means and all conditions, and all living images which are reflected in the mirror of truth, lapse in the one-fold and ineffable waylessness, beyond reason. Here there is naught but eternal rest in the fruitive embrace of an outpouring love. This is the dark silence in which all lovers lose themselves."

This is the rhythm of the universe. Everything comes forth eternally from the Father, the Ground of Being, in the Son, the Word and Wisdom of the Father and returns in the Spirit. The Father, the ground, is pouring itself out eternally in the Son, knowing itself and expressing itself in the Son, and the Father and the Son return to one another, unite with one another, eternally in the embrace of the Holy spirit. We are all enfolded in that love. One particular passage in Ruysbroeck brings this out well. "All things are loved anew by the Father and the Son in the outpouring of the Holy Spirit and this is the active meeting of the Father and the Son in which we are lovingly embraced by the Holy Spirit in eternal love." We are taken up in this communion of love in the Spirit. "This", he says, "swallows up every divine way and activity and all the attributes of the persons within the rich compass of the essential unity. To this the persons of the Trinity and all that lives in God must give place." He goes on, "The abyss itself may not be comprehended unless by the essential unity, so the persons and all that lives in God must give place, for here there is naught else but an eternal rest in the fruitive embrace of an outpouring love. And this is that wayless being which all inferior spirits have chosen above all other good things." This is the climax of Christian mysticism, as of all mysticism, where there is a return to the original unity of being beyond all distinctions and yet embracing all distinctions.

To conclude I would like to make some points about

251

Christian mysticism as a whole. First of all it embraces all creation, matter, life, time, history, man, woman. The whole of humanity is taken up in Christ into the life of the Godhead and is restored to unity. The whole creation is gathered into one and in and through Christ the Word, all things and all people return to the Father, in the Spirit. That is the total reintegration of everything, the recapitulation, or gathering into one, of all things. That comes at the end of the world.

Secondly, creation is not a fall and it is not God. Creation is often said to be a fall. Ken Wilber, for instance, in his very remarkable book *Up from Eden*, holds that ultimately creation is a fall from God, but in the Christian view this is not so. The world is created by God as the sphere in which human experience can be worked out, which is essentially God giving himself to the world in love and drawing the world back to himself in love. That is the essence of creation. So rather than a fall, it is an outpouring of love. Sin comes in, of course, and brings disintegration and death but the grace of God comes to restore it and bring us back to God.

Thirdly, the spirit of man is a capacity for God. It is not God. My *atman*, myself, is not God, but rather it is a capacity for God which can be filled by God and can be transformed into God and this is a gift of pure grace.

Fourthly, this capacity is fully realised in Jesus in the resurrection, and so made effective in the Church and the sacraments. In Jesus this outpouring of the Spirit of God was complete. In him, as St Paul says, "dwelt the fullness of the Godhead bodily."[8] In him human nature was totally transformed, and in and through him we return to the Father. The resurrection and the ascension release a power in the universe so that now it is working throughout the whole creation and the whole of humanity to bring back creation and humanity into life in God. The Church is the sphere in which this divine power is at work, particularly through the sacraments. The sacraments constitute the means by which this power, released at the resurrection, is made present to us, first in baptism, then in confirmation and then renewed each day in the Eucharist. In this way, through the Church, we are united as members of the mystical body of Christ and in that mystical body of Christ we return to the Father.

Fifthly, the human person is not lost in the divine but enjoys perfect oneness in love. Again and again the tendency is to lose the person in the Ultimate. In both Hinduism and Buddhism this tendency is always at work, so that ultimately there is no individual left and everything dissolves in the pure oneness of being. But in the Christian mystical understanding each person is unique. Each is a unique expression of God, a unique manifestation of the divine, and each is in all and all are in each. There is a total transparency. All are one in God and one in each other. But we are not lost in this oneness; we are found in our total being. "He who will lose his life shall find it."[9] When we lose ourselves totally in that abyss of love, we find ourselves. Perhaps the fundamental difference is this: that the heart of Christian mysticism is a mystery of love, whereas both in Hinduism and in Buddhism it is primarily a transformation of consciousness. *Brahman* is *saccidananda*, being, consciousness and bliss. It is not specifically love. Love is included, and was marvellously developed as *bhakti*, but this is not so central either in Hinduism or in Buddhism, whereas the essence of the Christian experience is an experience of love, not primarily of consciousness or of knowledge, though these, of course, are included, and love is self-communication. The nature of love is such that we become persons by loving. We have a capacity to transcend ourselves in love, to go out of ourselves and to experience one another in love, and grow as we communicate in love. It is all a matter of interpersonal relationship. In this understanding the basic need of human existence is growth in interpersonal relationships, in love,

253

and that is so basic that we are called into being by love. The love which is given to mother, father, husband, wife, children and friends, all this is simply a created manifestation of a love which created us in the beginning and is drawing us to itself. All created love is a manifestation of the uncreated love from which we come and to which we are moving. In this we do not lose ourselves, just as in a human relationship of love you do not lose yourself. If you love someone you become one with him or her and they become one with you, but you do not cease to be yourself. If that happened it would no longer be love. So it is a communion of love, an experience of oneness in love, and that is the end and meaning of life. This interrelationship in love is the reflection of the life of the Godhead, where the Father and the Son give themselves totally in love and are united in the Spirit in an unfathomable unity. So the interpersonal relationships within the Trinity are the model and exemplar of all interpersonal relationships on earth and ultimately also of all interrelationships in the whole creation. We saw in chapter one how the contemporary physicist describes the universe as a complex web of interdependent relationships. Everything is interdependent and interrelated on the physical level, on the psychological level and finally on the spiritual level; and the Trinity, as far as can be expressed in words, is the exemplar of all interrelationship and the unity of all being in love.

12

Synthesis: Towards a Unifying Plan

The intention of this chapter is to put together the ideas we have been considering, particularly the evolution of the world and the evolution of human consciousness, and to see how the whole process converges on an Ultimate Reality, a Supreme Being. It is important to have some kind of plan in terms of which to identify and unify our experience. It is also important that this unifying plan has a place for all the great religious traditions. Many Christians today feel the need to relate their experience to that of the Hindu, the Buddhist and the Muslim, as well as to the traditional religions, of, for instance, the American Indians and the tribal peoples of Asia and Africa. What follows is an attempt to articulate some kind of framework in which all these modes of experience can be related and seen in their inner unity.

We start with the explosion of matter at the beginning of time, around fifteen billion years ago. It is understood that in the original explosion of matter the forms which were to come into being in the course of the ages were all already implicated, enfolded together, and that these forms have gradually unfolded or become explicated in the course of the evolutionary process. We have to go a step further and say that not only was the matter of the universe implicated with all its forms but that consciousness was also already implicated in the original explosion of the universe because consciousness itself emerged from matter as the process advanced. This means that we have to conceive of a universe coming into being in which matter and consciousness are interwoven, and to speak about this I have chosen to use the Aristotelian terms, matter and form. Matter is the energy of the universe, an unformed, unstructured energy, which is behind the whole universe, while form is the principle of order. Form and matter are the two basic principles in the universe. Matter is indeterminate, unpredictable, unintelligible, a pure flux of energy without form. It is the principle of change, of becoming, of chance, of the absurd. All that element in life comes from matter. Form on the other hand is the principle of order, of structure, of intelligibility, of being in actuality. Matter has no being in itself. It is pure potentiality which is organised into being and becomes actual through the action of form upon it.

Matter and form are the two basic principles then and the whole universe evolves through the interplay between them. Part of the dynamic is that matter always tends to dissipate itself, to disintegrate, to become disorganized. Consequently at the very beginning of the universe there was an explosion of matter such that matter was thrown outwards in primordial expansion. It is believed that this principle of expansion is still operating and that the galaxies are expanding all the time as matter pushes itself out in that way. But at the very time that matter expands and tends to disintegrate, another force, the force of form, comes into play and begins to structure matter, organising and controlling it. The understanding is then that there were originally photons, electrons and other basic particles coming into being and dissolving, and then gradually forms began to be structured and the simplest atoms, those of hydrogen and helium, came into being. From that origin of organisation matter became increasingly more organised as the two forces were continuously operative, matter disintegrating and moving outwards and form drawing within, concentrating and centring the matter. So with the galaxies the matter expanded enormously while the forms began to structure

256

it, forming the stars, the galaxies and eventually suns, moons, and planets, including earth. We can understand then that the whole cosmos comes into being by the interaction of these two forces, one working on the other.

It is important to realise that matter is always in a state of disequilibrium. If it were to come into equilibrium it would become simply passive. It is always in disequilibrium as it moves out into a new phase, and from that a new form emerges. It is thought that this is how evolution takes place. There would be a particular form, a chemical, a plant or animal or whatever, and then something in the environment disorganises that structure and it has to reconstruct itself. In so doing a new form comes into being. In this process certain structures have been identified which Ilya Prigogine calls dissipative structures. Dissipative structures are found even in chemicals and still more conspicuously in plants and animals. These are structures which tend to dissipate their energy, destructuring themselves and then restructuring again somewhat differently. This, it is thought, is how development takes place, always a disequilibrium tending towards the organisation of a new structure. Rupert Sheldrake has suggested that what, following Aristotle, we are calling forms, or formal causes, act as morphogenetic fields. These are fields in which matter is moulded into particular forms. Evolution proceeds in stages as a new burst of formative energy is released and this takes place on a large scale. Recent research has suggested that new species come into being not simply by gradual stages but rather by a kind of explosion. This indicates that the matter has been prepared for it by changes having been introduced which make it ready for this explosion of new species. This is at the moment by no means proved but it does seem to be the pattern which is emerging.

There is then a gradual development. Atoms develop

into molecules, these develop into cells, cells develop into organisms, then to simple plants and animals, as organs are produced leading to the development of increasingly complex animal forms. All this is a continuous process. What is particularly interesting is that the elements of each stage, atoms, molecules, cells and so on, are each a whole in their own right and as they develop they integrate the other wholes within themselves so that the universe is composed of wholes within wholes. For instance, an atom itself is a complete whole, with its electrons, protons and neutrons and other elements. When that atom enters into a molecule it enters a new whole, and yet it retains its identity as, say, a carbon atom within the molecule, a smaller whole within the greater whole. Similarly, within a cell the molecules still retain their structure within the wider structure of the cell. And again the cells in the body multiply and grow and each is a whole within the greater whole of the tissue, the organ and finally the whole organism. So the whole of nature is composed of all these structures or processes built up one after another, one into the other, in such a way that nothing is lost.

In the course of evolution most processes simply follow mechanical laws. Rupert Sheldrake puts this down to a kind of force of habit, in that once a certain pattern of organisation has occurred it tends to repeat itself and so it gets fixed to a certain extent. This pattern appears as a kind of mechanical law. But at the same time there are also continual chance variations and the new form that emerges from these apparently chance changes integrates the chance elements, creating a new structure. So form and matter, order and chance, are working one on the other the whole time. At each stage the organism becomes more complex and the organising principle more powerful and more structured. This is what Teilhard de Chardin calls the principle of complexification. An atom of hydrogen is extremely simple,

258

consisting of one proton and one electron. But then as there arise more and more complex atoms, and increasingly complex molecules and cells, at each level there has to be a more complex deep structure to hold it together and the energy within has to be stronger. This is Teilhard's point of the within and the without of things. Atoms, molecules, cells, attain their structure from the outside, as it were, with regard to their matter but at the same time a force is appearing within each one which organises and maintains the structure. Matter is without; form, the organising force, is within. And so the form organises each thing in a more complex way and becomes more manifest as it develops, leading to increasingly greater and more complex formal order.

This process goes on continuously, through plants and animals to human beings. It appears that the same forces which are at work in matter and sub-human life operate also in the human person and in human consciousness. The same principle of matter and form working together can account for the whole evolution of humanity. But what happens in human beings is that this organizing power, this form, begins to emerge into consciousness. We have seen that there is an organizing power at every level and this organising power has the character of a mind. Mind, it has been said, reveals itself as "a pattern of self-organisation and a set of dynamic relationships". In this sense it can be said that mind is present in matter from the beginning. Form in Aristotle's sense of the word is a power of intelligence. It creates order. It causes the self-organisation of all organic structures and creates a set of dynamic relationships. So mind is present in matter, and in plants and animals, and that mind becomes conscious in us. And so, in a very exact sense, it can be said that matter becomes conscious in human beings. This process which has been going on from the beginning of time becomes conscious in us. It evolves into

259

consciousness. We are that stage of evolution at which the material universe is emerging into consciousness in each one of us.

At first this consciousness in us is, as we saw, a global consciousness. The child and the early man is each aware of himself simply as part of the physical universe. This is a beginning of a conscious awareness of oneself as part of this whole physical organism. Later there is awareness of oneself as part of a human organisation, of a human family, of human relationships. So the human person gradually emerges into consciousness. It is a fact, however, that all of us live in a state of half-consciousness for most of our lives. Most of our living goes on without our being conscious of it. All the activity of the atoms, the molecules, the cells in our bodies, for instance, functions of itself without our being conscious of it. And most of the physical functions of the body go on without our awareness. Only certain parts of all of this come into consciousness. We are emerging into consciousness all the time from the unconscious. Every night we go back into the unconscious. It is thought that in deep sleep we go right back to the original unconscious state, before anything emerged. In dreams we begin to come out into consciousness to some extent, and when we wake up we wake into a waking consciousness which is growing from the unconscious.

All this of course is a continual process. From childhood we are growing and our consciousness develops. Certain people develop their consciousness far more than others. Some remain at a very limited level of consciousness all their lives, while others gradually explore the further ranges of consciousness. This is what interests us now, that it is possible for consciousness to develop or expand beyond the present state. We at this stage have emerged into a certain level of consciousness. We can control our bodies to some extent and of course with modern medicine we have another dimension of physical control. We can also control our environment to some extent, but we are still exposed to the tremendous forces of the unconscious. In the same way, at the psychological level we have our emotional life and although to some extent we can control our emotions, they are very largely beyond our control most of the time. Emotions arise from infancy and from childhood habits and these are extremely difficult to control. Only as they gradually emerge into consciousness do we gain a measure of control over them.

In the evolutionary and developmental process, once we reach the level of language we have already crossed a barrier because with language it becomes possible to form symbols and an inner world comes into being. There is the outer world around us consisting of all the energies of matter and nature, and now with language and symbol we create an inner world where we represent, through the imagination, what we take to be the structure of the universe around us. Outside us are all these energies at work, but through our senses, feelings, imagination, reason and will, through all the faculties of our being, we structure a universe around us. It is a very limited universe and a very limited understanding that we have. It is always that we are structuring this appearance of the world around us. It is not as it really is. The world is infinitely greater than we perceive it. We only perceive those aspects of nature, matter and the energies of existence which are reflected through our senses, our feelings, our imagination, our mind and our will, through the whole of our human organism, and this is our particular way of perceiving the universe. So matter emerges into consciousness in us and we create this inner world by which we can represent the world around us and that can gradually be extended. The whole aim of pure science and of philosophy is to get a more and more accurate knowledge of the world around, but we know now that understanding

261

is always conditioned by the limitations of our minds.

As consciousness develops we become more and more self-conscious. First of all we are conscious of the world around us. Many people live in that world of external consciousness, being aware of the world around, of people, of events happening, of things to do and so on, but they seldom if ever reflect on themselves. On the other hand certain people, particularly at certain stages, develop the power of self-reflection to an extraordinary extent. Self-consciousness begins to grow and it becomes increasingly possible to be more and more aware of the universe around one in its relation to oneself, and of one's own human organism. This is self-reflection on oneself, and as far as we know it is a power unique to the human being. It appears that so far nothing else in the universe can reflect on itself as we do. The mind reflects on itself in such a way that we become conscious of consciousness. It is an inner reflection and that is where real growth begins to take place. That is where the universe now begins to emerge into a new mode of existence. When we begin to reflect on ourselves we can go back in consciousness, right to the beginning, to primeval, primordial consciousness. It is possible now by various methods to go back to the state of consciousness we have in the womb where each of us was one with the whole of nature. We can also go back in consciousness to our early childhood, to discover the emotions which we experienced then. Or we can go back to the stage where the imagination began to awaken, when our personal life began to come into being with the growth of language and all the developments which that brings. And then we can reflect on the functioning of the mind. Not only does the mind function, organising our experience, but we can reflect on the functioning of the mind. We come to know our minds and how they work, and from that we get the science of logic and epistemology.

In this way the whole realm of consciousness and the

degree to which that can grow is infinite. The important thing is that we now begin to experience ourselves as an integrated whole. This is the principle that we have taken from the beginning. We have seen that contemporary physics understands the universe to be an integrated whole, such that every part is related with every other part and no part can be explained except in relation to the whole. So the physical universe is an integrated, interrelated, interdependent whole and we can experience our physical being as part of the universe. The whole universe is in every part. That is the principle. Just as the structure of the whole human organism is present in every cell, so the whole universe is present in each one of us and we become conscious of the physical structure of the universe of which we are a part.

Secondly, as we become conscious of our feelings, our sensations, imagination and thought, we become conscious of ourselves as part of a psychological organism. None of us is an independent reality. We are all parts of a whole, experiencing ourselves through our heredity, our families, our language, our race, our traditions, our customs. In this way we come to be aware of ourselves as part of a psychological organism which eventually we realise stretches right back in time to the beginning of humanity and looks forward to the future. So each of us is part of this integrated whole which is both physical and psychological. And, just as the physical organism is an organic part of the physical universe, so this psychological organism is related to the psychic organism of the universe. We are all members of a whole, interrelated and interdependent. So far this is on a fairly ordinary level of consciousness but we can now go to a higher level of consciousness such that we go beyond our physical consciousness and beyond our normal psychological consciousness, and then we become aware of a transcendent or transpersonal consciousness. Different terms are used for this level of consciousness: transpersonal, suprapersonal, transcendent, spiritual, mystical, and so on. At this point we begin to discover a deeper dimension of being. So far we have seen ourselves as part of the physical universe, part of the whole psychological world, part of our family and people and the human race, but now we begin to discover that we ourselves are related to, and dependent on, powers and energies which are beyond us and above us.

It is at this point that meditation enters the scene, because in meditation we try to become aware of this physical organism and of the psychological level and then, as the mind becomes quiet and settled, we become aware of our transcendent consciousness. This was the great breakthrough in India in the fifth century, with the Upanishads and the Buddha: a breakthrough beyond the level of ordinary consciousness into transcendent consciousness. This has been explored in the East particularly but in many other parts of the world as well, through many ages. It is a part of human experience, as we now realise. We have our sense experience, our emotional and imaginative experience and the intellectual and moral experience of human life, but beyond all these there is transcendent experience which is just as real and well-established as any other. In the East particularly the exploration of the psychic universe has been particularly well developed, with Tibetan Buddhism probably going further than any other tradition. In Hinduism much of this psychic world has been charted and it has also been explored deeply in Christian and Islamic mysticism. It is significant that today scientists are recognizing that what comes out of this experience is a valid sphere of knowledge.

At this point an important distinction must be made. As long as we are in the realm of physical being our usual methods of measurement and quantification, of mathematical and logical thought, are all appropriate and ordinary

264

scientific knowledge results. But once we go beyond that order into the psychological, emotional or imaginative world those methods become increasingly less appropriate, and when we come to transcendent, mystical experience they are no longer valid at all. What is important is that we learn to interpret these transpersonal experiences. We have to evolve a consistent conceptual system by which we can interpret and integrate our experience of the transcendent. That is exactly what was done in Tibet and also in other Eastern traditions. Tibetan Buddhism is a completely consistent method worked out over hundreds of years, exploring how to interpret and integrate these phenomena of higher consciousness. This is in many respects a scientific method, just as valid in its own sphere as the methods of the physical sciences, but it does not come within the same frame of reference because the kinds of experience which are its data cannot be measured or quantified.

This higher consciousness has been present in humanity from the earliest times. A well-established example is shamanism, which has been investigated extensively by Mircea Eliade, Joan Halifax and others, and is found to occur all over the world. Shamans develop psychic powers and attain psychic knowledge, going beyond the physical and the ordinary psychological domains, to experience the early or lower levels of the transcendent. With such experience are associated what we call psychic phenomena, like visions and revelations, knowledge of the future and the past, and the ability to heal. These and many other parapsychological powers have been developed by shamans over the ages and continue to the present day. Such experiences are all part of what is called the subtle world and they were, of course, developed further in the great religious traditions. There is the gross world which is the world of the senses and of ordinary understanding. Normal Western science belongs simply to the gross world. But beyond the gross is the subtle

265

world, the sphere of the subtle senses, the subtle feelings, the subtle imagination, the subtle mind and the whole subtle organism, and all the forces of that world which are present and can be experienced. Many people today are more and more commonly having these experiences, and we know that in the past this was quite normal. The forces which are encountered in the subtle realm are depicted as both good and evil. Some assist the growth of the universe, of human evolution and of human persons while others prevent and counteract such growth. So when we enter the subtle, psychic world we are exposed, as we are in the ordinary human physical world, to both good and evil forces. These are cosmic and psychological forces working in the universe and in the human consciousness and we have to learn how to understand and how to relate to them. Again in Tibetan Buddhism this complete grasp of both positive and negative forces, and how to relate to and deal with them, has been worked out in great detail.

Not only shamans but all the prophets, seers and visionaries of the past were people who had these psychic powers and psychic vision. Today this whole area is being studied more systematically and the whole sphere of parapsychological phenomena is generally recognised. As we have more knowledge of this area we begin to see how it is structured. The experience of the subtle world depends on an intuitive insight. It cannot be attained by rational means. The ordinary, rational, mental level of mind has no access to this realm and ordinary scientific methods are useless to map it. It is important to remember, however, that in these investigations we do not discard our reason. The method is to open ourselves through intuition to these deeper insights and then to try to understand them, to relate them and appropriately to systematise them through the reason. Reason and intuition always have to be used together. Intuition by itself can be misleading. All sorts of weird fantasies can come up in flashes of intuition and these have to be corrected by reason. It is a matter of the right and the left brain, the right being the intuitive and the left the rational, and for a balanced understanding the two sides have to work in co-operation rather than one to the exclusion of the other. Even in the physical sciences intuition is recognised to be essential and it is well known that some of the greatest discoveries, for instance some of those by Newton and Einstein, have been made by pure intuition. It was by intuition that they caught glimpses of aspects of the inner structure of reality and then with the rational mind they were able to express this mathematically to show how it actually worked. So intuition has always been present but its use is limited in both science and ordinary philosophy. When it comes to the realm of the psychic, however, intuition is fundamental but, and this needs to be repeated, whatever is experienced in this realm always has to be studied in the light of reason. The attempt to understand with the reason is part of the process of gaining knowledge and it can never be dispensed with.

We have, then, the world of psychic experience, but beyond the psychic world there is a deeper dimension, the world of the transcendent. This we find in the great revelations. There what is revealed is not merely the physical or the psychological or psychic world but rather there takes place an intuitive insight into the ultimate, the transcendent. All the great revelations are, as it were, messages from that transcendent world. They are given in the scriptures of the various great traditions, the Vedas and Upanishads, the Quran, the Buddhist scriptures, and the Bible. These are all revelations of transcendent reality. Then again the process is that the revelations are interpreted by the rational mind and so there are the great theologians and philosophers, for example Sankara and Ramanuja for Hinduism, Nagarjuna, Asanga and Vasubandhu for Buddhism, Ibn al Arabi and al

267

Ghazzali for Islam, and St Thomas Aquinas, St Bonaventure and others for Christianity. These great thinkers bring the rational mind to bear on the transcendent mysteries which are realities of experience. It is important to realise this because so often the impression is given that these revelations are, as it were, dropped from heaven, and people tend to accept them uncritically and therefore to misunderstand them. The reality is that all religious truth comes from an original experience, that of the seer, the prophet, the saint. But the experience always has to be interpreted in the light of rational, conceptual thought.

see below (X)

In this way then we go beyond the physical, beyond the psychological, and beyond the subtle world of psychic experience to the infinite transcendent reality beyond. As long as we are in the psychic world it is a world of multiplicity. There are many gods, many angels, many spirits, many powers of various sorts and this is why the psychic world is always somewhat ambiguous. One can somehow come under the power of these different spirits and gods, and as long as they are diversified they can be dangerous, because they, like other entities, are only properly themselves when they are part of this integrated whole of which we have been speaking. Idolatry and superstition arise when some psychic or cosmic power is isolated and worshipped in such a way that one comes under that power. All the evils of religion come from that, when some aspect of the whole world, particularly the psychic world, is isolated and worshipped as if it were the ultimate. That is what we know as the worship of false gods.

On the other hand, just as the physical universe is an integrated whole and the whole psychological universe is an integrated whole, so the subtle world is an integrated whole. In the great religions it is always seen that all these powers, these gods and angels, are under the control of one supreme power. This leads to the sense of the cosmic Lord, the cosmic

268

(X) The danger of it being interpreted by a low-consciousness, conditioned 'Rational' mind - from the level where 'illussion' operates. The so-called 'Rational' mind will confine by it's interpretation. we have to find the

Person, who rules over all. In each religion, as we have seen, the point is reached when the cosmic Lord is acknowledged. But now the next stage is to go beyond that and to realise that in and through the cosmic Person the whole of this universe, physical and psychological, is being reintegrated into its source. When we come to the Supreme, everything returns to unity. Everything comes out of that original unity, exploding into a universe and evolving through all these forms that we see. That outward movement is called *pravritti*, the whole universe coming out from the Supreme, manifesting in all these worlds and in all these forms. But at the same time there is another opposite movement, the movement of return or *nivritti*. These two movements act together, sending forth the universe and drawing it back to its source. And so everything in the universe is all being drawn back to its source, back into its original unity. Or, using a different image, just as everything came forth from an implicated whole into explication, so now it goes back from explication to the implicate and everything is fulfilled in that One. The whole universe is implicated in this unity and exists eternally in a state of absolute oneness in this being. The whole universe, and everything and everybody in it, exists eternally in that one infinite being without any differences, in a total oneness.

In Christian understanding this absolute ground of being from which the whole universe comes is known as the Father, the One, the Source, the Godhead. These terms and others are used to signify the Absolute from which everything originates. The understanding is that from this ground, from this source, there springs a Word, a wisdom, an image of the Godhead, and that is this cosmic Person, who reveals the Father, the Source. In that cosmic Person, in the Word or Son, all the archetypes of all created beings are contained. The archetype of every being in the universe is contained eternally in the Word, in the Godhead; it is, as it were,

269

equivalent to the 'Rational' mind on the transcendent level. That is the next step before the quantum leap can be made.

implicated or enfolded there. These exist eternally in him and are implicated in his being, and of all these archetypes, which are in an integrated order, the supreme is the archetypal man, whom we have seen in Hinduism, in Buddhism, in Islam and in Christianity. The archetypal man contains within himself the whole universe and all humanity. He is the cosmic Person, who is recognised as the Lord of creation, the *tathagatha* of Buddhism, the supreme *dharmakaya* of the Buddha, the *purushottaman* or the *paramatman* in Hinduism and the "universal Man" in Islam. According to the Christian understanding he is that archetypal Son of Man, the supreme Person, who took flesh and was manifested in Jesus Christ. The understanding is then that from the original ground springs this eternal Word, this Wisdom, this image of the Godhead, containing the archetypes of all creation in himself and uniting the whole creation in one.

In Christianity we also speak of the Spirit, understanding that from the original ground there springs the Spirit which is uncreated energy. As the Word or Son is the source of all form in nature, so the Spirit is the source of all energy. It is the uncreated energy which flows forth eternally from the Godhead and which then brings into being the energies of matter and of nature. So nature and matter arise as created energies springing from the uncreated energy of the Spirit. The universe can be seen as coming into being as an overflow of this energy, which is love. The love-energy of God is precisely what the Spirit is, and that love-energy flows out to express itself in the universe. God calls into being all the creatures of the universe to express himself, to manifest himself, to manifest his love and to bring forth that love in them. And so the Spirit flows out in this love to cause the whole creation and the Word organizes all those energies of matter and the creation, gradually building up the universe as we know it and bringing it back to its source in the cosmic Person.

270

In the Christian understanding there are contrary forces both in the cosmos and in the human psyche which cause disorder in nature and disease in man. The question is often asked as to how there can be all this evil in the world if everything flows from the love of God and is organized by the wisdom of God. The answer is that there are forces of evil, cosmic forces and psychic forces, which are due to freedom. The Christian view is that God creates a world of free beings, because freedom is the greatest blessing one can have. Freedom is a condition of love and the world was created by love and for love. Without freedom there can be no love.

So the world is created with free beings, both angelic and human, but freedom means capacity also to fail, to fall away from love, to centre on the self and to cause disintegration. One way of talking about this is to speak of the fall of the angels resulting in negative, hostile cosmic powers which work against the order of the universe. These are the powers of darkness. In contrast to these are the powers of light, the angelic powers, which are responsible for organizing the matter of the universe. As a result of these cosmic and psychological forces human beings fall away from the life of the Spirit and centre on themselves, forming cells of disintegration like a cancer in the body, in this body of mankind. It must never be forgotten that mankind is one. The archetypal man contains in himself all humankind and all the universe. We fall from this order of the oneness of man into a state of disintegration. Through sin we fall away from the Spirit, from the Word, from the Truth, and we fall into ourselves, into separation, becoming isolated individuals in conflict with one another. That is like a cancer in the body; it is the disease of mankind. It is into this fallen world that we are all born. On the other hand, as the human race falls into disunity and disintegration the redemptive power of the Spirit is also at work. The one goes with the other. At the moment of fall the redemptive process already begins, to restore this unity. So the Spirit is also at work from the beginning. In every human being there is a presence of the Spirit which is drawing us back from our disintegration, from our self-centredness, into the life of the Spirit, the life of God. And the Spirit is gradually rebuilding human nature in the likeness of the archetypal man, the Supreme Person. We are all part of this process in which, even while we fall away from the truth, from the perfect man, into our disintegrated state, we are all being drawn back by the Spirit, by love, to the likeness of the perfect man, the likeness of Christ.

This process works throughout history. The Spirit is at work in all humankind, in all the different tribal peoples of the world and all the great religions of the world. It is part of the whole cosmic process that certain centres are formed, as for instance when a new species comes into being and there is a new centre of organization. In this way Israel was chosen as a new centre of organization in and around which the cosmic process of redemption should be consummated.

Through the history of Israel this cell is formed, as it were, in which the organizing power of the universe, the archetypal man, can manifest himself and overcome the powers of sin and death. In our understanding, Jesus is this archetypal man, the eternal man, manifesting in time and undergoing suffering and death so as to free the world from these powers of evil, sin, disintegration, disease and death, thereby releasing redemptive power, this power of the Spirit. So through the resurrection this power of death, of disintegration, in matter is overcome and matter is renewed. The matter of the body of Jesus is totally renewed and becomes spiritual matter, a universal spiritual body. Through that resurrection, which can also be seen as a new creation, the redemptive power of the Spirit is released in the world. The Holy Spirit coming on the church is the descent of that power of redemption at work now in the whole world. This does not mean, of course, that the Spirit is confined to the Church. The redemptive presence of the Spirit is everywhere and the redeeming power is present everywhere, but it is focussed, as it were, at this point, coming to a head in Jesus and in the community he establishes. He, in and with his community, is the centre for the regeneration of humankind. In this process the Holy Spirit is released as the energizing power overcoming the contrary forces in nature, rebuilding human beings into the likeness of Christ, the archetypal person, and uniting all beings in the love of the Father from which everything comes. In love the whole universe is pouring out and that love is drawing it all back to itself.

So, then, the universe and humanity return to the divine unity and each element and each person discovers its original archetype. We all have our archetype in God, our ideal form. As we grow out of sin, evil, limitation and all the infirmities of this world, we return to that archetypal form and we are reintegrated into the one. We are held together then in Christ, in the supreme Person, and we become persons in the Person. It is important to emphasise what Teilhard de Chardin says so frequently, that it is not a matter of simply dissolving into the one. It is very common in Hinduism to think that all individuality disappears and all differences in the creation disappear and dissolve into the oneness of the Absolute. This is a mistake, for in reality nothing is lost in the process. Every person and every thing is reintegrated into the One in a total unity transcending our present understanding. This is not, of course, something in time and space. It is an eternal and infinite reality and all of us even now are interwoven and interpenetrating in that one reality.

In this way the whole creation is restored and renewed. In the Christian tradition this restoration is understood as the new creation in Christ and the new humanity in Christ.

We saw that in Buddhism and in Islam, and in many Hindu doctrines also, there is a clear understanding that it is never simply a fusing into one. There is always a reintegration of the whole into the one. That is the final goal. How the many are in the one and the one in the many can never be explained or fully expressed, but we can get a glimpse of how it is possible.

Thus in meditation we seek to go beyond our personal consciousness into the sphere of the transcendent consciousness. Normally, though not always, that means going through the psychic world and problems can arise because of the presence of evil forces as well as good. On account of this one needs a guide, and a Christian needs the guidance of Christ, to take him through that psychic world. It is important not to stop in the psychic world but to pass on through it. It is good to remember that in that psychic world there are not only evil spirits and demons of all kinds, but there are also all the saints and angels. As we go beyond our limited human consciousness we become aware of the whole world of the saints and angels and other holy beings. Today we are generally much less aware of this than people were in the past. In the Eucharist we say, "Now with all the angels and archangels and with all the company of heaven we praise and magnify your holy name." This is a conscious relating of ourselves to the whole world of the saints and angels, which is always present although hidden from our normal mental consciousness. We need always to try to keep in mind that not only is the physical world around us, and the ordinary psychological world of our human experience, but also the psychic world of the saints and angels and the cosmic powers. This subtle world is more real than either the physical or the psychological world and enfolds both in itself. When the New Testament speaks of casting out demons or evil spirits it is speaking of realities.

In meditation then we go into that *mahat*, the cosmic order

274

or cosmic consciousness, and then we go beyond that to where everything is gathered into the unity of the one Person, the cosmic Lord. Then in and through the cosmic Lord everything returns to the transcendent unity beyond conception. The ultimate is beyond conception altogether. It is totally ineffable. That is why we constantly have to remember that all the words we use to speak of this are only pointers to that which is totally beyond. The Absolute itself is beyond all human comprehension and we use words, images and concepts taken from everyday finite experience in order to direct our mind, our will and our heart towards the Infinite and to allow that Infinite to enter into our lives and transform them.

The New Age

There is a general feeling today that we are at the end of an age, an age which began three centuries ago with the discoveries of Galileo and Newton and resulted in the gradual development of a materialist philosophy and a mechanistic model of the universe. This has in the course of time affected our whole society. The present industrial system and modern technology are the direct result of this mechanistic concept of the universe. The whole social, political and economic system of the West is governed by it, and even art, morality and religion are affected by it. So we live in a world which came into being in the last three centuries, and has come to a head only in the last century.

The basic principle of this world is its materialistic philosophy. This materialism is explicit in Marxism but it is implicit practically everywhere and it governs people's attitudes of mind and behaviour. Its basic principle is reductionism; it is the reduction of everything to certain material principles and to its material base. To take a simple example, all music can be reduced to vibrations on strings or in a pipe, mere vibrations in the air, and those vibrations may then be treated as being what music is, without concern for any other value which belongs to it. Fritjof Capra has shown convincingly in *The Turning Point* (1982) how this mechanistic system has come to dominate every aspect of science and of practical life today. He shows how modern physics was at first an attempt to explain everything in terms of atoms, where everything was reduced to material particles which obeyed mechanical laws and could be known by mathematical calculations. So the whole physical world came to be reduced to a machine. In biology the attempt still continues to explain all life in terms of physics and chemistry, and to believe that living beings are simply more complicated machines. More seriously for practical purposes, in medicine the human body is conceived from a biological point of view as a mechanical system obeying physical and chemical laws, and to be treated simply as a physical entity and manipulated by genetic engineering, without relation to the psyche or to the whole human person.

Psychology is obviously less amenable to reductionism than medicine. Nevertheless many of its methods are conspicuously reductionistic. Behaviourism, for instance, is a serious attempt to reduce the human psyche to the status of a machine by analysing it only in terms of external behaviour. Another example is the psychoanalysis of Freud and the tremendously influential method based on his work, where the attempt is made to explain the whole human personality in the light of the unconscious, which is seen in terms of repressed appetites, instincts and desires. In Freudian psychology all the higher levels of consciousness, the motives of the heart, morality and religion are explained in terms of the unconscious. This is typical of the whole method. It is an attempt to explain the higher in terms of the lower and to reduce the higher to the level of the lower, so that, to take a glaring example, religion is regarded as repressed sex.

In sociology the attempt is made to reduce society to individual persons who are either left free to seek their own advantage or have to be organised by the state. From this arises capitalism and communism, in both of which systems society is reduced to a multitude of individuals. Finally, in economics this principle is most obvious where the whole aim is to conceive society simply in terms of production and distribution. In Marxism society is deliberately reduced to the economic base, which is conceived as determining the whole. In capitalism society is judged in terms of monetary value so that the prosperity of a nation is evaluated in terms of its gross national product, by the money which is being circulated in it and the way it is being used.

This is a drastic system by which everything is reduced to the material level, and it has had extraordinary success. Scientifically it has led to great discoveries being made and it has undoubtedly produced an impressive system of technology. On a social scale it has produced states with tremendous power building up influence all over the world. But at the same time it is gradually producing inevitable evil effects, rapidly exhausting material resources, polluting the environment and leading to the build-up of armaments which threatens to lead to a nuclear war capable of destroying our entire civilisation and the whole planet. All this is the result of three centuries of materialism building up to its height in the first part of this century.

In the second part of this century we have begun to discover what has been taking place and in what we are involved, and a new movement has begun which is the opposite of all this. We are beginning now to be able to replace the mechanistic system and mechanistic model of the universe with an organic model. This is the beginning of a return to the traditional wisdom, the wisdom by which human beings have lived over thousands and thousands of years and with which the great societies of the past have been built up. In this ancient traditional wisdom the order of the universe is seen always to be three-fold, consisting not only of a physical dimension but also of a psychological and a spiritual world. The three worlds were always seen as interrelated and interdependent. This understanding of the three orders of being and of their interdependence is what is known as the perennial philosophy.

Materialism is correct in so far as it recognises the material basis of reality, and science has explored this basis further than has ever been done before. This is a positive achievement. The rational, logical mind has been used in the analysis of matter, and this has led to the organisation of matter to such an extent that it is hoped that by this means all human needs can be satisfied. This is why many people think that this age is in advance of any previous age. But it is only in this respect that the present age is in advance of others. In all other respects it is to be judged as being far below. A little exaggeratedly perhaps, Coomaraswami once made the remark, "From the stone age to the twentieth century,.what a descent!" There is something in this. The perennial philosophy was present in the stone age and human beings lived by that, In this view, as has been said, there was the order of nature, the physical world, then the psychological, social world and, highest of all, the divine spiritual world, and all three were seen as interdependent and integrated. If we want to see the decline of the modern world we cannot do better than to compare stages in the development of art.

Looking back on the history of art from the stone age onwards, you see how the ancient wisdom was embodied in every form of art. In the early stages art in whatever form was the expression of the religious instinct, the sense of the sacred. Everything in nature was held to be sacred, because it was pervaded by the universal Spirit. Art, whether in the form of stone implements, or burial places, or roughly carved figures, or paintings as in the palaeolithic caves, or pottery or clothing, was a way of expressing the sense of the sacred, of enacting the sacred mystery which pervaded human life. When the great civilisations arose in Egypt and Babylon, the temple became the centre of civilised life and all the arts were used to adorn the temple and to provide for human needs. Agriculture and pottery and weaving were no less sacred than the service of the temple. All alike were ways of expressing and manifesting the all-pervading mystery.

279

When the great awakening took place in the first millennium to the transcendence of the mystery with the Upanishads, the Buddha, the Hebrew prophets, art was less conspicuous. The Israelites were forbidden to make any image of their God and the early Buddhists made no image of the Buddha. The Hindu temple also had not yet come into being. But as these religions became established and as Christianity with its doctrine of incarnation emerged from Judaism, there was a flowering of art in every form over all the ancient world, in China, India, Persia, Greece and Rome. In Greece Athens was leading the way already in the fifth century before Christ and Greek influence seems to have been responsible for the development of Buddhist sculpture. Gradually throughout all these regions a marvellous synthesis of art and poetry and philosophy was achieved, which gave rise to Hindu sculpture and architecture, Buddhist painting and sculpture, the Chinese art of every kind and the cathedrals of Europe with their sculpture and stained glass and the painting of the icons in eastern orthodoxy. Everywhere art expressed the mystery of religion, the sacred mystery revealed in the Scriptures and embodied in every form of art and poetry, music and dancing, and even the simple articles of daily use. Even Islam, which had rejected all images, developed a style of architecture of the utmost refinement.

It was this period then, between AD 500 and 1500, that saw the great flowering of art and culture which took place all over the civilised world. After that the hold of the perennial philosophy with its holistic vision began to loosen. Individual geniuses arose but the sense of a cosmic vision and a cosmic whole was gradually lost and art and culture became more and more fragmented. Today we inherit this fragmented universe and we are as far as possible from the sacred universe of earlier times. The present system of industrialisation which emerged in the nineteenth century marked the death knell of traditional art. Yet, as we have seen, a renewal is taking place. As the cosmic vision of the new science and philosophy takes over we may hope that there will be a renewal of art, not merely in the sense of the fine arts, but in all the humble daily expressions of a sense of beauty, which is also a sense of the sacred in human life. We may therefore look forward to a new birth, another renaissance of art and culture in the New Age.

Many people today anticipate a great advance in humanity and I think that is perfectly right, as we shall see. In many respects we can look forward to a great advance but I think we also have to look back. We have to recognise that the summit was achieved in those centuries before Christ, and that with the coming of Christ the final fulfilment of this experience of ultimate Reality was reached. In other respects great developments took place and they can also take place again in the future. So there we have the perennial philosophy, with the physical base, the psychological development and the spiritual order transcending all and integrating all. We need to remember that it is the spiritual that integrates the whole reality.

We go on now to ask, what will the pattern of the new age be like? What can we discern in the light of our present understanding of the universe and of the knowledge which we have of Eastern mysticism and spiritual experience? How in our time can we look forward in the light of our present knowledge of what science has done both for good and for evil, and what are we to make of the past, its art and philosophy, its religion and its mythical experience?

The first thing is that human society will be based on a new relationship to the world of nature, arising from an organic understanding of nature in place of a mechanistic view of the universe. This is a major change which is taking place. We have to learn to see ourselves as part of the physical organism of the universe. We need to develop the

281

sense of the cosmic whole and of a way of relating to the world around us as a living being which sustains and nourishes us and for which we have responsibility. This will give rise to a new understanding of our environment and will put an end to this age of the exploitation of nature. At the present moment the whole movement of economics and politics is characterised and marred by the exploitation of nature at every level. The material resources of the universe are being grossly exploited in order to create more material prosperity for relatively few human beings, no matter at what cost that is done. That trend would be reversed by the new understanding that we are all parts of this universe, of this natural world, that we are integral elements in it and that we have to respect it. This would involve a new attitude to the earth and to the natural resources of the earth, to the sea and all the creatures in it, to the animal world as a whole, to the question of vivisection and the treatment of animals in general, and to our attitude to outer space, whether we try to exploit it for human gain or whether we look on it in another way.

Secondly, the sense of communion with an encompassing reality will replace the attempt to dominate the world. The different understanding of ecology and a greater sensitivity to its realities would revolutionise our understanding of nature and of the world in which we live. This would lead to a new kind of technology based on the new understanding of science, and an appropriate or intermediate technology as Schumacher conceived it, answering the needs of the vast majority of people in Asia, Africa and South America who live in rural communities. The present system of technology has been built up on the basis of mechanistic science and it savagely and indiscriminately exploits the world of nature. This has produced the terrible situation in which we find ourselves with its material conveniences for a minority but with its disastrous consequences of global injustice and destruction. We are looking for a new technology which Schumacher speaks of as appropriate or intermediate technology which builds up from the villages. It would build upon the economy of the village instead of destroying it. There would be respect for the basic crafts of spinning, weaving, pottery, carpentry, metal work and of course all forms of gardening and agriculture. This is very important. All these crafts were evolved in the millennia before Christ, from roughly the fourth millennium onwards, and they represent a summit of human achievement in this sphere. When we look back on the past and see the weaving, the clothing, pottery, woodwork and metalwork of the past ages, we put them in museums as something to marvel at because of their beauty. And that was the ordinary work of the people of those times. To discard those abilities in favour of the progress of the mechanistic system is to degrade civilisation and human life.

Respect for the basic crafts enables human persons to live in harmony with nature and with the world around them. Their art and their work express this harmony and therefore it is beautiful. Beauty is always due to this harmony with nature. When we have that harmony the products of our hands are beautiful, and when we do not have harmony the products may be useful and very helpful in other ways but they lose their beauty.

Thirdly, these new values would give rise to a new type of human community. This would be a decentralised society drawing people from large cities to smaller towns and villages where a much more total and integrated human life would be possible. I do not see any future for the huge cities of the present world, London, New York, Tokyo, Bombay and Calcutta. In such cities all over the world in every continent the population may be over ten million. Cities of millions of people do not provide a human mode of existence and depend on a whole economic system which will eventu-

ally collapse, for such societies cannot sustain their econom-
ies. So we have to look back beyond these industrialised
cities to find some kind of norm of human existence. Here I
would like to quote from Lewis Mumford, where in his book
The Myth of the Machine he describes the neolithic village.
This is a village the like of which lasted for thousands of
years, all over the world, and still exists to some extent to
the present day. This is how he describes it. "Where the
seasons are marked by holiday festivals and ceremonies;
where the stages of life are punctuated by family and commu-
nal rituals; where eating and drinking and sexual play
constitute the central core of life, where work, even hard
work, is rarely divorced from rhythm, song, human companionship and aesthetic delight; where vital activity is
considered as great a reward of labour as the product; where
neither power nor profit has precedence over life; where the
family, the neighbour and the friend are all parts of a visible,
tangible, face-to-face community. There the neolithic culture
in its essential elements is still in existence." That is to my
mind a model of wholesome human existence. All these
elements were present in the villages of India until recently
and are still basically there although they are being undermined daily. That Indian village life and culture which
existed for millennia is being systematically destroyed, year
by year.

Mumford's description of the neolithic village remains a
model for a human community. Science and appropriate
technology, building on that, may introduce improvements,
especially forms of transport and communication which may
link up the different human centres, but these will be based
on natural sources of energy, particularly the sun. Fritjof
Capra considers that the new age will be the solar age. The
sun provides all the energy that is conceivably necessary for
human existence. Such a society would be decentralised. It
does not require huge conglomerations of people in cities.

The sun is available everywhere and the energy can be made available. Also, of course, water and the wind are appropriate sources of energy. The new society would certainly exclude all forms of nuclear energy which is perhaps the supreme example of this mechanistic system and the most destructive form of it.

Education in the new society would be basic education, as understood for instance by Mahatma Gandhi. It would be an integral education of body, soul and spirit, relating each person to the world in an organic way and developing their personal capacities. Perhaps, following Rudolf Steiner's understanding, such education would centre first on emotional growth. Steiner held that during the first seven years the child has primarily to grow at the level of the emotions and the education given should foster this emotional development. During the next seven years the growth of the imagination predominates and education centres on music, art, dance and poetry. Only in the third seven years, from fourteen onwards, should the rational, logical mind be trained to develop seriously. To some extent obviously it is functioning before this but in the Steiner system the emphasis on it only begins there. The result of acting on these principles is an integrated education of the whole person, emotional, imaginative and rational, where each level, emotions, imagination and rationality, is properly developed, consolidated and stabilised. This is in marked contrast to our usual method of education, which concentrates on developing the rational, logical mind as early as five and so often loses out on these other aspects of human personality.

In medicine, rather than making use almost entirely of modern allopathic methods, there will be a turn to alternative methods such as homoeopathy, acupuncture, Ayurvedic and Tibetan medicine, and herbal medicine in general, all of which are concerned with the health of the whole person.

285

These forms of treatment always relate the body to the soul and the spirit and never regard it as something that can be treated in isolation. The human person is conceived as an integral whole, and it is seen that health, wholeness and holiness, being derived from the same root, are totally interrelated. The health of the body, the wholeness of the person and holiness itself are all aspects of the same reality and they cannot be separated.

This leads to the third aspect. We have considered first the physical, material growth of the world and secondly its psychological and social growth. Now we turn to the spiritual order and the place of religion. This involves a return to the perennial philosophy, the ancient wisdom which underlies all religion from the earliest times. It will involve a respect for the traditional wisdom of primitive people, the Australian Aborigines, the American Indians and the tribal peoples of Asia and Africa. More and more today we are discovering the wisdom of these people, the harmony they have achieved in their lives and the very profound understanding they have of how human life is related to the natural world about them and to the world of spirits beyond them. Generally such people evidence an integrated, holistic view of life.

Then we turn to the great religious traditions, Hindu, Buddhist, Jain, Sikh, Taoist, Confucian, Shinto, Zoroastrian, Judaic, Muslim and Christian. These are systems of religion which had their origin during the first millennium before Christ. All are based on the perennial philosophy, developed under different situations and in different circumstances, and all embody in their different ways the ancient wisdom and the wholeness of life. These different traditions will all be seen as interrelated and interdependent, each giving a particular and unique insight into ultimate truth and reality. In fact, of course, they all grew up apart and mostly without contact with each other for many centuries.

286

When they did make contact there was often rivalry, acrimony and conflict, and as a result we have the disastrous divisions of religion today. But we are learning, and we shall continue to learn, that all the different religious traditions, from the most primitive to the most advanced, are interrelated and interdependent, and that each has its own particular insights. For the Semitic religions in particular, Judaism, Christianity and Islam, it is important that they give up the exclusive claims which characterise them. This would free them to recognise the action of God in all humanity from the beginnings of history. For the Semitic religions this is a particularly difficult problem. All three tend to extreme exclusivism and on that account have brought so much conflict into the world.

For Christianity this enlargement of its horizons would involve a recognition of the limited character of its original revelation, coming as it did from within a Semitic culture in the limited world and thought-forms of the Ancient Near East. Emerging from that world it spread through the Roman Empire from Palestine through Greece to Rome. For centuries the whole sphere of Christianity was simply the Roman Empire centred around the Mediterranean and completely without contact with the greater part of Asia, Africa, America and Australia. Yet we have seen that Christianity is a unique revelation of God in Jesus Christ and that, although it was conditioned by the circumstances of its origin, this revelation has a unique message for the whole world. The Christian church began as a Jewish sect and only gradually realised its vocation as a universal religion. It developed its structures from the second century onwards entirely in the context of Graeco-Roman culture, with an extension which must not be overlooked in the Syrian East, in Egypt and Ethiopia. The doctrine of the church remains essentially based on a Semitic foundation developed by the Greek genius in terms of Greek philosophy, while the

287

organisation of the church remains a Roman structure built on the foundation of the original Jewish community.

In the course of the centuries these structures within Christianity have expanded and a whole system of theology, philosophy and morality, a sacramental order and an ecclesiastical hierarchy, have developed. Though it derives from Jesus and the apostles in the first century, the Christian church as such received its definitive structure in the second century, its evolution in the Roman Empire being determined by the circumstances of the time. All these structures which we have inherited are Western structures built on the foundation of the original Semitic revelation. These structures of doctrine, discipline and sacrament are thus historically conditioned. They are integral elements in a historical development which has taken place gradually over many centuries. In the course of its history – and this is the great tragedy – the Asian and African churches were separated from the main body. In Asia, where St Paul conducted his missions, the churches which were centred on Antioch were separated in the fifth century, while the churches of Africa, based on Egypt and Alexandria, were also separated. The result was that by the fifth century Asia and Africa were lost to the church. Then in the eleventh century Eastern Europe, centred on Byzantium, separated from Rome which was the centre of the Western church. Finally, at the Reformation the churches of Northern Europe were separated from Rome. It is this tragically divided church that we have inherited. The separations which have accumulated over the centuries are all still present today. It will be one of the tasks of the new age to see the reconciliation of these divided churches as each recognises the other as a particular expression of Christian faith and worship, and as each seeks to reconcile the differences. There are valid elements in every Christian church. Each is a way of expressing Christian faith and worship. There are obvious limitations and obvious differences in each but today we seek to discern the differences and overcome the divisions, in contrast to previous times when we were engaged in dividing from one another and in asserting our own values at the expense of those of others.

Reconciliation within the Christian church will involve recognition of different ministries. The present ministries of the different churches all derive from the second century or later. In the New Testament there is neither papacy, episcopacy nor priesthood. The only priesthood, properly speaking, in the New Testament is that of Christ himself and of the people, which St Peter describes as a "holy priesthood". It would be necessary to reconsider the different ministries in this light.

The present system of the papacy dates from the Gregorian reform of the twelfth century. It is important to recognise that this movement had its value at the time. One must consider that the Holy Spirit was present in each development of the church but each was limited to its particular historic horizon. It was only when the Eastern church separated from the Western that the papacy began to develop its present structure. It would be necessary to go behind the present structure of the papacy to the fifth century if a reconciliation is to be found with the Eastern churches. The Eastern church will never be reconciled with the present system of the papacy which is an evolution of the last ten centuries. In the fifth century there were five patriarchates: Jerusalem, Antioch, Alexandria, Constantinople and Rome. Already in the fifth century the primacy of the Pope, St Leo, was fully recognised but he was *primus inter pares*, the first among equals, and he normally never interfered in the affairs of the Eastern churches. There was a right of appeal to Rome and the right of intervention in grave necessity was recognised, but the patriarchs were responsible for the liturgy, theology and the whole conduct of their churches just as the Pope, as patriarch of the West, was responsible for the Western churches. At that time the Pope only appointed bishops in his own patriarchate. So this was a very different structure of the church from that of later centuries, and yet it was a unified church which recognised the primacy of the Pope. So we could go back to that point as a model for the reorganisation of the church today, particularly in the light of the Eastern churches.

With regard to the other churches apart from the Eastern church, it will be necessary to go even further back for a model. The person to go to is St Irenaeus, that great theologian and churchman of the second century. He was the most representative figure in the Catholic church at the time, being a bishop in Gaul, coming originally from Asia and being in close touch with Rome. He shows the Roman church at that time as the centre of Christendom. He speaks of it as being founded by the chief of the apostles, Peter and Paul, not Peter alone, notice, and he uses a very important phrase, *potiorem principalitatem*. This may mean "more powerful presidency" or perhaps "more powerful origin". The original was written in Greek and we only have the Latin translation so we cannot be quite sure of the meaning. But because the Roman church was founded by Peter and Paul it has a kind of primacy without a doubt. Then Irenaeus says in a very important sentence, "With this church it is necessary that every church should agree, or come together (*convenire* in Latin), every church, that is, the faithful from all parts (*eos qui sunt undeque fideles*)." This is an excellent model of the Roman church as a centre of unity to which people come from all parts. It seems to me that we have a model, there in the second century, of Rome seen as the seat of Peter and Paul, as a centre of unity to which people come from all parts and where the true faith is always preserved. That was St Irenaeus's point. It is to be noticed that the emphasis is on the church itself, rather than on the bishop.

290

The bishop became more important in the course of time but at this point it was the church that was important. This brings out further the function of Rome which is that it should be a centre of unity rather than a centre of power. Today many people in all churches see the possibility of a papacy which would be a centre of unity, of the pope as exercising a ministry of unity on behalf of the whole church. This would mean that Rome would no longer be the centre of power and domination which it had become in the Middle Ages.

This character of the Roman church is brought out further by St Ignatius writing in the second century to the Roman church, again not to the bishop but to the church. He speaks of the church as "presiding over the charity" (*prothestos tes agapes*) or, perhaps, "presiding in charity". Again it is a difficult phrase to translate, let alone know the exact meaning of, but it looks as though the church herself is considered as a charity, a school of love. The Pope has this function of "presiding over the charity" or "presiding in charity". The point is that it is a presidence of love rather than of power. That takes us back to the second century. But now we have to go further back still, because Irenaeus speaks always in terms of episcopacy which was fully developed by this time in the second century. But when we go back to the New Testament there is neither episcopacy nor priesthood in the usual sense. On the other hand we find a great many other different ministries. St Paul speaks of apostles and prophets but also of evangelists, pastors and teachers, helpers and administrators. So that was the structure of the church in the New Testament and it seems that we have to go back to the New Testament itself to restructure the ministries of the church. In that light the ministries of other churches which have no bishops could be reconciled with the church as a whole. We should also be aware that in the New Testament women played a very considerable part in the ministry of the church, and any attempt at renewing the

291

structures of the ministry of the church would involve women having ministries in equality with men. That would be the normal development that we would expect. So this is how the development of the ministries in the church could be envisaged, while remembering, of course, that in the New Testament the position of Peter among the apostles still remains a valid and unquestionable fact which has meaning for the church today just as it had then.

When the church has been opened in this way to a more universal structure of ministry it would be much more possible for her to open herself to the cultures of Asia and Africa and to answer the needs of the people in the Third World. So far the church has had a European structure. In its liturgy, theology, canon law and organisation it is a totally Western structure. We are only today beginning to discover the possibilities of structuring the church, not in the light of Europe, but in the light of Asia, Africa and South America. That is clearly where the future lies.

It may be that the basic communities in South America, particularly in Brazil, could provide a model for the church in the Third World. In these communities lay people, men and women, meet regularly to study the Scriptures, to celebrate the Eucharist, and to reflect on their life and experience in the light of the Bible and the Eucharist. They also relate their political and socio-economic problems to their experience of the Bible and the Eucharist and try to develop these aspects of their lives within this context. These basic communities, in Brazil in particular where there are tens of thousands of them, are all in communion with the bishops and the clergy, but they are lay communities. This kind of involved and committed community may well be the model for a renewed Christian church. Such communities could be compared to the monastic communities at the break-up of the Roman Empire. In many respects we seem to be entering a period not unlike that of the Roman Empire in the fifth century when the entire structure began to collapse. It was monastic communities, integrated communities with a physical, social base and a religious character, which were the sources from which the new civilisation emerged. As economic, social and political tensions increase in the present world there will be an ever stronger need for small communities, based on the new vision of life, which could in time form the basis of a new civilisation, like the monasteries in the Middle Ages. These communities would be communities of men and women, married and single, basically Christian but also open to people of other religious traditions and of other understandings also, where a new culture would gradually be formed.

Along with this a new theology would be developed, particularly as the church comes into contact with the religious cultures of Asia and Africa. Again we must remember that our present theology was first built up entirely in contact with Greek philosophy. The whole system was based on divine revelation in the Scriptures interpreted in the light of Greek philosophy. Today theology has drawn on modern philosophy, especially existentialism, but nowhere until the present time has the church succeeded in evolving a theology based on the experience and the wisdom of Asia and of Africa. Our present theology was evolved in Europe and we have to look forward to a theology which would evolve in contact with Hindu, Buddhist, Taoist and Confucian thought and at the same time a liturgy which would develop from contact with the art, music and dance of Asian and African peoples. It would be an assimilation of the cultures of Asia and Africa into the life of the church, just as in the early centuries there was an assimilation first of the culture of the Greeks and the Romans and then of all the "barbarian" peoples of Europe. That was how the church emerged in the Middle Ages. It brought its original Semitic wisdom, religion and faith and interpreted it in the light of the Greek and the

Roman world. Then later it assimilated the "barbarian" peoples with their wonderful gifts, creating that great church of the Middle Ages which we have inherited.

In this way we can envision the emergence of a new world culture as the present materialist and mechanistic system breaks down under the continued crisis of economic, social and political conflict. One of the characteristics of this new culture would be its feminine aspects. For three thousand years the world has been dominated by patriarchal cultures which overcame the ancient matriarchal cultures of the earlier ages. We have now reached the limit of this masculine culture with its aggressive, competitive, rational, analytic character. We are moving now into an age where the feminine principle will be valued, the *yin* in contrast to the *yang*. In the Chinese understanding *yang* is the masculine principle, *yin* is the feminine and as the *yang* reaches its limit it begins to move back again to the *yin*. We have now reached the limit of the *yang*, the masculine culture, and we are moving inevitably back to the feminine. The feminine will sooner or later begin to take its proper place with its characteristics of intuition, empathy and co-operation, and with its holistic approach. This will necessarily affect not only the economic, social and political orders but also spirituality and religion. The Christian religion has developed an entirely masculine concept of God. We always speak of God as Father, and of the incarnation of the Son. Even the Holy Spirit, which is neuter in Greek but masculine in Latin, we have conceived normally in masculine terms. In the Old Testament, however, the Spirit, the *ruach*, is feminine and in the Syrian church this same word was used of the Holy Spirit when they spoke of "our Mother, the Holy Spirit". That is found in the second and third centuries but it does not seem to have survived after that. The masculine character of the Godhead has always prevailed since then. There was however a feminine aspect in God in the Old

Testament and to some extent in the New, and in the Christian tradition we have particularly Julian of Norwich, who speaks of Jesus as our Mother. St Anselm of Canterbury does the same. So apart from a few exceptions the masculine character of God has strongly prevailed in the West. By contrast, in India God is conceived both as Father and Mother. Obviously theologically God may be conceived as both Father and Mother. Being neither masculine nor feminine he can be represented as either Father or Mother, or both, in masculine and feminine terms. In the Tantric tradition, which derives from the ancient matriarchal culture, the mother aspect of God is dominant. In that tradition the whole universe is seen to derive from the Mother and all worship is offered to the Mother. That is precisely the opposite of the Judaeo-Christian tradition. We may expect therefore a corresponding development in Christian theology recognising the feminine aspect of God and the place of women in the ministry of the church. There is of course no question of a return to a matriarchal society. It is a matter of the recovery of feminine values and the reconciliation of the masculine and the feminine.

It should be added that in Catholicism the feminine aspect is entirely centred on the Virgin Mary. It is the only way a Catholic, or indeed a Christian, can find a feminine figure in relation to God. So devotion to the feminine archetype centres on the Virgin Mary, but we should recognise that there is a feminine aspect of God himself and that the Virgin Mother is a manifestation of this. This means, in other words, that devotion to the Mother has its origin in God.

It is possible that the transition from a mechanistic to an organic society will come about gradually, without too much conflict. But it is more likely that there will be a general catastrophe as the economic, social and political structures of the present civilisation break down. We must remember, and this is important, that the conflicts of the present world do not derive merely from human failings and miscalculations. There has been a reversal of human values, a spiritual breakdown, which has brought into play forces beyond the material and the human. The present crisis has been prepared by the whole system of science and philosophy, affecting religion and leading to atheism. This is a systematic development where the previous spiritual values have been broken down and the materialistic system discussed earlier has prevailed. This has released forces beyond the material and the human. If a nuclear war takes place it will not be because anyone desires it but because people are being driven by forces of the unconscious which they cannot control. As St Paul says, "We are not contending with flesh and blood, but against the principalities, against the powers, against the world rulers of this present darkness".[1] When the truth of the transcendent order of reality is rejected we do not remain neutral. We become exposed to the hostile forces of the subtle world of which we have been speaking, forces which work in the unconscious and bring destruction upon humankind. Western Europe rejected the perennial philosophy at the Renaissance and has been led step by step to the materialistic philosophy which rejects fundamental human values and exposes humankind to the contrary forces at work in the universe. The only way of recovery is to rediscover the perennial philosophy, the traditional wisdom, which is found in all ancient religions and especially in the great religions of the world. But those religions have in turn become fossilised and have each to be renewed, not only in themselves but also in relation to one another, so that a cosmic, universal religion can emerge, in which the essential values of Christian religion will be preserved in living relationship with the other religious traditions of the world. This is a task for the coming centuries as the present world order breaks down and a new world order emerges from the ashes of the old.

NOTES

CHAPTER 3   *The Eastern Vision of the Universe*

1 Maitri Upanishad 6:17
2 Bhagavad Gita 15:14
3 Bhagavad Gita 3:12
4 Chandogya Upanishad 6:12
5 Brihadaranyaka Upanishad 1:4:11
6 Brihadaranyaka Upanishad 1:4:1
7 Rig Veda 10:90
8 Brihadaranyaka Upanishad 3:6
9 Brihadaranyaka Upanishad 2:1:20
10 Brihadaranyaka Upanishad 2:4: 1-5
11 Chandogya Upanishad 8:1
12 Katha Upanishad 3:10-11
13 Svetasvatara Upanishad 1:7
14 Svetasvatara Upanishad 4:14
15 Bhagavad Gita 9:4
16 Bhagavad Gita 9:5
17 Bhagavad Gita 10:19-20
18 Bhagavad Gita 11:9,13
19 Bhagavad Gita 11:4-5

CHAPTER 4   *The Christian Vision of the New Creation*

1 1 Samuel 28:13
2 Genesis 28:16-19
3 Genesis 32:30
4 Genesis 16:13
5 Genesis 21:33

297

 6 Genesis 14:18-19

 7 cf. Exodus 6:3

 8 Genesis 3:14

 9 Katha Upanishad 6:12

10 Wisdom 1:7

11 Wisdom 7:24

12 Genesis 2:9

13 Genesis 2:25

14 Genesis 3:8

15 Genesis 3:1

16 Genesis 1:1

17 Revelation 12:1

18 Genesis 4:2

19 Genesis 11:4

20 Genesis 12:1

21 Exodus 6:5

22 Ezekiel 36:28

23 Isaiah 11:1-9

24 Hosea 2:20-23

25 Exodus 12:25;14:24-25

26 Deuteronomy 7:2

27 1 Samuel 15:3

28 Isaiah 19:24-25

29 Isaiah 62:4

30 Isaiah 65:17-18

31 Hebrews 11:14-16

32 Romans 8:22-23

33 2 Peter 3:13

34 Revelation 21:1-2

35 John 17:21

Notes

CHAPTER 5   *The New Humanity*

1 Genesis 1:27
2 Genesis 2:7
3 cf. 1 Corinthians 2:14-15
4 Genesis 3:24
5 Genesis 3:16,18
6. Jeremiah 31:33
7 Isaiah 52:13 – 53:12
8 Matthew 15:24
9 Ephesians 2:14
10 Acts 22:3
11 Galatians 6:15
12 Galatians 3:28
13 2 Corinthians 5:17
14 1 Corinthians 13:12
15 1 Corinthians 15:45
16 Ephesians 2:22
17 Ephesians 1:19,20
18 Ephesians 1:20,21
19 Ephesians 2:2
20 Ephesians 1:22,23
21 Colossians 2:9
22 cf. Colossians 1:16-18
23 John 1:9
24 Colossians 1:16,17
25 Ephesians 4:13

CHAPTER 6   *The Cosmic Person in the New Testament*

1 cf. the word *theos* in the New Testament, in Karl Rahner, *Theological Investigations*. vol i.
2 John 20:28
3 Acts 2:22,24
4 Matthew 28:18

5 Ephesians 1:17,20-21
6 2 Corinthians 5:19
7 1 Corinthians 3:23
8 1 Corinthians 15:28
9 John 5:30
10 John 5:19
11 John 10:34-36
12 John 14:10
13 John 10:30
14 John 20:17
15 Mark 10:17-18
16 Acts 7:56
17 Psalm 8:4
18 Daniel 7:13
19 Matthew 26:63-64
20 Matthew 25:40
21 John 8:58
22 John 3:13
23 Philippians 2:16
24 1 Corinthians 15:47
25 Romans 5:14
26 Ephesians 4:22,24
27 Ephesians 2:14,15
28 Colossians 1:15
29 Colossians 1:16
30 Colossians 1:17
31 Colossians 2:9
32 Matthew 11:27; Luke 10:22
33 Hebrews 1:2
34 Hebrews 5:7
35 Hebrews 1:3
36 John 1:3
37 Ephesians 1:10

Notes

CHAPTER 7 *The Cosmic Person in Hinduism, Buddhism and Islam*

1 Colossians 1:16-17

2 Rig Veda 10:90

3 Rig Veda 10:90

4 Revelation 13:8

5 Brihadaranyaka Upanishad 1:4:1

6 Brihadaranyaka Upanishad 4:3:7

7 Katha Upanishad 3:11

8 Svetasvatara Upanishad 3:7

9 Svetasvatara Upanishad 3:11,13

10 Svetasvatara Upanishad 4:19

11 Svetasvatara Upanishad 6:7

12 Bhagavad Gita 10:8

13 Bhagavad Gita 11:18-19

14 Bhagavad Gita 11:47

15 Bhagavad Gita 15:16-17

16 Bhagavad Gita 15:18

17 I am indebted for this understanding of the Madhyamika doctrine to T.R.V. Murty's *Central Concepts of Buddhism*, (Allen and Unwin, 1960).

18 The philosophy of Ibn al Arabi has been studied with extraordinary insight and at the greatest depth by R. W. J. Austin in his translation of *The Bezels of Wisdom* in the *Classics of Western Spirituality* (Paulist Press).

CHAPTER 8 *God and the World*

1 David Bohm, *Wholeness and the Implicate Order* (Routledge and Kegan Paul, 1980).

2 Ken Wilber, *The Spectrum of Consciousness* (Theosophical Publishing House, 1977)

3 Michael von Brück, "Holistic Vision in Eastern Religions", *Indian Theological Studies*, 1985

4 cf. Exodus 33:20

5 John 1:18

6 1 Timothy 6:16

7 Ephesians 1:10

8 John 14:11

9 John 17:21

10 Beatrice Bruteau, "Prayer and Identity", *Contemplative Review*, 1983.

CHAPTER 9 *The Ascent to the Godhead*

1 Isa Upanishad 6

2 Katha Upanishad 3:10:11

3 Katha Upanishad 3:10:13

4 Katha Upanishad 3:10:13

5 Katha Upanishad 6:10

6 Mandukya Upanishad 7

7 Svetasvatara Upanishad 2:8

8 Svetasvatara Upanishad 2:8

9 Svetasvatara Upanishad 2:9

10 Svetasvatara Upanishad 2:15

11 Svetasvatara Upanishad 3:13

12 Svetasvatara Upanishad 3:13

13 Svetasvatara Upanishad 6:21

14 Katha Upanishad 2:23

15 Bhagavad Gita 3:30

16 Bhagavad Gita 6:10

17 Bhagavad Gita 6:12

18 Bhagavad Gita 6:13

19 Bhagavad Gita 6:14

20 Bhagavad Gita 6:15

21 Bhagavad Gita 9:34

22 Bhagavad Gita 18:65

23 Bhagavad Gita 18:66

24 Kena Upanishad 29-30

Notes

1 Genesis 12:1-2
2 Genesis 15:12
3 Genesis 15:17
4 Genesis 18:1ff.
5 Genesis 32:1-2
6 Genesis 28:12
7 Genesis 32:24-26,28
8 Exodus 3:1-5
9 Exodus 19:16-20
10 Exodus 33:9-11
11 Exodus 33:13-22
12 Deuteronomy 10:14,17
13 Svetasvatara Upanishad 6:7
14 1 Samuel 3:4-9
15 1 Kings 8:10-11
16 2 Kings 2:11
17 Amos 4:13
18 Amos 5:14,24
19 Hosea 2:19-20
20 Hosea 11:1
21 Isaiah 6:1-5
22 Isaiah 45:5
23 Jeremiah 1:5-6
24 Jeremiah 31:3
25 Ezekiel 1:4ff.
26 Matthew 11:27; cf. Luke 10:12
27 John 17:21
28 John 10:20
29 John 15:1-4
30 1 John 1:3
31 Acts 2:45
32 1 John 4:20
33 1 Corinthians 2:10-11

34 Galatians 4:6

35 Romans 8:15-16

36 Colossians 3:3

37 Bhagavad Gita 18:65

38 1 Corinthinas 6:19; 6:13.

39 Isaiah 65:17; Revelation 21:1

CHAPTER 11   *Christian Mysticism in Relation to Eastern Mysticism*

1 Micah 6:8

2 Matthew 11:27; Luke 10:22

3 An excellent account of Origen's teaching is to be found in J. Danielou's *Origen* (Sheed and Ward, 1955).

4 Colossians 1:15

5 The mystical theology of St Gregory of Nyssa has been studied by J. Danielou in *Platonisme et Theologie Mystique* (Aubier: Paris, 1944).

6 The edition of Dionysius, *Divine Names and Mystical Theology* from which these quotations are taken is that of C. E. Rolt (SPCK, 1940).

7 The quotations from Ruysbroeck are from *The Adornment of the Spiritual Marriage*, translated by Wynschenk Dorn (J. M. Dent, 1916).

8 Colossians 2:9

9 Matthew 10:39 ff.

CHAPTER 13   *The New Age*

1 Ephesians 6:12